YELLOW GRIZZLIES

A DECADE OF MY EXPERIENCES

Accounts of My Yellowstone Grizzly Bear Encounters, Observations, and Preservation Concerns.

Journey with me from the beginning. As a late starter, well into my senior years, I continue to hike hundreds of miles to photograph grizzly bears in the wild, in and around Yellowstone. Both on and off trail, each solo hike was memorable, often challenging, but always rewarding.

Exploring presented many grizzly bear sightings and several very close encounters. I am fortunate to share through my book's pages and camera lens, revisiting some of these adventures and experiences. Learn of natural, human, and political interactions that threaten the survival of our national iconic grizzly bear.

That Snap in the Timber?
Relax, it's only the Wind......Right?

By

Robert J. Nevens, Sr.

© 2023 by Robert J. Nevens, Sr.

ALL RIGHTS RESERVED.

No part of this book may be reproduced, duplicated, or transmitted in any form by any means, electronic or mechanical, including photocopying and recording, or by any information storage and retrieval system. Recording of this book is strictly prohibited, including but not limited to text material, photographs, and graphics in either electronic means or print.

Cover Design, Photographs, and Graphs ©2023

by Robert J. Nevens, Sr.

Cover Photo ©2023 Robert J. Nevens, Sr.

Entitled: *"A Conflicted Truce"*

Yellowstone grizzly bear feeding on a carcass.

Acknowledgments

*Yellowstone visitors, new and returning.

The majority of annual Yellowstone visitors, consistently express their "wants or must see" is to see bears, especially the grizzly bear. I know this very personally, as I too was one of them. Very often I hear from disappointed visitors, "So just where are all these bears that are supposed to be here?"

*The good citizens and businesses of Gardiner, MT.

Ravished by the June 2022 historic flood and destruction; this terrible disaster took place during the period in which this book was written. I've spent many of my journeys, in and around Gardiner and honor the courage and resiliency of its residents.

* Grizzly & Wolf Discovery Center - West Yellowstone, MT.

This was a launch pad in my journey. A must-stop for YNP visitors and returnees alike. The center provides an interactive setting for all age groups interested in Yellowstone's history and characteristics of grizzly bears, wolves, raptors, and otters. Visitors are amazed at the educational, entertaining, close-up, unobstructed grizzly bear and wolf pack viewing.

*Yellowstone NPS.

I also extend my profound gratitude and respect to the men and women of Yellowstone NPS. They collaboratively and tirelessly manage visitor safety, wildlife protection, and preservation. Without their valued expertise, dedication, and efforts, this book along with my personal experiences, would not have been possible.

CONTENTS

Part I: The Early Years 2008-2009

1. My First Visit to Wyoming Rocky Mountains   9
2. Back to Jackson Hole   12
3. Yellowstone at Last   15
4. The Grizzly & Wolf Discovery Center   17
5. Death in the Hayden Valley   23
6. My First Grizzly Bear Sighting   42
7. First Yellowstone Hike-Solfatara Trail   50

Part II: The Productive Years 2010-2023

1. Planning and Preparing the Trip   58
2. The Quad Mom   64
3. Three Feet Face to Face with a Grizzly   67
4. Turning Lemons into Lemonade   82
5. Grizzlies I've Known   96
6. A Bison Funeral Service   129
7. Tracking a Grizzly   136
8. There's no Bears Around Here   145
9. My Tribute to Legendary Yellowstone Grizzly #211   155
10. Grizzly Bear Characteristics   178
11. Hiking with Yellowstone History   199
12. My Hiking Equipment   213
13. The Shoshone Lodge Trapped Grizzly   228
14. The Tri-State Agreement -Trophy Hunt Grizzlies or Not?   278
15. Black Bear Hunter "Mistaken Identity"   291
16. 2023 and Beyond. Political Scorched Earth Policies   297
17. Closing/About the Author   317-320

Introduction

Every year the majority of 3.3 million annual visitors to YNP and the GYE, consistently list their "wants or must see" to view bears, notably the grizzly bear. I know this quite personally, as I too, was one of them. More often than not, disappointed visitors say, "Just where are all these bears that are supposed to be here?"

In my book, *Yellowstone Grizzlies-A Decade of My Experiences* the reader will have the opportunity to share my experiences and passion for hiking and amateur grizzly bear photography in Yellowstone National Park and the surrounding (GYE) Greater Yellowstone Eco System. I've restricted this book to Yellowstone grizzly bear encounters and related issues. I wrote this book for people like me, regardless of age, who are fascinated, or at a minimum very curious, about the prospect of sighting a Yellowstone grizzly in the wild. Some accounts of my grizzly bear journeys, adventures, encounters, humor, tragedy, and mystery await the reader. Insight is also directed to current natural, environmental, and human threats firmly aligned against a tenuous grizzly bear population.

My book is also written to enlighten those who share a common ongoing concern for the future preservation and sustainability of the grizzly bear population and observations of current natural and political issues posing persistent threats. Some opinions might be considered somewhat controversial by some. Others, who I believe would be the large national majority favoring enhanced grizzly protection, would hold the opposite views. Fair enough, as grizzly bears themselves are a complex iconic species, encircled by a complex and precarious future.

As a developing grizzly bear advocate, my introduction to grizzlies first commenced well into my senior years. It was a slow road to success, but then through years of self-dedication, education, and predominately solo hiking field experiences; my quest surpassed all expectations and introduced me to a great deal of adventure, learning, and achievement. And yes, it remains accompanied by times of risk and danger while hiking in grizzly country.

As my experiences and knowledge grew, I also realized the swirling adverse elements and direction of the federal (USF&WS) Endangered Species Act (ESA) and state grizzly bear management history and plans. Plans and actions that would hand over the management and protection of the GYE grizzly from federal protection back to state management. This would be the same state grizzly bear management policies that by 1975, brought the GYE grizzly population to the brink of extinction. The same three states again plan for "Trophy" Grizzly Bear Hunting. Seismic adverse impacts will likely result. In my book, I offer perspective into this renewed reckless paradox.

Whether as a Yellowstone newcomer, or a more experienced visitor, I'm compelled to share the path that brought me to this rewarding point. Through my story, I hope the interested public who may be passionate, or perhaps just curious about Yellowstone grizzly bears and the rugged beauty of the country they inhabit, will in their own way be entertained and enlightened.

All photographs contained within this book, with one exception, were taken by the author while inside YNP, or the surrounding GYE boundaries. None of my photographs were taken with long camera lenses that are often lined up on YNP pullouts and roads. Rather, I'm hiking in the field with a quality compact camera, which demands immediate access as wildlife opportunities happen very fast, often in a restricted visual setting. While this book concentrates on the Yellowstone grizzly, other wildlife encounters I've witnessed have a special relationship to the apex grizzly bear. Collectively they hold an intertwined common theme…. wilderness. For you see, without the grizzly bear, there can be no true wilderness. Yellowstone itself would be reduced to far less than its preserved true wilderness.

So, let's lace up, gear up, and head out into Yellowstone's beautiful and exciting backcountry, where risks and rewards abound.

PART I: The Early Years

Chapter One
My First Visit to Wyoming's Rocky Mountains

    The Jackson Hole, WY mid-winter weather forecast was quite challenging compared to the relatively mild winter weather in Nashville, TN my departure city. The exact year escapes me, but it was somewhere in the late 1990s. A short-term business trip was the reason for my trip where I would meet up with a business colleague at the airport. Even though I had traveled the country extensively on business-related matters, this was my first trip to Wyoming. There would be little if any time, for sightseeing or exploring this fantastic city or beautiful mountainous area. Besides, I was never a skier and the very thought of racing down a steep mountainside on two pieces of wood, dodging trees and people wasn't very appealing to me.

    The one thing that was never on my mind before, during, or immediately after this trip was the thought of bears, especially grizzly bears. Sure, in earlier years I had seen many bear movies, periodicals, and outdoor magazines featuring bears, but a real spark for bears had not yet been ignited in me. The media articles were just casual reference material.

    At that time, my main ongoing outdoor activity and interest was freshwater fishing for smallmouth bass and trout in Arkansas and Tennessee. The only time bears came to mind or were of potential concern was our wilderness unguided trips to northern Manitoba in search of trophy northern pike, lake trout, arctic grayling, and walleye. These are the only species of fish that can survive the harsh climate. Our small group would rendezvous in Winnipeg and eventually land via floatplane in the remote north and south Seal River areas northwest of Churchill;

the Canadian polar bear capital. Black bears and wolves were numerous in and around the inland lakes and rivers we fished. For that reason alone, we needed some form of protection. Bear spray had not yet been invented plus we were lodged in a primitive cabin, more like a very bad shack. There were no protections or people within a hundred miles accessible by floatplane only. Therefore, I was designated our camp Sergeant of Arms to have our only protection, my 8mm Mauser. Other than sighting it in, it never left my cabin bunk.

  My first arrival at Jackson Hole was memorable and quite impressionable. While walking out of the airport terminal to locate my rental vehicle, parked right next to it was a mid-size sedan that was barely identifiable. The front end was completely crushed back into the firewall. Thick brown hide and large bone fragments mixed with blood and gore encased the entire front end. You guessed it…I learned that the night before somewhere nearby on a dark black highway, the rental driver struck the bison at a high rate of speed. Seeing this destruction to animals, man, and machines was rather upsetting. I didn't know the driver's or passengers' condition, but I couldn't imagine anyone walking away from that accident unscathed. I've witnessed and experienced auto/deer collisions, but this one left a lasting effect and caution for traveling in large game country.

  After loading our bags into our vehicle, we left the airport for Jackson Hole. Shortly thereafter, I hastily pulled off the road and in wind-driven snow, got out of the car and stood there in a stout wind in absolute amazement. I couldn't believe my eyes at the thousands of elk across the road as far as you could see. They were bedded down or grazing at feeding troughs. The Elk Refuge was unknown to me. Right then on the roadside, freezing half to death in my business suit, I realized this was a very special part of the country that would undoubtedly, draw my further attention. Days later I departed for home, but strangely no thoughts whatsoever about bears had yet migrated into my psyche. Little did I know at that time, this Jackson Hole business trip would be the initial catalyst for my journey with the Yellowstone grizzly. Again, unknown to me, I just needed some yet-to-be-experienced event to light that fire.

    Somewhere north of here, a place called "Yellowstone" would change my world and open a new unimaginable journey of learning, adventure, and achievement coupled with occasional dangers. I was still far from reaching that inception point, but upon reflection, I sensed a developing feeling that something lay ahead but had no idea of just what or when.

Chapter Two

Back to Jackson Hole

Several years had now passed since my first trip to Jackson Hole. I remained a few years away from retirement, but my demanding work life saddled with never-ending business responsibilities, meetings, travel, etc., certainly never slowed down. Just the opposite. Reflecting on that time, however, I now realized that period held a silver lining and was instrumental in furthering my undiscovered journey with Yellowstone Grizzlies.

That silver lining came in the form of a September 2008 telephone call from a colleague in Idaho Falls, Idaho. He asked, "Bob, how would you like to come up to Jackson Hole in October and give a business presentation to my group? He went on, "The aspens will be in full color, perfect fall weather, and we want to invite your wife to accompany you." I had business responsibilities and multiple travels to Idaho Falls for several years.

Laughingly, I drew his memory to a previous late January evening flight into Idaho Falls. With a delayed airport arrival, I was met with a near blizzard. Temps had dropped into the low teens, and restaurants closed. What could go wrong? I failed to mention that my checked bag holding all my clothes and necessities, did not arrive, or was lost for our next morning business. Late in the evening, my colleagues dropped me off in the freezing Walmart parking lot in response to my travel dilemma. The store was closing in five minutes. Securing my necessities, I think the kind employees took pity on this wayward southern traveler. Upon exiting, I was greeted by an arctic blast of wind and snow. The parking lot was now empty! Perhaps there was some miscommunication between myself and my colleagues. The details of which, were bantered around for years afterward.

We both got a laugh at that prior event and reminisced about our other associations. I replied, "Of course I'll gladly help out, lock it in for October in Jackson Hole."

In early October 2008, my wife and I arrived in Jackson Hole for my business obligation. Indeed, the aspens were brilliant gold and quivering with the mild autumnal winds. Heading into town from the airport, I recalled from several years earlier, the incredible spectacle of the Elk Refuge. An enormous population of elk would start their winter migration here months later, nearly filling the spacious expanse of the refuge. Other elk in the surrounding mountains would head for lower elevations. In either setting, the elk would encounter two brutal survival threats. Wolves, and the unforgiving Rocky Mountain harsh winter weather. As the winter season continues to progress, the wolf grows only stronger; while the non-migrating bison and elk, weaken in the relentless cold, deep snows, and scant forage. The wolf pack has a superior tactical advantage over the old, weakened, sick, or injured prey; given their speed, durability, and coordinated pack hunting techniques along with their ability to traverse the deep snows and bring down their prey. At one time or another, most of us have watched this ancient drama take place on National Geographic or other outdoor media outlets. Most of this drama takes place in the Lamar River section in northeast YNP. During the coldest part of Yellowstone's winter, long lines of highly dedicated wolf watchers from across the U.S. and abroad, gather in the Lamar to view and video/photograph these eons-old acts of nature take place.

During this entire period, the grizzlies have been in hibernation and pose no risk or competition for the wolves. However, nature has provided the slumbering grizzly bears (and other predators) with awaiting winter kill rewards, as the final beneficiaries of the wolf's unchallenged winter predation. As the Yellowstone grizzly bear awakens from hibernation, usually in late March into early April, an early season source of protein awaits them. Buried deep in the early spring ice and snow are calorie-protein-rich elk and bison carcasses that succumbed to a variety of natural survival threats. But for now, I'm getting a tad ahead of myself. We will cover patterns and interactions in later chapters.

      Back to Jackson Hole. The third and final day of the conference allowed a mostly free day. I suggested to my wife, "Let's head north to see the Tetons and if we have enough time, let's go to YNP. We've never been there." She agreed and we were traveling north through Moose on our way to the Tetons by late morning. Later we came to the north end of the Tetons. Our trip through the Tetons was remarkable! This was the country I could only dream of and had so very much to study and learn about. No doubt, I just had to press on to Yellowstone. For me, this was a game-changer. Heading north to the YNP South Entrance, the brilliant mountain skies were turning cloudy as the early October temperature was gradually dropping.

Chapter Three
Yellowstone at Last

We excitingly entered YNP On October 9, 2008. I did not know much about Yellowstone and knew far less about YNP grizzly bears. My only knowledge was casual information from news periodicals, outdoor shows, advertisements, etc. That day, and decades later, I realized that I made a good move as we entered the Moose Road en route to Grand Teton National Park. I was about to pay our NPS entry fee at the entry gate. The Ranger noted that I was a senior citizen and advised that we were eligible for a Senior National Park Pass. He recommended that I buy a Lifetime Senior Pass for twenty-five dollars, good for life, at all United States National Parks. That sounded good, but I paused for a moment thinking maybe I wouldn't need such a pass, much beyond this one short trip. Thankfully, however, my better half wisely took charge and replied to the Ranger, "Oh yes sir, that's wonderful, we will take the pass." Looking back, what a smart decision she made then and so remains today. During subsequent years I've made countless trips to Yellowstone and never paid a single-entry fee. I understand the fee for a current Lifetime Senior Pass, is eighty dollars. Some seniors and others balked at the amount of the August 2017 price hike, but in my opinion and experience, I wouldn't bat an eye for the value, especially in the hyperinflation period we currently find in our country.

Proudly displaying my receipt for our new Season Pass, we drove through the South Entrance Gate. On October 9, 2008, I was in Yellowstone National Park for the very first time. I had little clue where we were, or what to do heading into the park. Once I received the Fall 2008 Yellowstone Visitor Guide and YNP map, I at least now had some bearings to visit, within the restricted time we had to spend here. I recall how enormous the size of YNP appeared in the guide. On top of that, I had no comprehension of the effects of time and distance, for traveling from one spot to another. From the map, the park looked enormous, compared to the tiny segment we had traveled. The travel map itself does not convey the real-time distances to travel the "figure eight" and adjoining park roads.

The initial plan was to visit the Lower Falls and then just take it from there. Not much of a plan, but after seeing my first bison slowly walking in the middle of the road north of Grant Village, I knew I would return to this treasured place at some point to see more and maybe, find new adventures.

Chapter Four
The Grizzly & Wolf Discovery Center

The Lower Falls of the Yellowstone River was awe-inspiring, stunningly beautiful, majestic, and powerful. Pictures or videos I had seen were simply inadequate and could not convey the grandeur of the ever-changing colors, the depth of the canyon, and the torrent of the Yellowstone River as it swiftly winds 692 miles north/northeast to the confluence with the Missouri River. The name of this river has various historical names. The most commonly held name by the Minnetaree Indians was "Mi tse a-da-zi" or Yellow Rock River. The Crow called it the "Elk River." In the 1840's French trappers and early mountain men called it "Roche Jaune" or Yellow Rock. The YST River has its headwaters in Wyoming, down the slopes of Yount Peak which then flows through three states: WY, MT, and ND. Here it then flows into the Missouri River and heads south into the Mississippi River. As the longest undammed river in the United States, I found it somewhat amazing that the waters of the great YST River eventually wind up in New Orleans and eventually flow into the Gulf of Mexico.

The weather continued to be questionable as we departed the Lower Falls. The winds were gently picking up and the skies turned grey as we contemplated our next move. As newcomers, we decided on the obligatory visit to Old Faithful. It was at that point; I first experienced the mistaken realities of time and distance traveling within YNP.

Two beautiful sights, my wife Anita & the Lower Falls.

Arriving near Old Faithful much later than anticipated, I exclaimed to my wife," I can't believe it's taken so long to travel this short section of the map to get here. It just doesn't look that long on this map." Of course, I've never traveled to YNP before; all I knew was that it seemed much longer than traveling "Tennessee" map miles. And that was without disruptions from bison/bear jams, heavy traffic, or road construction projects. Valuable lesson learned.

Given our remaining time restraints, we decided visiting Old Faithful would take far too long. We still wanted to see more of the park itself, so I consulted the park map on a whim and decided to drive to West Yellowstone and check that area out. Little did I know, that spur-of-the-moment decision, turned out to be a pivotable moment in my future journey with Yellowstone grizzly bears. Passing the Madison Junction, a few snowflakes were sporadically hitting the windshield. I paid no attention. I was greatly enjoying seeing all this new spectacular scenery.

Heading west toward town, the views were even more impressive, with the flowing Madison River on one side of the road and the towering Purple Mountain on the other. However, on the entire trip so far, I was expecting to see more wildlife than very sporadically appeared.

As we passed out of YNP at the West Entrance you immediately enter the town of West Yellowstone. After driving around the streets for a while, I needed a cup of coffee. Spotting a McDonalds, I pulled into the drive-through window. As I awaited some fresh brew at the service window, I noticed a large sign across the street..... something about bears and wolves? "Why not stop and see what this is," I said to my wife. Closer to the sign I read, "The Grizzly & Wolf Discovery Center." I still didn't know what this was, nor ever heard of it, but it had my full attention. I said to Anita, "Let's go in honey. After all, we have come all this way, and at least jokingly, we could say we saw a bear." As she put on her scarf she said, "Why not, but remember we have a long drive back to Jackson Hole." As I opened the entrance door for her, I knew I had stumbled upon something pretty awesome! This first visit to the GWDC turned out to be another major catalyst that would eventually take me into the backcountry and stand in awe of grizzlies in the wild. But yet there were future events or steps to be taken to turn my quest into a reality.

Entrance to the Grizzly & Wolf Discovery Center.

At the very onset, I highly recommend to all YNP visitors; first-timers, or seasoned returnees, at some point during your trip, visit the Grizzly & Wolf Discover Center. Don't leave YNP without experiencing a close encounter with grizzly bears or wolves. Regardless of your individual experiences with bears or lack thereof, since you are reading my book, clearly you have some interest, curiosity, or desire to view grizzly bears and interact with them close up, with only the naked eye and unobstructed views. After all, a large majority of YNP visitors rank very high up, seeing a bear is a priority experience. So many people I meet are disappointed they haven't seen a bear, much less a grizzly, during or when their trip to YNP is completed. To some degree, a visit to the GWDC may temper that disappointment and offer encouragement and renewal to pursue bear sightings. Keep in mind, things in Yellowstone, especially wildlife viewings, often happen spontaneously, you never know when or where. Oftentimes, minutes indeed matter to a great degree. The adage, "If only you were here, five minutes ago you would have seen the most amazing thing!"

In my opinion, what GWDC *is not*, as opposed to *what it is;* represents a key element of attraction, authenticity, and source of knowledge. It is not a zoo, tourist trap, or a "drive through/see a bear" location. Without belaboring the multiplicity of what the Center is, i.e., a not-for-profit, wildlife sanctuary for grizzly bears deemed as nuisance bears, orphaned, or otherwise displaced bears in close viewing natural and educational settings. Please feel free to inquire about information and planning via their website.

You will not be disappointed if you stay for an hour, half or a full day, or return the next day. The experience is amazing for young and old alike; to intimately view and learn about grizzly bears, wolf packs, raptors, and otters. Beyond the main attraction of seeing grizzly bears and wolves, the Discovery Center has many attractive and very educational exhibits.

Wolf curls up for a nap at the Grizzly Wolf Ctr.

Through the ensuing years, I've spent many enjoyable days and hours viewing and studying the grizzlies. I never tired of learning from their interactions with one another and witnessing their incredible strength. One morning while I was there, various manufacturers of "bear-resistant" waste containers were being studied. Suffice it to say, many containers failed the important element of being "bear proof" and did not pass due to the intelligence and strength of grizzlies finding ways to break into the waste containers. I watched in near disbelief, as one grizzly effortlessly overturned and broke into a large chained and sealed metal dumpster with a single swipe of his left paw. Watching the chained dumpster tumble over several times and also viewing grizzlies wrestling around in playful, but rough engagements; it became very obvious to me that it would

be impossible for any human being attempting to fight off a serious grizzly bear attack. If a grizzly wanted and intended to kill a person with no protection, nothing could stop a grizzly bear from effortlessly doing so. Closely watching the bears play fighting, I was intrigued by their tactics in approaching the other, who then engaged with quick feints and head positioning to throw the other off balance and gain an early positional advantage. Once the grizzlies engaged each other, sheer strength and rapid positioning occurred for dominance. Once an exhausting series of play fighting was over, it was amazing to see how fast the bears ran off, chasing each other. I viewed the combinations of strength, intelligence, determination, and speed would be collectively overwhelming to a human being. Watching the two young grizzlies jaw and wrestle about on the ground and in the trout pond, provided clear evidence why the experts strongly advise against attempting to fend off a grizzly bear.

After watching these grizzlies "having fun" with each other, I wasn't too sure that in the future I wanted any part of traipsing around in their Yellowstone habitat. It certainly made a hesitant impression on me at the time. I had so very much to yet learn before I could reach a reasonably cautious level of entering their domain.

A few captivating hours went by as the weather finally caught up with us. Paying little attention to the increasing cold and now steady snow from earlier flurries, it was time to head back to Jackson Hole. Anxiously, we followed a snow plow out over the Continental Divide. No question whatsoever, my spur-of-the-moment decision to venture to West Yellowstone was a fortuitous event that lit a spark in me to later develop into a seasoned and successful ambassador of Yellowstone and a backcountry grizzly bear enthusiast. The journey towards accomplishing that would jump-start at a later time. Even though I had an amazing and captivating experience at the Grizzly & Wolf Discovery Center, I still had not seen a free-roaming grizzly bear in the wild. Little did I realize that that situation would wildly change within a few more years.

Chapter 5

Death in the Hayden Valley

John Wallace

Before moving on from the Grizzly & Wolf Discovery Center, I want to share some factual knowledge I learned several years later involving a certain pair of then, grizzly cubs and the circumstances in which they were involved; tragically resulting in placing them in the GWDC sanctuary. I bring this up as just one example, to highlight the great sanctuary service and compassion the Center provides for shall we say, repeat compromised or nuisance grizzlies, that otherwise would suffer elimination via euthanasia by state wildlife agencies. This event also reflected an ongoing degree of interconnected YNP grizzly information and experience that I was acquiring.

Most unfortunately, the following account involves rare and extremely troubling events involving the fatality of a seasoned YNP hiker by a grizzly bear. It also serves as a measure to remind people that there are levels of risk and danger with wildlife encounters coexisting, alongside the adventure of exploring YNP's backcountry.

Arriving alone by himself into Yellowstone from his home in Michigan, fifty-nine-year-old John Wallace established his camping site in central YNP Canyon Village campground. According to his family, Mr. Wallace was an experienced backcountry hiker, and outdoorsman, and had previously hiked in YNP.

According to the National Park Service U.S. Department of the Interior, Supplemental Case 11-4555: Mr. Wallace checked in on August 24, 2011, as a guest at the Canyon Village campground front desk. He was checked in by a campground representative who stated, "He didn't want to hear the "Bear Speech" which is part of our check-in process." Looking her in the eye, he said that he was a grizzly bear expert. She replied, "Fine, then you can critique my Bear Speech. So, he got the Bear Speech and after reviewing the rules, I gave him his map." Displaying his outdoor experience, Wallace set up a neat, organized campsite. The next morning, he would drive south from Canyon to the Mary Mountain Trailhead in the Hayden Valley.

South of the Canyon Village campground lies the sprawling fifty square-mile Hayden Valley. It is an expansive area of open hilly terrain, with scattered islands of timber, geological features, marshy intersecting creeks, and bordered by deep forest. The Hayden Valley was once a submerged arm of Yellowstone Lake and transformed into its current terrain by retreating glaciers thousands of years ago. The Hayden Valley is also prime habitat, attracting rich diverse wildlife and waterfowl. In addition to large bison herds, elk, and other ungulates, the valley is also a prime wolf and grizzly bear territory. Black bears are rarely seen in the valley's open area. They are more restricted to the deep forest surrounding boundaries. The Mary Mountain Trail is one of two, extensive backcountry trails transecting Hayden Valley's numerous creeks, ponds, sagebrush, and marshlands. It is also a beautiful area and an engaging landscape for hikers and photographers.

The summer morning of August 25, 2011, started with promising clear weather, a perfect hiking day. At about 7:30 am, Mr. Wallace arrived at the east trailhead of the Mary Mountain Trail. As an experienced hiker, he geared up with the most essential day hiking necessities, except *one critically important item* for recreating in grizzly country. Departing alone, he headed west into the open expanse of the Hayden Valley. Later in the day, as often occurs during Yellowstone summers, heavy thunderstorms and hail altered the pleasurable morning. That night, Mr. Wallace did not return to his vehicle or campsite at the Canyon Campground.

The following early afternoon on August 26th, a young woman and her father also departed the east trailhead of the Mary Mountain Trail. They too, as did Wallace, headed west on the trail to Mary Lake, their destination. The lady was in the lead, followed by her father. About five miles in, the trail left the more open ground and into some sparse timber. She reported seeing "birds circling" and crossed a log over the trail as she approached. Seeing a drink container and a backpack, she cautiously moved closer. The young lady was horrified to see boots sticking out and the upper part of a body covered with dirt. Running back to her father, they both returned to look at the scene. They did not approach the body any closer and quickly left the area, fearing that a bear may still be nearby. Her father believed a bear was feeding on the body and had covered it with dirt. Scurrying as quickly as possible back to the east trailhead, arriving at 1:20 pm, they drove to the Canyon Ranger Station to report the harrowing finding. Multiple rescue and investigative agencies were immediately deployed to the location. The trail and surrounding areas were posted and closed. A search team by helicopter was sent to locate the body.

After a careful approach from the west (not to disturb the trail or possible tracks) at 6:00 pm, the search team located the body. The team reported," The body was surrounded by grizzly bear tracks, *five bear scats*, and some bear hair. According to Ranger David Page team leader, "Small logs (tops of fallen trees) that lay between items and the body had what appeared to be blood stains on them as if something had contact with the logs. There appeared to be at least one partially bloody/dirt-soiled bear track on one of the downed trees. Although a partial track, it appeared it may have been from a medium-sized bear. Two areas of pushed-down vegetation extended from the body in a westerly direction. The pushed-down vegetation appeared to be a path made recently by animals that came and went from the body." Ranger Page further reported that a large bull bison carcass about a week old was found 330 yards from the fatality site. Furthermore, Ranger Page reported, "Upon arriving at the fatality site, *small bear tracks* were observed on the trail and on the disturbed soil where the body was discovered. The *track size was a cub of the year*. These tracks were new from the time that we left the area the night before, at about 8:00 p.m."

Ground investigation revealed that two bison carcasses were located in the area. Bears will often create a day bed near a carcass to rest and protect the carcass from other unwanted predators. In this case, a bison carcass was located 360 yds southeast of the body. Surrounding the carcass, 16-day beds were discovered. A second bison carcass was found 1.5 miles away. On August 22nd, three days before the Wallace attack, nine individual grizzlies fed on the carcass. A female grizzly known as the "Wapiti Sow" and her two cubs were among the bears feeding on this carcass.

Travis Wyman, Bear Management Biological Technician, discovered a recent day bed about 220 feet from the fatality site. Near this day bed, he discovered additional blood-soiled tracks on downed logs. He described the tracks as, "To be from a medium-sized bear and a *cub of the year* due to their size."

What happened to Mr. Wallace and what circumstances were present during this tragedy? The exact details may never be known, as Wallace was alone, without any witnesses. According to National Park Service-Yellowstone, Case Incident Record 114555; an extensive investigation concluded that at some time that morning after he left and before the afternoon storm, Wallace had stopped along the trail for something to eat or drink. Perhaps sitting on a log, he was attacked by a grizzly bear from the front or back. It remains undetermined if the attack was a defensive attack (sow protecting her cubs, and/or a bison carcass) or alternately, the nature of a predatory attack viewing Wallace as prey. It is noteworthy that two bison carcasses were near the fatality location. Unquestionably, a bison carcass, much less two, is a strong attraction for grizzly bears and other predators. The area of attack also supported other abundant ground bear foods including yampa, elk thistle, wild strawberry, and clover. This was quite evident as sixteen bear day beds were around the bison carcass.

However, investigating authorities along with post-mortem findings support that at some point, Wallace fought for his life. Defensive wounds were evident on his hands and arms. Thomas L. Bennett, MD, forensic medicine concluded, "The majority of his wounds appear to be postmortem." The bear (or other bears) fed upon his remains.

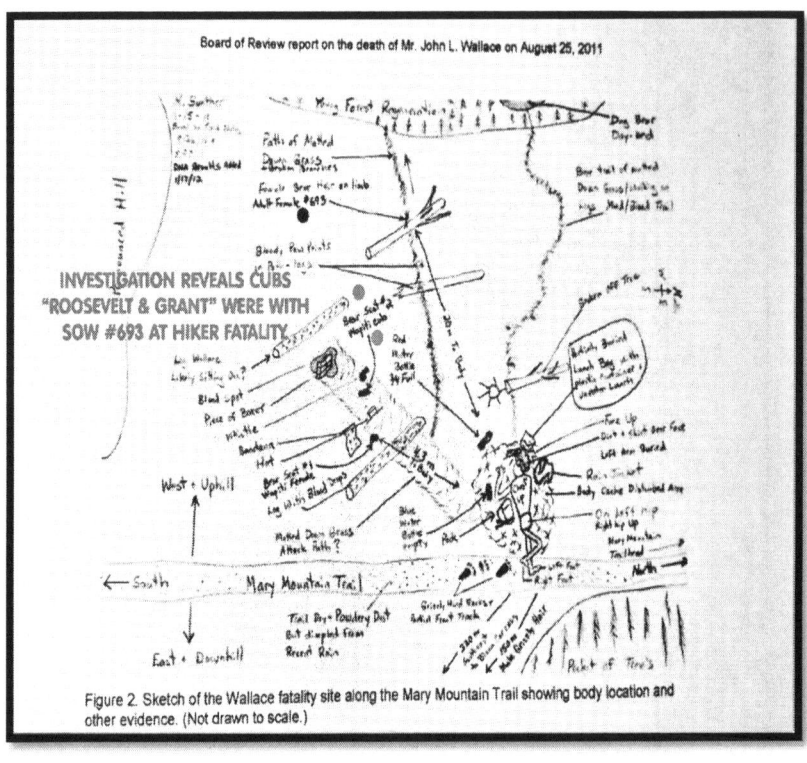

Figure 2. Sketch of the Wallace fatality site along the Mary Mountain Trail showing body location and other evidence. (Not drawn to scale.)

January 12, 2012, Forensic Report prepared by: Kerry Gunther, Wildlife Biologist (Bears) Yellowstone National Park.

    The day after the discovery of Mr. Wallace's body, aerial reconnaissance was conducted in the Hayden Valley to assist in identifying grizzly bears in the vicinity. Nine recon flights were deployed during a thirty-three-day period through September 29, 2011. During that period, recon flights established a significant presence of grizzly bears. Thirty bear sightings and/or radio telemetry contacts revealed at least 19 individual documented bears.

    Of later significance on August 30th, a female grizzly known as the "Wapiti Sow" and her two COY (cubs of the year) were spotted in the Sour Creek drainage on a bison carcass with four wolves. Also, for a later chapter reference, *grizzly bear #211, a/k/a "Scarface"* was radio located. In 1993 he was first captured within YNP after bluff-charging some park visitors. After the Wallace fatality, I had several memorable close encounters with this Yellowstone legendary grizzly. Again, on September 29th, aerial recon observed the Wapiti Sow and her two cubs in the Sour Creek drainage.

Bear trapping operations were also initiated on August 27, 2011, at the Mary Mountain trail fatality site and other locations in the Hayden Valley. These live trapping operations lasted until October 16, 2011. As aerial reconnaissance confirmed, significant grizzly bear trapping activity took place. Authorities placed ten different trapping locations in the broad Hayden Valley area. In addition to the fatality site, these locations included areas around; Otter Creek, Sour Creek, Wapiti, Crater Hills, Natural Bridge, Grebe Pit trap site, and several others.

Overall trapping efforts involved 25 captures of 13 individual grizzlies. A week later on September 2nd, the first grizzly was captured at the Otter Creek trap site. The bear was identified as formally collared bear #155, a 25-year-old male; first captured as a two-year-old cub for killing sheep in the Targhee National Forest. He was released after examination of canine width and foot pad widths were both inconsistent with evidence from the fatality. DNA testing further cleared him of any involvement. *Again, for a later chapter reference: *Grizzly Bear #211* during this period was captured three times. On September 15th the 21-year-old, 453 lb. male was first captured at the Grebe Pit site. He was released as physical and DNA testing also cleared him of involvement. On September 16th one day later, "#211

Scarface" was recaptured at the Otter Creek trap site and released. Three days later, on September 19th, he was again captured for a third time at the Crater Hills trap site and freed at the capture site without physical handling.

Further bear trappings revealed a capture at the Wapiti site, on September 28th of an uncollared, six-year-old, 249 lb. adult female, known as the "Wapiti Sow." She was the only female in mid-2011 with COY's inhabiting the Hayden Valley, primarily on the east side of the Yellowstone River which intersects portions of the Hayden Valley. One of her male cubs had a distinctive blonde coloring. The following day on September 29th both of her 43lb. male cubs were captured at the identical Wapiti trap site.

Testing and forensic evidence of the three captured grizzly family confirmed they were present at the Wallace fatality site. DNA from the Wapiti Sow (#2011030) matched the DNA from the female bear scat 4.8 yds from Wallace. DNA from the blonde cub (#2011032) matched DNA with DNA from the male bear scat near the victim's possessions. The other dark-colored male cub's (#2011031) track prints were consistent with width measurements on a dusty trail next to where the body was cached.

<u>Kerry Gunther's, Wildlife Biologist (Bears) YNP
January 12, 2012, Conclusionary Report</u>

Reported in part, "Evidence indicates the Wapiti Sow and her blonde cub were both present at the Wallace fatality site and deposited scat there. By association, the Wapiti Sow's dark-colored cub was likely present as well, as cubs are usually accompanied by their mothers." Cub tracks at the site indicate that a female with cubs were present at Mr. Wallace's body.

Death in the Hayden Valley

Brian Matayoshi

Just who, or what significance are the "Wapiti Sow and cubs?" Again, most tragically and sadly, we need to step back nearly two months before the John Wallace grizzly bear fatality, and head 8.1 miles northeast across the Hayden Valley to the Wapiti Lake Trail. There on July 6, 2011, a park visitor and his wife were attacked by a grizzly bear and a cub. Only his wife survived the fatal assault.

This was the fourth visit to YNP that Brian Matayoshi and his wife Marilyn, came to enjoy on a sunny early summer day in Yellowstone. The California couple set up their camp at Grant Village on July 5th. During prior visits to YNP, the middle-aged couple never saw a single bear; grizzly, or black bear. They prepared for their day hike, basically in a populated area of the front country of YNP, with the *exception of one critically important item,* while recreating in grizzly bear country.

They began their 8:30 am morning hike at the Wapiti Lake Trailhead near the Chittenden Bridge parking area in the Canyon area of YNP. Their first leg was a hike to Clear Lake, and from there they hiked toward Ribbon Lake on the Wapiti Lake trail. They intended to hike a loop trail. One mile from the trailhead they met another park visitor overlooking the Hayden Valley. They joined the visitor in watching and photographing a female grizzly and two cubs in the far distance. Notorious Yellowstone summer mosquitos altered their hiking plans half an hour later. Retracing their steps back to the trailhead, they again saw the grizzlies that they had previously seen at a far distance.

The bear was now close to their return trail, approximately 100 yds away on the far side of a dense line of trees. At this point, the couple turned back away from the bears and headed east. Seeing their movement, the grizzlies moved in their direction. Mrs. Matayoshi stated she saw the bears pop up about 20 yds behind them and told her husband. He responded, "Run." As the bears approached, they both ran away from the bear; yelling and shouting down the trail as the bears gave chase to the fleeing people. At 173 yds (1¾ football field lengths) from the point they saw the bears, they caught up with them. Mrs. Matayoshi recalls the cubs were running and growling behind their mother. She did not see the adult sow attack her standing husband but, heard it just as she dove for cover off the trail behind a small downed tree five yds away from her husband. Sensing a period of quiet, she looked up and the sow was looking directly at her as she tried to get to her knees. Dropping facedown, the bear picked her up by her backpack and then dropped her to the ground. The bears then suddenly left the area. She walked over to her husband and attempted to use a jacket as a tourniquet on his bleeding leg. He was unresponsive and had expired. The cause of death was listed as blunt force trauma and blood loss from femoral artery injury.

On September 9, 2011, the <u>Conclusionary Investigation Team Report</u> was conducted by various state and federal Bear Management Authorities.

Concluding in part, "The incident was initiated by a surprise encounter followed by the bear chasing two fleeing people for over 270 yards and attacking one person and not injuring the other. What possibly began as an attempt by the bear to assess the Matayoshi's activities became a sustained pursuit of them as they fled running and yelling on the trail. In addition to the unfortunate circumstance of being at the wrong place at the wrong time, a possible contributing factor to the chase that ensued was the victims running from the bear screaming and yelling. The bears left the area rapidly after the chase and attack. The bear was unmarked, had never been captured, and had no known history of conflicts with humans. The bear was not removed after the attack because the encounter was characteristic of a surprise encounter."

According to the Wallace Report, the first casualty involving the Wapiti Sow's presence at the fatality site, "DNA evidence indicates that the Wapiti Sow was responsible for the death of Mr. Matoyoshi on the Wapiti Lake trail in the Hayden Valley on July 6, 2011." Furthermore, "DNA from the Wapiti Sow is a DNA match from the hair snagged on Matayoshi's eyeglasses and from a bear scat collected at the Matoyoshi fatality site." The report goes on to state, "DNA collected from the Wapiti's dark-colored male cub is a match with DNA from the male bear scat collected at the Matayoshi fatality site."

The Wallace case investigation concludes in part, "In the Wallace case, it remains unknown by investigating authorities the roles that the Wapiti Sow and adult female grizzly bear #693 played in the Wallace fatality and/or consumption of his body. Given the large number of bears utilizing nearby bison carcasses, DNA and track evidence suggests that several bears were present close to the fatality site, and with the lack of an eyewitness, it is not possible to precisely determine the identity of the bear or bears responsible for the death and/or consumption of Mr. Wallace."

What are the factual similarities and differences between the two grizzly bear fatalities involving the same female grizzly known as the "Wapiti Sow" and accompanied by her two young cubs?

In my opinion, while both the Wallace and Matayoshi grizzly bear fatalities held some common elements, factually they are quite different. Both tragedies took place in the Hayden Valley, both attacks were hiking-related and both trailhead locations displayed hiker information and warnings of potential danger of hiking in grizzly bear habitat. Neither location at the time of the hikes, had any official red signs posting "Warning BEAR Frequenting Area." Both fatalities involved middle-aged men, 59 years old. Both extremely rare hiker fatalities also demonstrate what I often describe as "the risks and dangers" while hiking in grizzly bear country. As with these two cases, whether you may be less than a mile from a busy trailhead, or miles away in the backcountry; grizzly bear attacks may occur. There are also other Yellowstone fatalities which exhibit that distance from a trailhead may be immaterial to the risk or danger of hiking in grizzly country. Among other issues, the most obvious opposing facts between the two encounters remain that Wallace was a seasoned hiker, outdoorsman, solo hiker in the Hayden backcountry, and a self-described, "grizzly bear expert" with previous hiking/camping in Yellowstone backcountry.

On the other hand; Matayoshi was hiking with a partner, and of much less experience. He wasn't hiking in the backcountry, but rather in a populated section of trails, about a mile and a quarter from the parking lot. The likely catalyst of the Wallace encounter was the close physical presence of two bison carcasses and a large number of bears in the area. A grizzly will aggressively defend a carcass. A hiker coming close to a carcass is one of the most dangerous situations a person can encounter. The catalyst for the Matayoshi encounter appears to simply be in the wrong place, at the wrong time. Undoubtedly, the encounter was greatly escalated by their running and screaming as the bears approached. Per autopsy findings, Wallace had many defensive wounds on his hands and arms, indicating he faced the bear or bears attacking him at some point. His body was consumed and scavenged by bears. Matayoshi also faced the bear and was killed in part by blunt trauma from the charging bear, however, there were no defensive wounds, nor was any part of the body consumed.

    I do not intend, nor is it my place, to judge the behavior of either situation. Based on my experience and opinion, I'm content to conclude that best practices for hiking in grizzly country were not followed in both cases. Lack thereof may have avoided or at least, minimized the severity/morbidity of both outcomes. However, I cannot minimize the most critical, priority number one factor relative to my observations of the missing "*the exception of one critically important item.*" According to my review of the entirety of the investigative reports, neither of the victims carried or had possession of bear spray. That is the crucial hiking item that may have saved the lives of one, or both individuals. Bear spray may have also minimized the morbidity of their physical injuries. I'm especially at a complete loss to understand why Mr. Wallace, an experienced hiker in grizzly country, and a self-described, "grizzly bear expert," failed to carry bear spray when he stepped foot on the Mary Mountain trailhead on Aug 25th and entered the grizzly bear inhabited backcountry of Yellowstone's Hayden Valley. I don't want to speculate on the reason(s) why bear spray was absent from his hiking items. Furthermore, it's unknown if he previously carried bear spray during other grizzly country hikes, or even if he knew how and when to properly use it. In the end, all that mattered was that bear spray wasn't present when he desperately needed it to help save his life. We know he faced his attacker in a futile attempt to fend it off was in vain. Verifying this act are the defensive wounds he suffered. Based on the thorough investigative reports, Wallace appeared very organized and paid attention to detail in his campsite and surroundings. It will never be known if he would have survived if he had bear spray on that fatal day. Statistically, data and research support that his odds with bear spray would be appreciably improved. At a minimum, the absence of bear spray resulted in a loss of opportunity, to employ defensive tactics in case of such an encounter.

As to Matayoshi, there was also an "*exception of one critically important item*" scenario. Neither he nor his wife carried bear spray. Here again, I don't want to speculate the reason(s) behind that decision. The same general trail warnings were present at their departing Wapiti trailhead in a northern section of the Hayden Valley. However, in this case I suggest that the use of bear spray had a much greater chance of neutralizing the oncoming grizzly as it first approached the couple on the trail. Once they turned and ran screaming down the trail, sparking the grizzly into full pursuit, the efficacy of bear spray may have been diminished to some extent and effective deployment reduced. Regrettably, the outcomes of both attacks if bear spray was available will never be known. The same holds true if either victim followed the last effort to bear attack defense by falling to the ground, covering up, and not fighting back the grizzly.

While certainly both incidents are tragic events; fatalities caused by bears in YNP are historically, exceedingly rare. According to the current 2023 Yellowstone National Park, NPS data: since Yellowstone's 1872 establishment, eight people were killed by bears in the park. The earliest fatality occurred in 1916 inside a roadside camp. Others involved hikers, a photographer, and campers, including a 1972 fatality happening in an illegally established camp. Put this in further perspective since 1979, Yellowstone accommodated over 118 million visits. However, the data supports the fact that while statistically rare, hiking in grizzly bear country is not without personal risk or exposure to possible harm or death.

In conclusion, as far as the Wapiti Sow and her two cubs of the year were involved in these two Hayden Valley hiker fatalities, occurring less than two months apart; evidence reveals that the Wapiti Sow killed Mr. Matayoshi and her two cubs were present during the attack. It remains unknown which bear or bears, actually attacked and killed Wallace as there were no witnesses, and many grizzlies were in the vicinity of the fatality site feeding on two nearby bison carcasses.

How do these two 2011 summer hiker fatalities by grizzly bears relate to the beginning of this chapter with the Grizzly and Wolf Discovery Center?

GWDC grizzly bear enclosure early signage on 5-22-2016.

The Wapiti Sow was euthanized by Bear Management authorities. Her two surviving cubs in essence, received a death sentence after their mother was euthanized. The remaining young cubs of the year (COY) had no chance of survival in the wild without their mother. They likely faced the same fate as their mother, until most fortunately, on September 30, 2011, the Grizzly and Wolf Discovery Center accepted them in to live among other young and older grizzlies that had some history of some prior troubled circumstances. After they arrived at the Center, the two cubs were named "Roosevelt and Grant." For eight years, the brothers romped around, wrestled, and chased trout together in the grizzly bear enclosure pool. During portions of those years together, I had the repeated pleasures of closely observing them and watching them grow into young adults. While observing these now 5-year-old former cubs playfully wrestle and chase, I was convinced, that it would be futile and only escalates the severity of an attack, for a human to try to fight off an attacking grizzly bear; rather than following expert advice of what to physically do, and what not to do if attacked. The bears' significant tactics and level of aggression, were only engaged in friendly competition. In a real-life hostile encounter, I could only imagine their overpowering aggression and devastating outcome with a human.

I was also present at the GWDC one year when the sanctuary was used for real-time "grizzly bear test" effectiveness of newly developed bear-resistant waste and dumpster containers provided by various manufacturers. The test waste containers were composed of various materials, sizes, latches, doors, hinges, etc. They ranged from coolers to large metal dumpsters and were placed in varied positions throughout the grizzly bear enclosure. Multiple bears were then released to the scent-attracted containers. I was amazed to watch the grizzlies quickly open and/or destroy some of the rugged-appearing test containers, while others proved to be much more resistive. Reverting to my observed view of the strength and power of "playful" grizzlies, I stood in amazement, as I witnessed a medium-sized grizzly's attraction to the largest, chained-down metal test dumpsters. At first, the bear cautiously circled the dumpster, his keen nose testing the source of the scent. After sensing the dumpster posed no immediate threat, he made multiple attempts to gain entry on all fours and standing. He was unable to do so. His frustration was visibly growing, as the dumpster's interior food-alluring scent evaded his hungry efforts to break in. His pacing increased, when suddenly he raised on his hind legs, and at the same time, with one powerful, lighting-fast swipe of his left front paw, overturned the extremely heavy dumpster sending it tumbling to rest. I recall my fears and amazement envisioning the disastrous impact if that same swipe was inflicted on a human. The quickness, power, and strength of just one swipe with those four-inch claws, would be disarming and overwhelming with massive or fatal injuries.

At a very early age in 2019, Roosevelt (the lighter blonde cub) passed away from an aggressive form of cancer. However, the GWDC advised that his brother Grant (darker colored cub) has adjusted and interacts well with other grizzly bears at the Center. Yet the reality of their initial and current thankful presence at the GWDC remains that both former one-year-old, 42 lb. cubs, whose mother was euthanized, according to the investigating wildlife agency's evidence and conclusions, both cubs were present at the Wallace and Matayoshi fatality sites in the Hayden Valley.

While that fact remains, I suggest that it's very important to keep in mind that at the time, both cubs were very young cubs of the year, likely less than six months old. Furthermore, instinctively and naturally, grizzly cubs remain extremely attached and protected by their mothers. They follow mom's every step of the way as they navigate and learn during their early months and short years through their mother's guidance. In my own experience, I've witnessed these grizzly bear mother with cubs behavioral traits many times. They are all vital means of teaching survival, instructive, behavioral and protection to her cubs. These lessons are paramount to the cubs in very short order. Nearly 50% of all cubs do not survive past their first year of life.

Roosevelt (L-lighter blond color) and Grant wrestle in GWDC trout pond.

      Each time I visited the Center and had the wonderful opportunity to closely observe them for hours in their new environment, I could not shake feeling sad about the circumstances and losses that brought them here from the wild. Yet, as a staunch grizzly bear preservationist, I celebrated their existence. When I hike around in the Hayden Valley to photograph grizzlies and other wildlife, I recount these fatalities and still experience sadness for the victims and their families. As I hike the valley's ground, traverse her rolling hills, cross the winding creeks, and look at the magnificent sky; I prayerfully pay my respects to them.

  Rare tragedies like these are always in the back of my mind whenever I venture into the backcountry. Various sounds, field conditions, forest density, and wind-blown meadows along the way, will inevitably test your psyche. In reality, I believe those are favorable stimulates to occur, as they may provoke momentary reflection to help focus your attention on your surroundings and reinforce safety and preparation for a potentially adverse situation that may arise. In my opinion, a reasonable balance between adventure and situational risk is a smart policy.

Chapter 6

My First Grizzly Bear Sighting

June 8, 2009, 4:39 pm.

A typical Nashville, TN long hot, humid summer in the south had passed since our return home from the Grand Tetons and our very short venture into Yellowstone. My growing interest in Yellowstone and grizzly bears had now developed into more than just curiosity and captivating sightseeing. I recall spending a lot of time reading about both the Park and wildlife. I just knew when time permitted, I needed to return to Yellowstone on my time and itinerary, to see places that I had only read about that summer. The seasons continued, as did my early growing interest and YNP self-education. I could not pass up any television program or nature production about Yellowstone and its wildlife. Also, as sort of a historian, I supplemented my early efforts with interesting historic and geological education. Even then, I was well aware that I had a long road ahead of me to absorb a fraction of what Yellowstone was all about. It was a starting point and that is all that mattered. I didn't have the faintest idea or thought of all the adventures, encounters, pleasures, and hardships awaiting me as I now formally embarked on my journey into grizzly country. After all, I have yet to have seen a grizzly bear in the wild. At the time, all that I felt was a growing impulse to become a living part of all things Yellowstone.

Soon after a cold TN winter, my thoughts and journey evolved into planning my first solo spring trip to Yellowstone. During the past months, I gathered very basic equipment, clothing, and materials I thought necessary for such a trip. I found the initial planning, gathering, and preparations to be fun and part of the journey itself. Please note that as a newcomer to Yellowstone, I didn't say all the forgoing activities and items were adequate. But then again, it was yet another first and that's all that mattered. Now as a navigator, I was prepared with a fancy Nat Geo topo detailed map. With its display, YNP just got quite larger again from the visitor map.

Since I had been in West Yellowstone on my first, oh so very brief, visit to Yellowstone, I decided to make that my destination. Hotel accommodations and airline and auto rental reservations for Bozeman, MT were secured.

Packing was completed as our two beloved Golden Retrievers; Goldie, and Sandy, circled sniffing my bags and flashing at me that guilt-ridden look again, "Where are you going now and when are you coming back?" I think our very best friends have an innate ability to sense when "something is up," before that something is present. They both succeeded, with their self-imposed guilt factor routine on me. It always worked.

God love them, as I had the same feelings of, "I'm sorry and I can't wait to get back to you." That's one thing through the years making my return trips from Yellowstone more acceptable. Homecomings were always so sweet and special. Forward many years to today, those exact feelings reside with my inseparable, "Daisy the Beagle."

      It was now June 2009. The Delta jet landed in Bozeman, baggage arrived, and the rental car was ready. After picking up some provisions, with the aid of my portable GPS, I was headed south en route to West Yellowstone. The sights were all new and exciting, especially the further south I drove. I was anxious to see West YST again, this time unrestricted, with much more time to visit this YNP's quaint border town. As I approached Big Sky, I was enamored with the growing new sightings of mountains, deep valleys, and awe-inspiring wide-open vistas.

      Once entering the YNP boundary I passed through the northwest portion of YNP and noticed some trailhead sites. Little did I know back then, that years later this area alone, both within YNP and adjoining Montana backcountry; would find me hiking extensively, photographing grizzlies as well as other adventures in the backcountry. But at this time, for the most part, I was nothing more than a new tourist excited to be in Yellowstone. Passing through the Hebgen Lakes area, I soon reached my destination. After unpacking at my destination, I could hardly wait to enter the West Entrance to the park. As the daylight slowly diminished and the temperature fell, I flashed my NPS Senior Pass and ID to the gate ranger. Like General MacArthur's return to the Philippines, I too fulfilled my ambition and objective, as, "I too shall return." This trip was the beginning of my journey with Yellowstone Grizzlies, but not quite yet.

For the next several days I drove around YNP taking in many of the fantastic obligatory tourist locations and being in awe of the landscapes. However, on my own, I saw very little wildlife, maybe a bison or two, at least as to my novice expectations, and certainly no bears whatsoever. In that regard, reality began to set in. I recall a sense of some disappointment bucking up against my newcomer's wildlife viewing expectations. Maybe it was just bad luck, or not being in the right spot at the right time? What was I doing wrong? However, at that time I didn't even know, what I didn't know. It also became very clear to me that it's nearly impossible to see or experience, to any reasonable degree, most of YNP or even one quadrant of YNP in days, or a bare minimum of a week or more.

Maybe the next day would bring me better luck with spotting wildlife. I also recall a YNP event by a coworker, that perhaps I was unrealistically using a measuring stick for my expectations. A year or so earlier, he and his wife drove to Yellowstone as first-time tourists. They had absolutely no experience, or information, nor for the most part; even knew where they were during a short two-day drive-through visit. Well, "right spot/right time/you never know" Yellowstone luck was with them. As they drove on one of the roads, twenty feet away a wolf pack brought down an elk right next to their car. Following that analogy, please don't make my rookie expectation mistake a source of self-frustration. I don't advise any visitor to use such an awesome sighting, or other incredible roadside wildlife viewing as a goal. Yes, such occasions happen, but they are minuscule in number compared to the annual tens of millions of viewing manhours. Simply enjoy the journey and await what might be ahead around the next curve.

Well, the next day came and I tried to employ the very same advice as above. I set out early in the morning with high hopes. Other than seeing some bison, and a few elk off in the far distance, I was again skunked seeing any other wildlife. The same doubts and questions were persistent as I headed back into West Yellowstone after an uneventful morning. At the top, I wanted to see a bear, especially a grizzly bear followed by other animals. Frustrated, I had to do something much different. Back at the hotel, I thumbed through some brochures advertising some local one-half-day wildlife tour guided van trips. What did I have to lose? I called and signed up for a tour starting in an hour. Climbing aboard the van I was greeted by our driver/guide and seven other new tourists. We all had the same interest, to see wildlife.

Settling in the back of the van as we departed into YNP through the same West Gate; I must admit I felt comfortable in not having to both drive and look for wildlife. I could listen to passenger commentary and share in some enthusiasm when we would see something. As we reached the Madison Campground intersection (still only saw a few bison) our guide turned north up toward Norris Junction. It was quite pleasurable seeing the mountains, meadows, and thermal features, but no new wildlife.

Reaching the Norris Geyser Junction, we continued north towards Mammoth Hot Springs. Passenger optimism waned a tad over the near-approaching two-hour trip. Our guide announced our turnaround destination in the evening was the Lamar Valley where "we might see a few bighorn rams." I recalled reading about or hearing of the Lamar Valley, but at the time, I lacked any informed information about it. During the tour, our old-timer guide would call out certain points of interest and offer a brief description. This was all new ground to me from my prior day's travels. We did not disembark the tour van for any of the features, but as a newcomer the announced information and locations were helpful. I could now relate to the territory we were covering to the positions on my outstretched Nat Geo map on my lap.

As tourists, we enjoyed group conversations and shared our first impressions of Yellowstone. We all came from different backgrounds and parts of the country, with varied levels of interest in Yellowstone. I was the only passenger to express that at some point in the future, I wanted to explore these mountains, valleys, and meadows to see just what is around the next corner and safely locate and photograph bears in the wild. Quite an ambitious proclamation from a guy that's never hiked anywhere within 1,400 miles of Yellowstone and has never yet seen a grizzly bear!

Our van continued north past several small lakes/springs to our left. Our driver announced traffic ahead was slowing down. Up to this point, we had not experienced any of the infamous long delays with Yellowstone "bison or bear jams." Is that what's up ahead? As we slowly advanced, I could see through the side window, indeed there were slowly moving vehicles, some stopped alongside the road. On my map and visually I could see that we were approximately near Roaring Mountain with steam vents bellowing out of the large hillside.

Rolling past a few people along the road, our driver exclaimed, "Folks I think we have a bear jam going on." For the passengers, it was a full Red Alert! Cameras were prepared for the ready as we all waited our turn to bail out. We were like paratroopers over Germany. Stepping off the roadside opposite Roaring Mountain, the first response was, "What bear?" Finally, after minutes of looking in vain at a distant hillside, one hawk-eyed tourist yelled out, "There it is, it's a grizzly!" My adrenalin ramped up as I asked for a reference to focus on in the deadfall lacing the hillside. With the aid of my binoculars, I located the grizzly. It was simply a dark spot in the timber with its rump facing us. Despite the bear's distant position, I celebrated as I finally arrived. My first Yellowstone grizzly bear!

June 8, 2009, 4:39 pm/My First Grizzly Bear near Roaring Mtn.

      Unfortunately, the grizzly never gave us a better view. Yes, it was technically a roadside far-off grizzly sighting, but it was like adding jet fuel to my prior days of dampened spirits searching in vain without seeing anything but a few bison and elk. And now I was being rewarded with none other than a grizzly for switching my search tactics. The driver was now our old-timer "Wild Kingdom" hero. The bear never turned sideways or toward us. All we got was that rump shot, but importantly it was my rump shot! With the bear lumbering off into the forest, the bear jam thinned out as quickly as it probably started.

We piled back into our tour van abuzz with what we just saw. Our spirits soared as we departed northward into YNP with renewed hopes of seeing additional encounters. Our driver/guide was grinning ear to ear with our cheers of success. We continued to Mammoth and then east to the Yellowstone Picnic pull out where we did see several bighorns bedded down in the dusk and now rain. The cold rain was now mixing with snow as we departed back to West Yellowstone. Our guide turned left at the Tower Junction as we began our climb up Dunraven Pass. The light snow had now turned heavy, as darkness was spreading over the mountains making the turns seemed a little dicey, with steep mountain drop-offs on either side. The snow abated as we cleared Dunraven Pass. It was a relief to later return to West Yst. and recount the entire day. I was emboldened by the trip and thrilled to see my first grizzly. But yet, I had another first to accomplish during my first solo trip to Yellowstone.

Chapter 7

First Yellowstone Hike-Solfatara Trail

The next day June 9th, emboldened by seeing my first grizzly bear the afternoon before with the tour van, I set out driving again with my Nat Geo map on a combined trip to discover wildlife, geothermal features, and other attractions within the park. Well, the solo wildlife viewing once again did not pan out very well, however, I was in wonder about the other new tourist attractions. Furthermore, I was beginning to better sense and experience Yellowstone's "time and distance" traveling factors, influenced by weather, traffic, and wildlife jam issues. It was a good learning curve for future incursions into the park. I did not explore or travel outside YNP boundaries except for the Bozeman travels. For me, the park itself remained mostly undriven. As a first-timer, I sure didn't need to absorb any more surrounding wilderness. Yet, those very same surrounding wilderness areas would later become a vital part of my journey with Yellowstone Grizzlies. That night I nervously spent considerable time reading about hiking trails and NPS warnings about hiking in grizzly bear country. I knew that I had yet another important "first" to accomplish on this inaugural solo visit. I was determined to take my first solo hike on a Yellowstone trail.

Slugging down coffee, the next morning, I peered outside my hotel room with my hiking book and map spread out on the table. The day dawned clear and rather chilly. Let's put it this way, it wasn't like an early June morning in Nashville, however, it was vigorously refreshingly, a perfect morning for my first hike in Yellowstone. Consulting my map, I decided to make the Grizzly Lake trail my destination. The trail name was perfect. After all, this wasn't a very difficult decision to make. I had just seen my first grizzly bear the other day and the Grizzly Lake trail was about one mile north of Roaring Mountain. Seemed like a logical selection.

It was now 6:30 am, and I somewhat nervously placed my primitive hiking gear and backpack into the trunk of my rental car. Finishing a quick inventory of my hiking and sightseeing materials, I nearly spilled my coffee in the cupholder. Soon I was headed out of West Yellowstone into the park. All sorts of thoughts, excitement, and fears accompanied me as I reached the Madison Campground Junction and turned north towards Norris Geyser Basin. Continuing north I passed Roaring Mountain. Several miles ahead the Grizzly Lake Trailhead awaited my arrival. Looking at the mountains still capped with snow and the forests in between, my excitement and yes, apprehension took on a new level. Am I really doing this and, am I ready for this? Seeing the Grizzly Lake trailhead sign-off to my left, my doubts subsided. Let's do this!

Pulling off the side of the road, I saw an unexpected sign at the trailhead. No other vehicles were in the vicinity as the morning clouds were thickening. The sign read, "Trail Closed Bear Frequenting Area." My excitement lessened as my apprehensions took over. After all, I was a first-time rookie heading alone into an unknown area and environment. Fighting off my apprehension, but fully complying with the trail closure, I decided to get in the car and continue to the very next trailhead, whatever and wherever it was.

Heading further north, in short order I came upon the next trailhead sign to my right. It read, "Solfatara Trailhead." I parked in a very small vacant pullout near the trailhead. Spreading my map out on the trunk of the car, I could readily see this trail appeared significantly longer than the closed Grizzly Lake trail. Facing south, the map revealed some small geothermal areas, a small Lake of the Woods, and Solfatara Creek further south as it made its way south to Norris Campground.

My First Yellowstone Hike-Solfatara Trail.

Even with the bear closure notice, for some reason, I was disappointed that I wasn't going to embark on the Grizzly Lake trail. Maybe it was perception or fixation on my part, for my first rookie hike into Yellowstone. Nonetheless, as a few snowflakes floated down, I was here now and it was time to head into the forest and explore.

Geared up, I headed up on the trail finding myself embedded in a forest stamped with patches of lingering winter snowfall with no sight or sound of any human activity. I remember it as a liberating feeling that I made it this far. At this point as far as hiking was concerned, I wasn't looking for grizzly bears. I had absolutely no experience or ideas of how, where, or what to do. Of course, I carried bear spray just in case, and even then, had never deployed it or knew the proper way to disperse it.

View from Solfatara Trail north to distant Gallatin Mountain Range.

I guess more than anything else, I was just getting my first taste of exploring the Rocky Mountains. Looking back, I have to chuckle at myself, envisioning that I was part of the Lewis & Clarke Expedition. The wilderness setting must have awakened the 1950s kid still in me. The scenery was incredible, every new trail curve or hill brought new expectations, and my confidence was increasing.

Cresting a high hill, to the northwest I could see a distant part of the Gallatin Mountain Range. Little did I know at the time that years later, I would be spending a great deal of time hiking, exploring, and photographing grizzly bears and other wildlife in those majestic mountains.

Mother Nature had a surprise for me on my inaugural Yellowstone hike. An hour or so after leaving the trailhead, those few previous scattered snowflakes were now falling heavier.

I wasn't prepared to be out in the snow for any length of time. However, captivated by hiking this Yellowstone trail, I continued. After a while of climbing, brushing several inches of snow off a log, I sat down to rest and scan a small draw below me. There in the snow, I saw my first animal while hiking. It was a large coyote working a small acidic creek. Of course, at first, I thought it was a wolf. It didn't matter whether it was a coyote or wolf. I just succeeded with another first event in my long quest of spotting grizzlies. Besides, in later years both coyotes and wolves were often spotted taking down prey or scavenging during my grizzly bear quests. It also dawned on me for the first time, who is to say that the grizzly bear, or bears from the Grizzly Lake trailhead closure, might now roam over here just a few miles away? At that point of my fledging growth and lack of experience, an encounter with any bear would not be a good thing.

Shortly after spotting the coyote, snow was falling hard and getting deeper. Again, foolishly I wasn't equipped for such snow. I pulled lightweight rain gear over my clothing. Temps were falling and the snow was getting deeper. It was time for me to get back to the trailhead. I had a decent sense of direction of where I was, but the now heavy snowfall was making the identity of trail features more difficult and had completely covered up my tracks. I didn't panic, but alone, I was growing concerned. The footing, especially downhill had become difficult. With the aid of my walking pole, I traversed the now slippery hillsides. I was further aided with my portable Garmin to secure my egress path, now buried a foot or more under the snow. By the time I arrived back at the Solfatara trailhead, nearly two feet of snow had fallen. Bundled up I walked across the road to check traveling conditions. My concerns now switched from warming up to driving conditions. There I encountered a close-up sight that I had only seen on Nat Geo type of programs. A single very large male bison was standing in the now deeply buried forage, swinging his massive head back and forth like an excavator and grunting, trying to reach down to the ground level to graze on the grass or early sedges. Well, maybe the bison wasn't surprised by this sudden deep spring snowfall, but I sure was.

        As a then-novice Yellowstone hiker, very valuable lessons were learned that day for many future spring and fall trips. Eventually, I made it back to West Yellowstone as afternoon temps started to rise and road conditions improved. There I critiqued what I did wrong, what I did "sort of right" and the proper equipment needed for backcountry hiking and taking near-instant photography opportunities. I knew that I had a long way to go, but now more than ever, I was determined to learn and continue my journey with Yellowstone Grizzlies. Even today, I also wonder what would have happened if I were able to hike my first choice, the Grizzly Lake trail. Perhaps that question doesn't need to be answered, as even today, that trail is one of few Yellowstone trails I have not traveled. I simply have no explanation for that.

        The next several days I spent further exploring YNP and acquainting myself with different park sectors, along with visiting in astonishment, several must-see geothermal areas and geyser basins. Walking the boardwalks of Old Faithful on a very cool overcast late afternoon, I stopped to read the sign below Grand Geyser which rests in very close proximity at the foot of the geyser itself. The sun was soon fading, when I decided to head back to West Yst. Just then I heard and saw a gurgling, low spurting of water around the geyser cone. In short order, the pool began to fill as I watched in wonder. In a minute or so, Grand Geyser fully erupted, cascading twin cones of water very high in the sky and surrounding hillside. Pulling my raincoat hood tightly, I was treated all alone with a prolonged geyser eruption enveloping me and the boardwalk with sheets of mineral-laced water falling high from the grey and dimming skies. Grand Geyser is the tallest geyser in the world with eruptions over 300 ft, surpassing that of Old Faithful.

I marveled at the majestic Yellowstone Inn and the storied history behind it. In the Canyon area, I hiked to Cascade Lake with a very light pack, then huffed and puffed my way up the awesome views from Observation Peak. For areas I was able to visit, I relished the enormity, beauty, and variance of YNP. These non-wildlife days were wonderful and most enjoyable. My spirits were certainly renewed as I immersed myself more into the Yellowstone Eco System and was feeling a developing sense of belonging. I capped off my last day of the trip by spending many hours at the Grizzly Wolf Discovery Center observing and recording grizzly bear behavior and interactions. This first solo trip introduced me to so much; including realizing my limitations and need for much more study, experience, and exploration. Several accomplished "firsts" set my path in the right direction for my ultimate objective...locating and photographing grizzlies in the wild. My longing to know what rests around that next curve, over the next hill or mountain pass/drainage was now in full gear. I immediately knew this was a venture that I needed to do wholly on my part. I was firmly determined to establish an informed relationship with the awe-inspiring land and the great grizzly bear surviving in this last vestige of true wilderness.

I later returned to Yellowstone in late September for a follow-up fall visit. I hiked several new trails and while I did not see any grizzlies, I now discovered grizzly bear tracks, scat, and bear hair embedded in the weeping sap from fresh bear tree scrapping. Taking a small victory from these findings by executing previous map study, grizzly seasonal habitat, and other readings, I was now inching forward to piece together relevant information for locating Yellowstone grizzlies. Along the way I was now spotting in the wild, other large animals i.e., elk, bison, moose, etc. As the mid-October Yellowstone snows began to fall, I was back in Nashville and already looking forward to my next spring trip with rising hopes that my current progress, coupled with another eight/nine months of research and study would pay dividends with my grizzly bear quest. Despite my minor advancements, I could not envision in my wildest dreams, what would happen to me in Yellowstone the next spring.

PART II: The Productive Years 2010 to 2023 (present)

Chapter 1

Planning and Preparing the Trip

2010 was just around the corner and I was determined more than ever to proceed with my journey. The past year had been one of initial growth, but also frustrating in the sense that I was far from realizing my goals and desire to photographically capture grizzlies in the wild. I knew for certain this would be a multi-year process heavily dependent on continuing self-education, field experience, and a healthy dose of plain old-fashioned good luck. My hopes were high for next year, but then again, hope is not a strategy.

At home, I continued to add to my library every book, video, and periodical associated with Yellowstone and grizzly bears. Increasing the collection of detailed topo terrain maps of Yellowstone and bordering national and state forests, my familiarity continued to grow. Spending endless hours of detailed map study, I acquainted myself with numerous new promising areas, both on and off trails, which appeared to be favorable grizzly bear habitats. Ruling out certain seasonal unproductive areas is as important as identifying favorable locales. For example, finding on a map a lower elevation feeder creek with adjacent small meadows bordered by forest tree lines where in spring with the bears out of hibernation, grizzlies are creating unmistakable rotor tiller like "grizzly digs" feeding on early vegetation and ground squirrels, voles, etc. Or productive open areas of greening sage brush searching out, nose to the ground, newborn elk calves hiding motionless in the sage. Yet another example of thorough map study is locating once-frozen ponds or small lakes where bison or other ungulates may have crashed through the ice leaving a highly prized ice-covered carcass loaded with early protein for famished grizzlies just out of hibernation. Yellowstone NP in its own right, is an enormous place with over 3,468 square miles and 2.219M acres of mountains, rivers, plains, and forest. It is reported four-fifths of the park is forested land. In my opinion, any advantage you may secure by pre-planning is worth the effort. Studying the topo map elevation lines will immensely help your tentative backcountry hiking plans into select areas you wish to concentrate. Reading various grizzly bear and expert books along with watching videos, I was able to correlate positions, names, and seasonal locations. All of which, might be favorable allowing me to identify and locate in the field.

The months continued to pass toward spring as I invested heavily in Yellowstone self-study, education, trip reports from the field, and purchase of higher quality equipment and durable clothing for weather extremes which were all but certain during spring in Yellowstone. I didn't need a reminder of my first solo hike last spring on the Solfatara Trail hike. The trail was clear and later buried in 2 feet of snow. I learned that lesson quite well ever since.

My research and personal experience convinced me that mid-late May and early June, on average were the prime times to locate bears in Yellowstone. Many years later with extraordinary sightings, I still maintain that exact position. The weather may still be dicey, and intermittent snows are a given, but travel is usually unaffected. Earlier, in late March or early April, the big males are first to come out from hibernation, followed by the females, many of which would be accompanied by their new (COY) cubs of the year. Normally two cubs born in the den would get their first look at the world from the darkness of the den and mom's dominating protection. Depending upon the weather, mid-late May in Yellowstone was also a reliable period for the emergence of post-hibernation food sources i.e., early vegetation, tubers, sedges, and plentiful ground gophers, voles, etc. Also, to be found would be frozen trout around the perimeter of lakes and winter-killed bison and elk carcasses. Soon thereafter, bison would be dropping their newborn calves aka "little reds" followed by elk dropping their highly prized newborns in expansive sagebrush areas. In short, this period would signal an approaching time of plenty for bears and other wildlife after surviving a long arduous Yellowstone winter. It's estimated by the experts, that inland grizzly bears annual diet is comprised of 90% organic vegetation, insects, etc., and only 10% protein from meat. This fact alone helps explain the grizzly's massive shoulder hump, comprised of muscle from constant digging organic sources aided with their long straight claws serving as shovels. Through the ensuing years, I have witnessed many grizzlies tearing up large sections of ground aka "grizzly digs" in pursuit of nutritious bulbs and tubers, along with spending extraordinary efforts to track and dig up a meager mouth full of pocket gophers. Watching them work the ground for extended periods before catching a morsel, I had to wonder why such a large animal expends so much energy and calories for so little in return. Perhaps, the answer simply resides in the fact they are incredibly hungry and determined to find and devour what's before them.

     Spring is a great time to witness grizzly bears transitioning from surviving on the fat/caloric reserves that have sustained them for months in hibernation as the frigid Rocky Mountain winds and snow endlessly swirl above their dens. Watching them search for the source of an underground ultrasonic sound and then pouncing on the location and start digging and shoveling up the ground to get a fist-sized food reward, is very entertaining. I have viewed them determinately, with a quarter of their body immersed head down in the dig to capture their target. It's especially rewarding and amusing to see a newborn cub mimic Mom's teaching moment by warily peering down the excavation to see what this is all about.

Grizzly heads down in the ground searching for a pocket gopher.

Success! 12 minutes of labor for a meager return on investment.

Into late January or early February, I completed my May flight and lodging reservations early as they are usually the most economical, and availability is better. I don't enjoy packing the least bit, but I do find planning for upcoming trips, including necessary reservations a fun part of the trip. All the months spent scouring over maps, absorbing useful and critical safety information, regulations, and books revealing adventures and encounters with grizzlies, were well spent in final preparation for my upcoming spring trip. My confidence was increased that I would have a successful solo venture finding the bears as I planned to explore new promising regions of Yellowstone.

No sense in worrying about long-term weather forecasts. Most of the time, it's simply the luck of the draw the week(s) that may afford a better outlook. In my opinion, it's best to take the calendar window of opportunity for locating bears, rather than rely on a weather forecast that may or may not pan out. I've learned it's like the stock market; you can't reliably time when to get in or get out. Still, it is very wise to adjust your short preparation with a comparison of local and national short and long-term weather forecasts. However, in the mountains expect wide swings of weather possibilities, especially during spring.

      I started packing a couple of weeks before my departure. And then started repacking several times as I bounced between over-packing and under-packing. The adage "every ounce matter" really means what it said, particularly when headed into the backcountry. Furthermore, I face several handicaps resulting from two back surgeries including a failed two-level spinal fusion. Even today, I go through flip-flop decisions, "Do I really need to carry this item, or should I better pack this along." In the end, the final decisions are based on compromise and experience. However, every year I still struggle with packing and finding that elusive sweet spot between necessity and excess. Try as I may, over-packing seems to always win out.

Chapter 2

The Quad Mom

Arriving at Bozeman everything was going well. My baggage arrived, the rental car was secured and soon after purchasing bear spray, I was heading down to Yellowstone. Sunny but cold weather greeted me as I entered Hebgen Lakes northwest of West Yellowstone. I was optimistic that on this trip, I would advance and turn a corner in my growth to locate grizzly bears. That would be a major leap from the past couple of years of my development. I could not imagine at the time, what heart-throbbing encounter this trip had in store for me.

After several days of exploring, my advanced studies paid off handsomely. I located and photographed a grizzly bear scavenging the scattered bison bones on the edge of a prior frozen pond. Unlike my prior trips, traveling to different areas of the YNP I saw plentiful wildlife on the move; bison herds with their "little reds" elk, moose, coyotes, and more.

Things were about to get even much better. One day I was traveling to hike a new search area from the Mammoth Hot Springs area south. Several vehicles were parked alongside the road, with a few people glassing something in the distance. I pulled over and learned they had spotted a grizzly with cubs deep down a hillside at the edge of the woods. I grabbed my binoculars and identified it was a sow with three young cubs visible. Standing close by to me were two men. From their conversation, I could tell they were both highly experienced and knowledgeable grizzly bear enthusiasts or experts. From one of my library books, one gentleman appeared to be somewhat familiar. He was shorter and less stocky than his accomplice. More distinctly, he had an eyepatch covering one eye, and his face was visibly scarred. I couldn't help but hear the excited tone in their voices as they expressed words to the effect, "We finally located her, the Quad Mom...this is fantastic." Just then, the sow and her cubs left the tiny meadow below and headed south into the timber. "Come on, let's try to see where they might come out," they exclaimed. They both started walking very fast to a trot, south down the road with the bears hopefully below them still hidden in the dense woods. Out of reaction, I too started a fast walk considerably behind them. After a quarter mile or so, I began to wonder if I should break off as the unseen bears could be anywhere by now. I had gone this far, so continue on, as their stated plan was to locate a position on the road where the grizzlies might come out and cross.

Sure enough, as the two guys ahead of me came to a halt about fifty yards from a curve, the sow emerged from the timber with three (as I saw them) cubs in tow. She led them safely across the road and into a large formation of giant boulders on the other side of the road, which I later learned was named the "hoodoos." It was a remarkable thrilling sight to both my eyes and the camera lens. Across the road, the two men were ecstatically high-fiving each other and remarks i.e., "We got great pics of her, mission accomplished." There were only the three of us at the crossing. I too was excited and exhausted, as I now had several photos of the famous sow grizzly, the "Quad Mom." I also felt the pursuit of a possible crossing wasn't crowding or harassing the bears in any way. They were concealed far below in the timber before emerging very quickly to climb and cross the road. Within ten to fifteen seconds, they were totally out of sight. I only saw them beyond the hundred-yard mark and before that, several hundred feet far below in the tiny meadow. Above all, my intentions are always to respect all wildlife safely.

But just who were the two men that I followed on their crossing pursuit? This wasn't something in my very early years that I would not have done on my own, or even given a second thought. My only regret is that I never approached them or introduced myself. Events were happening quickly and I didn't want to interfere.

I go back to my library of grizzly bear and Yellowstone books which now nearly fills a bookcase. In my library is a book that I have read many times over, entitled: *BLINSIDED Surviving a Grizzly Attack and Still Loving the Great Bear*. Authored by Jim Cole with Tim Vandehey, ST. Martin's Press, New York. The book is about Jim Cole's amazing story of survival and perseverance after a severe mauling by a grizzly and cub while hiking in the Hayden Valley. I too, hike this area and I'm always aware of the many grizzly bear encounters, some tragic, that occur here. I cannot say with any knowledge or certainty whatsoever, that Jim Cole himself was there with the Quad Mom. The only direct familiarities toward such possibility were his voice, eye patch, and visible facial scarring, along with his expressed knowledge of grizzlies and his excitement of now finding the Quad Mom. I mention his voice as it sounded nearly identical to song recordings and interviews, he had given. I may have missed an opportunity to meet him in person if indeed that was Mr. Cole. If not, nonetheless I pay my great respects to him as a staunch grizzly bear advocate and adventurer that survived twice being mauled. Sadly, Mr. Cole passed away at the age of 60, on July 30, 2010, from natural causes, unrelated to the Hayden Valley severe mauling from a female with a cub.

Chapter 3

Three Feet Face to Face with a Grizzly

May 24, 2010

The past several days of this trip were splendid and so far, greatly surpassed my expectations. Beyond the grizzly bear sightings, excellent wildlife viewing occurred just about where ever I ventured. Most of the park and the sectors I had traveled to were both new and productive. On top of that, the scenery itself was nothing short of superb.

Yet, ahead of me, I had years' worth of exploring new areas in pursuit of my quest. I had earlier decided to restrict my ventures to three of four quadrants inside Yellowstone and the park's surrounding wilderness. The quadrants included the northwest, northeast, and southeast. I omitted the southwest as I viewed that area as more of a geyser basin with heavy tourist traffic, even though bears inhabit it. The areas I would devote my searches to are enormous in size with complex terrain that would be impossible for me to even try to venture into. I believe it would take over a full lifespan to minimally scratch the surface of new discoveries. With that reality, I planned to hone my travels and exploration to what I believed would be the best seasonal locales and opportunities for finding grizzlies. My plan would grow and adjust as I gained more experience and knowledge from field ventures and continued self-education.

On the morning of May 24th, I decided to explore and hike new ground, out east past Yellowstone Lake toward the East Entrance Road. I was under the impression it held a more limited number of trails within the park itself, combined with the bear-rich diversity and more heavily forested habitat would be a productive, if not challenging area.

Reaching Fishing Bridge, I turned east skirting around the north shore of still mostly frozen Yellowstone Lake. It appeared that year, winter's cold air still held a grip on mid-southern Yellowstone. The mountain tops were still buried in deep snows and the descending valleys and drainages were slow to green. A stout southwest wind blew cold air across the lake as I fully zippered up my jacket and put on warmer gloves. Still new to Yellowstone, I wondered if it was like this every spring. After all, June was just a week away.

What unthinkably happened next would dangerously test my newfound grizzly photography hiking to the core!

Passing Cub Creek, I decided to get out and start hiking the rolling hills and forest dotting the landscape, with 9,000 ft mountains dominating the scene. After hiking east off trail for several miles I felt a pressure-like feeling over my left shoulder. I spotted a grizzly bear paralleling my path about several hundred ft above me, and to my left as I neared a small pullout area. I immediately stopped as the grizzly continued his path forward. I was aware there was a nearby pond still frozen over, with early vegetation emerging around the banks. Good available early season bear food. I had a hunch perhaps he was heading for that pond. A photographic sequence of events follows.

The above first photo is the grizzly above my trail, passing above me.

I maintained my composure and relied upon the retention of expert information on what to do, and more importantly what *not to* do, if encountering a bear. My response seemed to work as the grizzly continued ahead of me. I felt that he would eventually drop down, cross my path, and then further descend several hundred feet to the pond. Well, I was correct on two of the three anticipated movements.

Looking ahead, the grizzly bear turned right and descended the hillside well ahead of me and down toward my path. I was relatively certain that once he reached my path, he would continue straight down, cross a ridge line and then go downhill toward a ponded area. I was in for a big surprise. The grizzly was in control of this developing big problem, not me.

Grizzly looking down before coming down to my path.

However, instead of crossing my path and dropping down a small ridge to the pond, he made an abrupt right turn and was now headed directly toward me. He did not charge but kept a steady unbroken gait locked on me. My level of response was escalated and my nerves were now really being tested. As I very slowly backed up, I drew my bear spray off my shoulder harness with the safety cap removed, ready to deploy if needed. I had earlier positioned my spotting scope on a tripod on the very path the grizzly was moving. He kept approaching and I saw his body brush up against and wobble the spotting scope. Still locked on me, it was clear he wasn't stopping. The distance between us shortened considerably. Every fiber in my body is now screaming for me to run, get away fast as I can. Which is exactly what you should never attempt to do. Any quick movement or running is likely to trigger the bear's predatory nature and view you as prey.

I can't explain it, but something calming just automatically clicked in with me. Perhaps my feeling of calmness internally arose from all my prior research and self-education. I knew I was in potentially deep trouble. I recall thinking, "Don't screw this up and concentrate on the things *not to* do."

In less than a half minute, the grizzly had now advanced, still maintaining his steady unbroken gait, within twenty-five feet from me.

Grizzly at 25 ft. quickly closing in.

Instantly I started panning my surroundings, looking for anything to put something between me and the approaching grizzly. There was no time, or suitable tree to try climbing. Glancing behind me and to my peripheral left, my eye caught a brief flash of blue.

Instantly retreating to the yet unidentified object, I now saw it was an old long-bed pickup truck on a slight angle. With no time to spare, I quickly advanced to the driver's side of the pickup bed. In a sparse matter of seconds, the grizzly reached the passenger side of the pickup bed and raised on his hind legs. We were now facing each other, eye to eye, across the truck bed around six feet apart!

I was in disbelief at how the series of events at this point, led to this dangerous unnerving predicament. While trying to concentrate on just what to do next, I recall thinking some crazy thoughts like, "If this bear doesn't kill me, my wife will, for getting myself into such a situation." Quickly dismissing that fleeting thought, I broke off eye contact as I recalled direct eye contact may be processed by a bear as a challenge and promote an outright charge. Moments later, I turned my eyes again toward the bear. He was no longer across the truck bed. I distinctly recall thinking, "Oh my God, where is he....is he going around the front of the truck, the rear, or had broken off?

With this development, my anxiety was now at the highest level of the encounter and the instinctive human reaction to "run" again flashed in my subconscious. Promptly rejecting that feeling for the second time, I had to find just where the bear was now. Do I remain or move? I wasn't satisfied just holding my position under the existing circumstances.

Waiting about six seconds, bear spray at full ready in my right hand, I ever so slowly, moved with my body against the truck bed toward the raised tailgate. Looking behind me towards the front, I didn't see the bear. As best I can recall at the time, I was thinking (hoping) he had broken away. Cautiously with apprehension, inching my way, I was nearing the rear of the old blue truck. With one last fast glance to the front,

I was sort of hunched over to my left on the tail bed as I reached the raised tailgate.

Looking down and to my left, the least favorable scenario was already in full motion. The grizzly had already moved across the tailgate with his body tightly up against the raised tailgate with his head very low to the ground. As I peered down to my left, we both immediately froze a couple of feet apart.

I did not deploy my outreached bear spray. Strongly feeling I needed to do so, I decided against it at that time. We were only mere feet apart, he had not charged, and above all else, I felt very strongly at this ridiculously close distance, discharging the loud bear spray 45-degree cone blast of a red-orange pressurized hell in a can, would immediately result in the grizzly taking a single lunge ripping into me.

Whether a right or wrong decision, it was my split-second decision made at a time of duress, for both me and the bear. Looking back to this timeline of now a fully developed intense grizzly bear encounter, I had to process and act upon several situational challenges since this escalating encounter began. I could not afford to make any mistakes in hopes for a good outcome for both myself and the bear. The moment of truth was staring at me three feet away. If I had reached out, my hand would have touched the grizzly on his nose.

Actual photo of the grizzly standoff three feet away. We both froze, eye to eye.

In the above photo, I didn't even realize I had taken a picture. Things were moving quite fast. Without knowing it for some time later, I must have pushed the shoot button, as we faced off for the first time. The only thing I recall at this decisive time was not wanting to drop the camera in close range for fear the bear would react and charge to the sudden movement and noise of falling to the ground.

Within seconds of our face-off, some of my research studies spontaneously just kicked in. While still eye to eye, I started to very calmly talk to the bear. I understood if done properly and calmly, this may help diffuse a close encounter. I remember making phrases like, "It's all right Mr. Grizzly, it's going to be all ok, etc." For about twenty seconds he listened without any reaction. He continued to stare at me with beady brown penetrating eyes. Suddenly, he exhaled all his air with a frightening visceral "humpff" and started to shake his head from side to side. The grizzly was done listening and I was done talking. He remained low and hidden by the corner of the truck as I moved back toward the front of the truck while facing the rear. I then firmly decided, if he came tearing around that corner at me, I would deploy the bear spray and drop to the ground, assuming the attack position, and hope for the best. As I continued to slowly back up with my left hand on the side panel, the bear had not broken around the corner, once again, was he now moving to the front, under the truck, or broken off somewhere? I didn't know, but now my focus was trying to get inside the truck. Inching backward, with my left hand on the truck, and my right hand with my bear spray, I felt the driver-side door handle. A fleeting moment of salvation now filled my spirits. As I pulled the door handle……it was locked! My spirits fell as quickly as they had arisen. I had no idea where the grizzly was now. Not knowing where he was at this time was extremely stressful and my heartbeat was once again pounding. Apprehensively I moved back to the center of the truck bed. There were still sizeable patches of snow on the ground. Peering over the other side, I saw fresh grizzly tracks leading away towards a ridge. I now had the first sense of relief since this encounter started. I maintained my position and defused my nerves, for fifteen or so minutes.

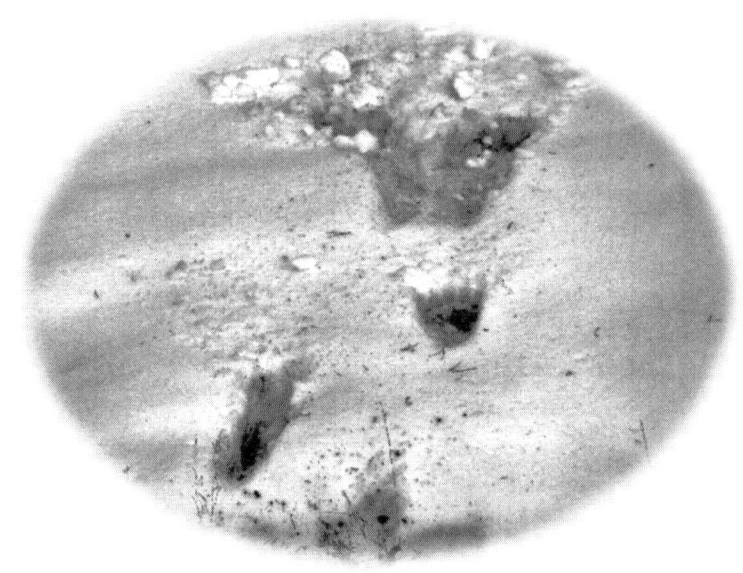

New Grizzly tracks heading away. Time to relax?

With my adrenaline still on overdrive, reliving what happened, whether right or wrong, I strongly felt the things I had studied and acted upon, helped me avoid a very uncertain or perhaps, tragic outcome. However, this eye-to-eye encounter wasn't over. A second stage would soon develop.

Convinced the grizzly indeed had broken off with fresh tracks leading to a ridge, the frozen pond was below. This was the exact location I first believed he was heading until he turned on me. Checking my gear, with my bear spray remaining at the ready, I ever so slowly followed his tracks as they disappeared at the ridge line.

Peering down the hillside to the pond, my hunch was correct. Far below, the grizzly had his back to me as he clawed up tubers and emerging plants. I maintained my position high on the ridge. Without a doubt, he knew I was up above on the ridge as at one point, he very briefly glanced up at me. At this point and for quite a while, he paid absolutely no attention to me, nor anything else as he contently fed. Everything appeared well under control, as I proceeded to observe him at a safe distance of over a hundred yards from the ridgeline.

After ten minutes or so, something triggered an abrupt change in his demeanor. I don't know what it was, but he raised his head from foraging and appeared to be looking (or smelling) something towards a distant tree line. In a split second, he spun around on his hindquarters and did a pirouette in my direction.

Grizzly at the pond, spins around at me on the ridgeline.

This really can't be happening again! My first thought was perhaps the correct one. Unlike the first eye-to-eye encounter, where the grizzly sought me out, perhaps I had pushed the envelope following his breakoff tracks to see where he was headed. On the other hand, my curiosity, still in an early learning stage along with the outcome of the first encounter, dictated my pursuit of photographing Yellowstone grizzlies. It would be hard to walk away from a now-second golden opportunity to do just that.

Again, right or wrong, or perhaps somewhere in between, I faced another uncertain close encounter. Except, this time it appeared the grizzly meant business. The hillside up to the ridge was a steep fifty-degree slope. The slope itself was strewn with boulders, logs, and deadfall. With dirt and rocks flying, the bear was now in a full charge upslope straight at me. Looking down at the charging grizzly I could easily see his raised silver tips. His speed going up this steep slope was incredible; I thought he had no intention of stopping

The second close encounter. Looking down from the ridge, grizzly charging me upslope.

This time, I was forced to quickly retreat backward on the ridge, out of his sight, as he raced uphill. I made it back only twenty feet from the ridge, standing my position, bear spray armed with clear intentions to deploy it this time and if necessary, hit the ground assuming the proper cover-up position and hope for the best. Looking back, I subconsciously realized, when my mettle was put to the acid test; I was a "Stayer," not a "Runner" well, at least for this first challenge.

Perhaps that was my most important untested behavioral reaction when faced off with a grizzly bear. I held my ground. Even though internally, every fiber in my body, cried out, "Run, run, get out of here fast." Within a matter of seconds, I saw him crest the top of the ridge. With this view, he appeared enormous, even though I would describe him as a medium-sized, robust adult. He continued his advance as I was about to discharge my bear spray.

Suddenly, stiffening his front legs, he slid to a quick stop. I believe it was a bluff charge. I'm glad I deferred to hit him with the bear spray as he was now stationary. No telling how he might initially react to the canister blast. However, without a doubt, I would use it if he took one step closer or acted aggressively. So unbelievably, here we are again in a second faceoff after a charge with around 25-30 feet between us. Adrenaline still racing from the initial charge, I contemplated my next move. This time, I would not "talk to him" as I had previously done. Deciding to simply await his next move, I remained poised, doing my best to conceal my nerves and fear, to hopefully avoid an escalation. Facing each other again, now at twenty-some feet, instead of three feet, I think we both awaited the other's next move.

Following nearly a minute of the second eye-to-eye encounter, the bear once again shook his head from side to side and then turned broadside to me. At first, he lumbered away slowly, then broke into a fast run. In mere seconds he reached another steep forested hillside and disappeared into the snowy timber. These twice eye-to-eye encounters and a bluff charge were now over. In total, I estimate the entire ordeal lasted about 40 minutes or so.

Needless to say, I was exhausted and ever so lucky, that neither the grizzly nor I suffered any physical injury or worse. This was a day that I'll never forget and often relive. I firmly believe that had it not been for my prior self-education on what to do when facing a grizzly bear; this story would not have a good ending. I couldn't

The second faceoff, grizzly turned broadside after charge.

believe that in just one single year, I had gone from seeing my first grizzly, the distant "rump high up a hillside" to the mind-blowing twice, eye-to-eye encounters. That was something completely unimaginable. Well, indeed it happened and I never want to be in that position again. Yet, on the other hand, inherent risks and uncertainties are part of venturing into grizzly bear country. Later I discussed this entire situation with several YNP rangers. The rangers indeed felt I could have done several things differently, but they were unanimous in their assessment. "The fact that neither you nor the bear were hurt, means that you did the right things, you were there, at the times you had to make decisions," concluded the rangers.

I certainly learned from this experience, and hope that others that might find themselves in a somewhat situation, might benefit from some of my actions. I can only conclude that under duress, my psyche took over control, rapidly extinguishing the normal human flight response. Many years later with all sorts of bear sightings and encounters, I feel this incident prepared me for other wildlife encounters. Four words sum it up; "*Don't Run-Don't Panic.*" However, lest I forget, there are no outcome guarantees, the only thing you can control, is yourself and your reactions.

Brushing aside the duress of the encounters, the remainder of this spring trip afforded terrific grizzly bear sightings, including females with new emerging cubs of the year (COY) from their winter dens. The weather had turned sporadic with rain and snow intermingled with fog. Wildlife was on the move and places I thought might hold grizzlies, panned out. My fledging journey was not only continuing, but it was also super energized by all events. As sure as the aspens would gorgeously turn yellow, I'd be back in the fall.

Chapter 4

Turning Lemons into Lemonade

Summer quickly passed, as my tentative fall, Yellowstone trip was now drawing close. It was a busy period with ongoing work commitments and hefty multi-state travel. I still had a couple of years to go before retirement from my career of thirty-plus years. As would often happen, I could be called away on very short notice to attend to important business responsibilities. This turned out to be the case as I had to be in Boise, ID around the same period my trip was scheduled. Scheduling conflicts, fortunately, worked out to accomplish both.

I would first fly to Bozeman for Yellowstone and then drive over to Boise. By this time, colors out West were reaching their peaks and temperatures were dropping. Very soon the YNP roads would be seasonally closing as the brilliant aspen leaves were dropping and the roadside snow polls were all in place.

Packing accordingly, I had very high hopes in anticipation of further outstanding grizzly bear sightings and fall hiking in new locations that I had researched. The bears would be in the hyperphagia phase packing on all the vital pre-hibernation calories and switching their seasonal intake from summer patterns to remaining organic sources and the all-important, whitebark pine nut harvest.

Once inside Yellowstone, I was greeted with many grizzly bear sightings. The new areas and trails held a great degree of promise. Several of the trails that are closed in the spring because of emerging bear concerns, were now open. They were new ground for me. The bison and elk rut seasons were all but over, with a few remaining, and entertaining bulls jousting with whatever testosterone-fueled dominance remained. I quickly learned that daylight in the mountains at this time of the year, dwindles quickly. The backcountry landscapes were awesome and I could just sense there was a feeling in the air with wildlife movements. While at times the air was acrid, with the skies cloaked with smoke from sporadic forest fires, it made for awe-inspiring sunsets. Yellowstone displays its ever-changing natural beauty, season to season, with wisps and sometimes enormous changing weather patterns. So, what possibly could go wrong with this trip that started so promising?

Strapping on my backpack at the Hayden Valley trailhead, the morning dawned overcast and seasonably cold. I intended to hike a new area of the valley with most of my travels off-trail. I find hiking in this expansive grizzly bear habitat easier in the fall compared to the spring. While I believe spring is the most productive season to locate grizzlies and wildlife in general, hiking is more difficult due to substantial marshy and wet areas.

****

Traversing the stillness of the vast panorama was awe-inspiring. Again, what could go wrong on such a pleasant hike with nature's showcase abounding on a beautiful Yellowstone fall day?

****

The lower landscape is riddled with small springs and abundant rivulets flowing downslope from the undulating rolling hills. While quite passable, some areas can be more slogging than hiking. However, the dry fall season makes for easier hiking. Regardless of the season, the Hayden Valley is crossed by a maze of game trails, oftentimes misleading from portions of the faint Mary Mountain trail.

On this hike, unlike the Lamar Valley, the Hayden was void of bison, save for a few post-rut solitary huge bulls. I took my time hiking and would often stop and glass the tree lines lining the fall golden brown terrain for bears. As the cold morning eased into a pleasant afternoon, I didn't see a single other hiker the entire day. Traversing the stillness of the vast panorama was awe-inspiring. Again, what could go wrong on such a pleasant hike with nature's showcase abounding on a beautiful Yellowstone fall day?

Having hiked approximately four miles in, mostly off trail, I was now situated in a valley bordering a forested area. Stopping for rest, hydration, and some great trail mix, I decided to head back to the trailhead taking a different return route. Rejuvenated, I moved on. Well, just then something indeed went very wrong. As I was clearing some deadfall timber, my foot snagged on a tangle of ground roots. The pain in my knee was instant. I knew this most unwelcome pain from a prior accident. Within seconds, I couldn't place any weight on my affected leg. Grabbing a spare tee shirt from my backpack, I hobbled over to a nearby tiny stream. Tearing the shirt into strips and soaking them in the clear cold water, I rolled my hiking pant up. Wrapping the cold compresses around my leg with tape from my first aid pouch afforded some short-term relief. But I was alone, miles away from the trailhead. This is one of the risks of solo hiking, especially in grizzly country.

With the aid of my hiking pole, I began my ever-so-slow and difficult egress. Each little bump or snag while hobbling only made matters worse, but I had no other alternative. I must have looked pitiful, or even worse…. like a wounded animal a predator would single out. In addition to grizzlies, the Hayden Valley is home or passing ground for several wolf packs. I know first-hand at least one wolf den in the area and have personally viewed a pack of seven wolves single out a limping elk from its herd and take it down. I could just hear observing peering yellow-eyed predators from the forest, "Nah, you take him, Fred, this looks too easy for me!"

Minutes turned to hours, as I limped my way back to the trailhead. Before reaching the trailhead, I recall coming across some very fresh grizzly scat on the trail. This was new scat and wasn't there before as I made my way into the Hayden. Spotting my vehicle several hundred yards ahead, I seemed to be moving a tad faster, like a horse when it gets closer to the barn.

Leaning against the car door for balance, I removed my gear and gingerly, positioned myself behind the wheel. Well, "lemons number one-what could go wrong," certainly came to fruition. Debating what to do next, I decided to return to West Yellowstone and rest, icing down my knee. After a while, my hopes were dashed that I would be able to hike. Rather than wasting further precious Yellowstone time, I decided to drive back to the Hayden Valley. Placing my spotting scope and tripod on the passenger seat, I set out in the mid-late afternoon to a favorite pull-out to glass the Hayden Valley for wildlife. Frustrated that I could no longer hike, glassing was my only outdoor option.

The pull-out was empty when I arrived. Balancing on one leg, I set up my spotting scope high up, out to the distant east, overlooking the valley's wide expanse bordered in part by distant forested high ground. A few vehicles arrived, people jumped out and took a brief look at the valley, then quickly raced off down the road. While uncomfortable, I concentrated my glassing on a high distant meadow between two patches of timber. Closely scanning the area, I caught some movement at one of the tree lines next to the down-sloping meadow. Adjusting the magnification settings on the tree line, there they were! A large grizzly sow with a cub emerged out into

Sow and new cub of the year (COY) emerge from the forest.

the meadow. At this distance, the grizzlies were nearly undistinguishable without a spotting scope or super-quality binoculars. Shortly after I had acquired the bears coming down the meadow slope, several new vehicles pulled in. Several families with young children intently viewed the valley with straining eyes. I overheard one of the excited youngsters ask a parent, "Daddy are there any bears here?" He responded, "I don't think so honey, we haven't seen a bear yet."

I turned to the parents and said, "Well, I can fix that for you right now, you are most welcome to take a look. I have sighted in two grizzlies." Peering into my scope eyepiece, they were ecstatic, "Can the kids take a look?" I replied, "Of course," as the young boys and girls jockeyed for position. "Just don't touch the scope or bump the tripod so I can keep the bears in focus for you," I replied.

One of the parents brought out a cooler for the kids to stand on, and the problem was solved. Adjusting the field of view and focus, I had a near-perfect position on both the sow and her cub as they slowly moved down, pausing occasionally to sniff and paw the ground. "Holy cow, look at the bears!" the kids yelled out in happiness. Other cars pulled in with adults and children alike wanting to see the bears. Periodically adjusting the scope, I was more than happy to oblige them all, as long as I could keep the moving grizzlies in sight.

Grizzly sow and cub continue to descend Hayden Valley meadow.

My injured knee was now throbbing as the afternoon sun was lowering above distant mountains.

The grizzlies had reentered the timber and were no longer visible with the scope. But, despite what happened to me during my hike, this turned out to be one of my best days in Yellowstone. Helping people see their first bear, especially a grizzly sow with a new cub, they would not have ever seen, was very uplifting. I cheered along with the excitement of the youngsters and the endless questions they would ask. I'm quite sure they would go back to their homes in the many states they came from and tell all their friends about seeing the bears. I'm pleased my misfortune brought about an opportunity for others, to enjoy what they so badly wanted to see in Yellowstone. Lemons into lemonade!

But wait, this trip wasn't over yet, far from it...the "lemonade" part was great, but more lemons awaited me. The sun was starting to dip down toward the western edge of the expansive Hayden Valley, as I limped over to put my scope into the car. I still had reasonable time to make it back to West Yellowstone before the fall sunset abruptly fades into deep ink blackness. I didn't enjoy the ride back, especially with a bum knee, wondering about physical limitations for the remainder of my trip. My immediate goal was to get back, raise, and ice down my swollen knee, hoping it was just a strain and tomorrow would be a better day.

Tomorrow started, not as a better day, but got worse with a potentially serious event. Unfortunately, the next morning my knee didn't improve at all. As much as I hated wasting field time, I decided to keep icing the knee and wait until the afternoon and then make a decision on what to do. Early morning turned into noon, then approached decision time. Any thought about hiking was quickly dashed away, as I struggled to get dressed. Reaching the door, I was greeted with a beautiful clear crisp fall day. My goal for the rest of the day and the trip itself faded to only driving the park to help dimmish my disappointment with my knee injury. I wasn't even sure how far I could drive and keep my leg in position.

Departing West Yellowstone, my final decision was to test my capabilities with a drive to the Canyon area. If I could halfway do so, perhaps I might be able to stake out a promising area and glass again for bears and other wildlife. By far, it wasn't a comfortable drive as I approached the Norris Junction at about 3:00 pm. I was aware that by mid-October, many if not most, YNP services were closed, or would be closed by day's end. All the more reason to proceed.

Road traffic was very light as I turned east on Norris Canyon Road. My nerves had settled down as I began to accept my situation and enjoy this day as best I could. Since departure, I had not seen any wildlife on, or near the roads. Crossing the Solfatara Plateau I started to gradually descend the high ground with Canyon several miles ahead. As I approached the bottom of the hill at 40-45 mph, the area was thickly forested on the right side of the road. The trees were only a few feet from the road itself. Suddenly, literally, in a split second, three blacktail deer (buck with two does) hidden in the tree line next to a meadow, bolted out. Instantly, the two-doe peeled off into the meadow, and the buck slammed into the front right of my sedan. It happened so fast, that I never had a chance to hit my brakes.

I watched as in slow motion, the deer crashed and rolled over the hood, with hooves slamming into the windshield and over the roof. The deer was airborne as it crossed both lanes and landed somewhere out in a field. The car hood and front end were crumbled up like an accordion. The vehicle immediately lost all power and control as it continued spewing lime green anti-freeze and other fluids. Steering and braking were gone as the car came to a stop. With my seat belt secured, I was puzzled. Strangely, the airbags never inflated! How could that be in an accident like this? The buck's full body went over the front end and I saw his eyes stare at me as it slammed into the windshield. Fortunately, there weren't any oncoming vehicles that could have been involved. I sat stunned but felt no injuries from the collision. However, I felt horrible about killing that deer and remain so to this very day. Somehow my knee escaped without any further trauma, but not my psyche.

    I was unaware there were any vehicles behind me. After my car came to rest, I recall a gentleman running up to me from a vehicle behind. Luckily, he had been following me downhill at a distance and saw the collision. His wife and children were with him. Another car slowed to stop. With no cell phone signal, his wife went with another car to contact park rangers in Canyon, as he kindly attended to me. About half an hour later, a ranger pulled up with the lady that summoned him.

    He checked my physical status, asking what happened. After I explained the accident, he left to locate the deer and dispatch it. I recall informing him that I was certain that would be unnecessary. Walking back to the point of impact, mercifully, he found the deer laying in the opposite lane ditch where the collision took place. Returning, he advised there was no need to put the deer down. Still very upset about the loss of the deer, which I prized as all Yellowstone wildlife, I again expressed my sadness for the deer. Looking me in the eye, the ranger responded, "Well, the bears and wolves will eat well tonight." I'm not so sure at the time, I was very consoled with that image, though it is part of nature itself. Nothing goes to waste in Yellowstone. The ranger finished his investigation, including interviewing the driver behind me, who confirmed I was traveling within the posted 45 mph speed limit and there was nothing I could have done to avoid the accident.

The westerly sun was now fading, as the ranger left to contact the park wrecker service. I was now alone pondering what next, as a few roadside flares illuminated the wrecked car. The sun had now set when a wrecker with flashing lights appeared coming from the direction of Canyon Junction. With the sun down, it was turning cold as I sat on the passenger side with my bum knee extended out the door of the wrecked car. I couldn't generate any car heat, as the engine was completely dead and would not turn over. I was about to learn yet another Yellowstone traveling issue.

I soon learned from the experienced and friendly wrecker driver, how lucky I was to be reached, as the YNP wrecker service was closing down for the season. He informed me that he was minutes from leaving Canyon to the off-season storage garage, just as he received the radio call from the ranger. My vehicle needed to be hauled out to West Yellowstone. Then came a surprise. I was informed the wrecker fee was $300.00 and they did not accept any wrecker insurance coverage from a rental agency or individual towing coverage. Furthermore, any outside YNP wrecker companies from surrounding communities were not allowed, per contract, to tow within YNP. I had no choice as payment in full was required at the accident scene. It's up to the individual to seek towing reimbursement from their insurance company. In this case, I had two full towing coverages, one with the rental agency, and the other with my auto tow coverage. For whatever it's worth, my attempts for reimbursement from either insurance were unsuccessful for some obscure technical issue hidden within the bowels of insurance jargon. The bottom line, towing inside YNP can get pretty dicey, restrictive, and pricey.

I jumped up (oops, crawled up) with my bum knee in the wrecker as we departed to West Yellowstone. By now it was completely dark as we twisted our way up and down the inky-black roads. During the one-and-a-half-hour drive, I enjoyed our conversation along the way. It certainly was another "lemon day." I was unable to hike with a painful knee from each movement and then wound up totaling my vehicle. All I wanted or could do, was go out and glass/scope for wildlife. Even high up in the wrecker, I felt quite nervous and jittery that something would bolt out from the woods and another wreck. I still had a few days left for my Yellowstone stay and more concerning, I still had to attend to business a long way away in Boise. The headlights brightened up the unattended gravel area behind my hotel. Dropping off the car, I bid farewell to the YNP wrecker driver as I stood in the unused lot wondering just how things were going so consistently wrong. However, looking at the totaled-out vehicle, I was so thankful that I wasn't injured, or worse. Counting my blessings, surpassed the tribulations of the past few days.

I labored up the stairs to my hotel room and immediately called my car rental company and reported the accident. They were terrific people. They would shuttle down a replacement vehicle tonight from Bozeman and the flatbed would return the wrecked car. At about 2:00 am I saw truck headlights pull into the graveled area. In no time, the driver unloaded a new vehicle and winched up the wreck to return to Bozeman. I finally had some time to settle down and would wait until later in the morning to decide what to do.

That next morning, I decided I would just try and put away the events of the past several days, a new start if you wish. I attended to some ongoing business matters and communications. Being a horse lover, I would simply employ the adage, "If you get thrown off a horse, get back in the saddle." I would try the same as the day before but in a different area. I very cautiously drove out to the west entrance and for the next twenty-five miles or so, felt reasonably comfortable. Nevertheless, I found myself tensing up whenever I passed a wooded area. After driving further, my palms became sweaty and I had a death grip on the steering wheel. My eyes would dart back and forth to the roadside timber. I wasn't responding to my self-advice," to just "relax." It was apparent to me, that while I wasn't physically injured in the collision, my psyche was. Short of panic attacks, I would envision something jumping out at me from behind every tree. Pulling over several times only offered temporary respite. I was still obsessing and somewhat distraught with the deer I had accidentally killed. My day plan wasn't working, but more so, my sense of safety and reactivity cautioned me to discontinue what I was doing. I never set up the spotting scope as planned and I dared not travel further to a good wildlife location I knew of.

    I turned around back to West Yellowstone, abandoning my further plans. My confidence and joy were out of it. I didn't feel at ease whatsoever until I reentered the wide streets of the town. Perhaps, I just needed a tad more rest from all I had been through the past few days. Returning to my hotel, I did something that I never do, much less in the grandeur of Yellowstone. I took a nap.

    As I awoke late afternoon, my thoughts quickly flashed back to, "Get back on the horse again." I gave it another try, but the same results. Unquestionably, I knew that it was fruitless to remain in Yellowstone though I still had several more days on my itinerary. I was more concerned about the long drive I had ahead of me through Idaho. It turned out, my concern was well taken.

Cold rain and spats of light snow were falling as I packed my bags and loaded the car for my trip tomorrow morning. Deciding to leave early was in my best interest. A tore up knee from hiking, followed by totaling out a car, accidentally killing a deer, and near panic attacks would ruin it for just about anyone. Grabbing a last cup of coffee to go, I pulled out for Idaho. Shortly after leaving wide paved streets, I was soon back on mountainous and forested roads. The white-knuckled pattern soon followed. I kept wishing the road would just widen out some. I still felt something hidden in the tree lines would bolt out again. With the rain continuing, the further I traveled away from Yellowstone, my reactions would relax somewhat. That was some progress from yesterday.

After a while, the tree line wasn't standing next to the road, but now the rain changed to mostly snow. I recall feeling with each mile traveled, I would be out of the difficult part. I longed for a four-lane highway with open terrain. The further I went, despite the snow, the more the road opened up. Traffic was quite light, ahead of me was a white car. I followed in his tracks for a while. All of a sudden, he hits his brakes and I see to my right, a gigantic bull moose looping across the road! I thought for sure the white car would hit the running moose, but he missed it by only several feet. But now, the moose was directly in front of me at a very close range. The moose might as well have been a train car. I hit the brakes as the moose ran between our two cars, crossed the road, and disappeared into the woods to my left. A couple of seconds were all that kept me from hitting the moose. I could have been the first person in Yellowstone to total out two vehicles and kill a deer and a moose, in less than twenty-four hours.

An hour after that hair-raising near collision, the road finally expanded to a wide-open four lanes of traffic. My heart rate returned to normal and my white-knuckled grip had eased. The snow had ended, and I headed south and then west across Idaho to Boise. The weather warmed up and except for my leg, I was feeling much better. Still, I was highly disappointed with the circumstances ending my Yellowstone trip.

Reaching Boise near evening, I was never so glad to vacate a vehicle after this trip. Meeting my business associates the next day, they wanted me to see their orthopedic doctor for my knee. I just knew there was something seriously wrong with it, so I decided to wait to see my orthopedic doctors in Nashville. I completed my business trip in a few days and with some assistance at the airport, I made it back home. My doctor promptly diagnosed a severe complex meniscus tear requiring surgery. By the way, my fear of something jumping out behind each tree persisted for many months afterward.

Lessons learned from this trip? Reinforces expert advice on increased risks when hiking solo. Carry emergency first aid medical items. Expect the unexpected. Road travel in Yellowstone can be quite dangerous, you don't know what dangers lie ahead at the next curve, hill, etc. Oh, and be sure you can cover on-the-scene towing costs. In my opinion; yes, lemons can be turned into lemonade, but I'll settle for lemonade any day of the week.

Chapter 5

Grizzlies I've Known

Through the years I've had sightings and encounters with a substantial number and varied grizzly bears including; large boars, sows, subadults, cubs, and cubs of the year (COY.) Most of the grizzlies were located within the three YNP quadrants that I devote my time in. Others were located in the Gallatin Mountain Range outside of YNP to the northwest and outside the East Entrance in the Shoshone National Forest bordering the Absarokas. My photo and video library of Yellowstone grizzly bears alone is extensive. Each recorded sighting or series of sightings, holds a memory etched into my mind of time, place, and circumstances. For the sake of brevity, I'm restricted to highlighting only a sampling of grizzlies. I would be remiss to not point out, that each grizzly bear viewing, in its own right, was an exhilarating awesome experience. Locating the magnificent iconic grizzly in the wild is truly a remarkable and memorable personal experience. A memory that will most likely be retained, as other pleasurable or significant experiences.

My full intention for this book is my focus solely on grizzly bears. That is not meant to dimmish in any form or manner, Yellowstone black bears. Along with my grizzly bear success, black bears were often located in what I refer to as, cross-over terrain i.e., more forested land than open terrain, in which both grizzlies and black bears (the majority) cohabit. That's another topic for another writing. Both Yellowstone bear species provide ample opportunities for adventure and interaction. The following is but one example.

On a mid-spring day, I was hiking off trail through a moderately open forested area. Movement between the trees off to my left caught my attention. In close range, a spotted a black bear sow with a black and a cinnamon cub in tow. Halting, the bears passed above me approximately 35-40 yards. I remained at a standstill as the bears quickly moved into the high grass cover ahead of me. As the three bears quickly ran into a clump

of high grass, an unseen fox jumped up from the grass. The fox bolted about 50 feet and then turned around to gaze back at the bears to see just what the heck just happened. Everyone was trying to figure out just where they stood in this little ongoing drama, Including me.

The displaced fox looks back where the bears rousted him.

The bears and the perplexed fox stared at each other, each trying to figure out what was going on. While the stare-down continued, momma black bear then turned her focus to me, standing twenty-five yards

behind the startled fox. She was also grunting out orders

to her two nearby cubs, who appeared as confused as the fox.

Suddenly, the fox had enough drama with the intruding bears and sprinted directly to me. Stopping two feet next to me, he sat down at my feet, looked up at me, and then turned to look at the staring bears, as Momma slowly nudged our way. "Thanks, Mr. Fox!" I mumbled to myself as I unholstered my bear spray just in case. I had difficulty deciding whether to laugh or be concerned with the situation.

Sitting at my feet, the fox keeps an eye on the approaching black bear.

I enjoyed the encounter with the three black bears and the spooked fox. As so often happens, it was a random unexpected event in the backcountry that occurs while hiking in Yellowstone. However, had the bears been grizzlies, instead of black bears, the encounter would have taken on a much more serious risk with my reactions handled much differently. It is reported that a grizzly is greater than twenty times as dangerous as a black bear. A startled black bear will most likely run to a tree. Whereas, a startled grizzly bear will also run but is equally prone to charge or attack. This observation is substantiated by my own field experience.

As I mentioned above, few things can match the exhilaration and awe of seeing grizzlies in the wild. However, the majority of people visiting grizzly country in the lower forty-eight, never or only rarely, see a grizzly. There are several factors influencing this observation. First, only a very small fraction of Yellowstone visitors ventures on trails or extend into the backcountry. Secondly, the law of large numbers comes into play. What do I mean by that?

Consider the following. Excluding Idaho which has a very small and restricted population of grizzlies, the two other states, namely Wyoming and Montana combined, have the vast majority of a very limited grizzly bear population. The state of Wyoming is 97,813 square miles. Montana is comprised of 147,164 square miles. Combined the two states, encompass 244,977 square miles. Grizzly bears inhabit a very small percentage of those square miles. According to the most recent data from state wildlife agencies, the Greater Yellowstone Ecosystem (GYE) reveals a grizzly population of 1,070 bears in northwest WY, parts of Montana, and a very small part of Idaho. In the state of Montana, the Northern Continental Divide Ecosystem (NCDES) which encompasses 16,000 square miles, reports a 1,000 grizzly bear population. Thus, within an enormous amount of combined square miles of habitat which may support grizzly populations, approximately only a total of 2,100 grizzlies survive in this vast supporting terrain. Despite a rising grizzly bear population from the 1970s due solely to the enactment of the Endangered Species Act (ESA), I suggest the purported recovery numbers of grizzlies, while helpful, are currently woefully inadequate to claim as a "success story." Based upon the accuracy of these subjective numbers of bears, Federal and state regulators are clamoring once again, to remove the grizzly bear from ESA federal protection. More about this in a later chapter.

In any event, my point is this. When you experience the thrill of a sighting or an encounter with a grizzly bear(s), count yourself fortunate and treasure the experience, whether you are experienced or a first-timer. Too small of a bear population, within tens of thousands of square miles of habitation, coupled with an ever-increasing human expansion into or bordering the remaining grizzly bear's natural habitat productive areas, are in my opinion, major obstacles. Of course, there are many other fluctuating natural and human-impacting elements as contributing factors.

With the above in mind, the following samples are just a few of my grizzly bear sightings and encounters. Each is a most valued experience and a lasting memory of my presence with Yellowstone grizzlies in the wild.

The mid-late May winter snow was quickly retreating from the mountains as the lower elevations and flats were slowly greening up with scattered patches of remaining snow. I was hiking in the Gardner's Hole area in northern YNP. The elk were also in the general area, with signs the females were having, or about to, drop their spring calves to initially hide them from predators in the sage flats. This is a fortuitous and expected annual occurrence, not unnoticed by the hungry post-hibernation grizzly bears that moved down from their high dens above, and below the receding snow line.

Spotting movement at a distance in the low sagebrush, I cautiously and slowly moved to investigate. With binoculars raised, I saw a large female with what I thought were two new cubs, playing around in the sage near Mom. Holding my ground, I didn't advance, as I was at a very safe distance. The sow had her nose to the ground as she gradually drifted in my general direction.

Grizzly sow advances toward me with two new cubs.

I was confident she was seeking out an elk calf. As she approached, I could see a huge wide open, oozing gash just above her right eye and forehead. I could visualize the open white shine of her skull and the deep red open wound and blood-matted hair. Her muzzle was streaked with large vertical scars. I immediately knew that the only thing that could inflict such damage, was another grizzly. Perhaps, just one powerful swat of a paw by a large male inflicted the damage, as she undoubtedly fought to protect her cubs. After all, this is the prime time of the year when the large dominant boars will seek out a sow and kill the cubs to promote the sow to breed with her cubs gone.

Grizzly sow with a large gashing wound to the head and muzzle.

I've witnessed this behavior on several occasions. I was quite concerned that the very recent dreadful head injuries impaired her ability to forage, thus posing a great survival danger to her and the newborn cubs. After observing her move about, I was relieved to see her raise her head from the ground while chewing without any apparent difficulty. Based on the precise location of her gaping injuries, if the assault had been a few inches lower, she would have certainly lost her right eye, along with, perhaps fatal, impaired jaw and mouth function. The results of such injury would also pose serious, to certain survival risks for both new cubs.

My youngest adult son Michael Nevens, is an avid hiker, camper, growing equestrian, and amateur photographer in Middle Tennessee. I was happy to take him along with me into grizzly country for his first trip into the Tetons and Yellowstone. He learned quite a lot and together, we experienced some adventurous times with Yellowstone grizzlies. Sadly, similar to the above sow incurring significant injuries defending her cubs from a large male, on a recent spring trip, we witnessed the harsh, before and after results of a mating pair of grizzlies resulting in the attack and fatality of her several year's old large cub. However, in this encounter the facts were both alike in nature, but different in tactics.

Observing a very dominating male and smaller female in a meadow laced with grizzly bear digs, from the mating pair of grizzly bears, was also a growing several-year-old cub that the sow had unsuccessfully, attempted to drive off, parting ways for good.

Courting pair grizzlies (L sow, R male) in a meadow among grizzly digs.

Her adult cub kept coming back to this area. The female ran her cub off repeatedly. On the final attempt, while the female was futilely trying to run the cub off, the large male had enough. He aggressively charged the cub, violently throwing it around like it was a stuffed toy. The sow also inflicted injury on her cub. The injuries ultimately proved to be fatal.

The large, near-sub-adult cub painfully struggled to leave the area. Alternately losing balance, while falling and crawling, it was able to agonizingly travel about a mile from the adult pair. The cub was later located by YNP rangers, immobile and profoundly suffering from severe spinal injuries and pain. Humanely, the rangers had no other option, other than to put it down on site.

The courting male that mortally injured the cub, rests in the meadow.

Sadly, research indicates that less than one-half of new grizzly bear cubs of the year, do not survive past their first year of life. Large males killing cubs to promote mating opportunities, as reflected in the above, is a major mortality factor in this alarming statistic.

In my experience, there are few, if any, more awe-inspiring encounters in grizzly country, than coming in backcountry contact with a grizzly sow and her cub(s) whether newborns or up to three-year-old cubs. In addition to the initial heart-thumping sighting, it's incumbent to quickly analyze your proximity to the bears and employ the utmost safety practices. After all, one of the most dangerous hiking scenarios you can inadvertently venture into is an encounter with a female and her cubs. I can't emphasize this enough, as your first reaction may be to visually lock on to the cute cubs, and not pay immediate attention to assess the situation you find yourself in, especially if the encounter happens to be within close quarters. Of course, whatever you do, never run, nor make any quick movement. Whether the sighting is at a long distance, or an unexpectedly close distance, observe the same "Safety Number One" practices. Too many variables with the bear's behavior could ensue and happen very quickly. While the new cubs will stay close to mom, they often are very playful and quickly roam about, curious about their new surroundings. And that could include you, potentially triggering a not-so-pleasant reaction from a nearby mom.

I believe deferring to take pictures or video until you are certain that you are well within safe boundaries and circumstances, is the best and safest policy for your well-being and equally, that of the grizzly bears. I've experienced both long and short-distance encounters with female grizzlies and their cubs. The longer distance sightings were indeed less stressful and importantly, presented far less risk of any adverse incident. Two personal examples of each scenario follow below.

I was hiking mid-central YNP in early May. It was fairly typical of early/mid-Yellowstone spring weather. After gearing up, I started my hike on trail.

Consulting my map and GPS after several miles, I decided to make a short detour off trail to an area with small pond-like lakes. This was new ground for me as I enjoyed the hike in fairly open and forested, small rolling hills. A gentle light rain was beginning to fall as I pulled my parka hood down over my cap. As I hiked, the ground was very soft and silent with early emerging vegetation. An occasional beautiful mountain bluebird flittered by through the woods, a sure sign of a Yellowstone spring.

  I came to a small saddle opening and decided to climb up on one side to get a better view of where the ponds were. It was a very easy and short climb up. The gentle rain had now mixed with spats of snow. In no time I neared the crest of the hill, stepping one foot over the crest, I came to a sudden complete stop. At the bottom of the slope directly in front of me, a female grizzly with two newborn cubs were foraging next to a small creek. I had no idea they were there and by their initial activity, I doubt they knew I was there. I don't know if they heard me coming, or smelled my scent as I walked up the side of the saddle. I had no idea there was a bear in the area as I had not come across any signs of bear activity i.e., tracks, scat, grizzly digs, etc. So yes, this was a surprise encounter, fortunately at a safe good distance. Still, my adrenaline was in overdrive as I processed the situation.

  My initial attention and concern focused on the female. Would she charge when she sensed my presence? Likewise, would the cubs let out an alarm bawling, imparting to her the highest level of danger? Except for slowly removing my bear spray from my chest holster, I remained motionless while deciding my next move.

  The bears remained foraging as the rain/sleet mix continued. As the grizzly family had not exhibited any aggressive behavior toward me, I planned to get one quick photo at the exit edge of the slope and retreat down the saddle slope and then exit the area.

Surprise encounter sow with two new cubs.

I watched them for a brief period and took this photograph as the cub on the left standing up, had spotted me. The female was just turning to see what was going on. Her splendid dark black coat glistened with the falling rain and sleet.

Keeping a very low-to-the-ground profile I backed down the slope and was now out of sight of the grizzlies. My bear spray remained armed as I continued my downslope retreat. My only concern was she might come tearing over the crest. Luckily, this did not happen, as all turned out well. Still, the sighting once again exemplifies both the risks and random events, as well as the rewards and adventures of hiking in grizzly bear territory. It was critically important how I reacted to this surprise encounter. I remained calm, quiet and didn't make any provocative movements. I believe by treating the bears with respect and by not further intruding on their area, the grizzly sow in turn; while acutely well aware of my presence, did not view me as a threat to be neutralized as a direct danger to her cubs. At least for this encounter, it was a good strategy that diffused a potentially serious situation.

Below is another short, but very safe distance encounter with a female and her two yearling cubs. This took place in a more open, unobstructed landscape and did not involve any potentially threatening behavior. This sighting presented near-optimal grizzly bear observation for both safety and clear visual opportunity. I watched the trio roam the landscape, foraging early season food opportunities, while the two yearling cubs romped around wrestling. In my mind, it was a perfect grizzly bear family outing, enjoying a great spring day. However, the female was ever vigilant, constantly panning her surroundings and testing the air for any scent of a potentially intruding male grizzly or humans. Nature has its boundaries and limits. In another couple of years, if the cubs continue to survive, they too, will be kicked away by mom to fend entirely for themselves against the threats and risks from nature and humans.

Sow with two yearling cubs.

Through the years, I've been very fortunate to witness many grizzlies with cubs. If you are a grizzly bear enthusiast, watching those cubs' heads pop up in the sagebrush with front paws playfully swinging in the air, is a memorable experience.

For me, on the opposite side of that endearing experience, is the nagging realization, that the odds of survival to adulthood for these cubs are extremely tenuous. So much in nature and human activity, is stacked against them. Newborn cubs have a fifty percent mortality factor within their first year of life. This is a dreadful mortality/morbidity rate, especially considering that grizzly bear reproduction itself is quite low and of long duration. If that's not enough bad sustainability news, factor in the unyielding attempts by special interest groups to promote Trophy grizzly bear hunting. More about that, in a later chapter.

A final example of mothers with cubs is encountered at a longer distance. By terminology alone, this scenario depicts safety and less stress for both bears and humans. I've had more of these sightings than closer ones and I'm very pleased with that fact. In reality out in the field, for the greatest part, the hiker in grizzly country has little to do with the onset of the initial type of experience. The bottom line is safety and adherence to distance rules and regulations. You may not be able to control the initial development of a short-distance experience, but you can and must, do your best to adjust your position and activity accordingly. Always keep close in mind, any encounter with a female grizzly with cubs is unquestionably, one of the most precarious situations a human, or other wildlife can face. While I have never encountered or sighted a cub or cubs, appearing to be alone without their mother in immediate sight, you can be certain the mother grizzly is in very close proximity to her cubs. Any attempt to move closer toward the cubs or even remaining in place, is all but certain to result in a fierce charge with great risk and danger to life and limb.

Sow with COY foraging at a long distance.

      The above sighting was at an initial long distance with steady rain, snow, and fog. I was in the Turbid Lake area of central Yellowstone when at a distance, I caught a glimpse of a large female and cub of the year emerge from some heavy deadfall while traversing a hillside. At first, I wasn't even certain there was a cub in tow, due to distance and weather factors. Suddenly, the little cub emerged from under a fallen tree near the ground, as he closely followed Mom. The grizzlies turned up a hillside, foraging their way up. The cub would imitate whatever his mother was teaching him, like staying close to me and using those new claws for digging up a pocket gopher or tender emerging flowers, bulbs, or tubers.

Despite the persistent lousy weather, I enjoyed watching them as I often cleaned my binocular lenses of fog, before they crested the hill and disappeared into the forest. From his mother's efforts, this little cub was learning fast where the food might be. I watched with amusement, as he located a good size hole in the ground that Mom had dug up. Sniffing and walking alongside the dig, he either tried to imitate the art of the dig or had fallen head-first into the hole. Quickly, those cute little cub eyes popped up at ground level, with legs racing like a four-wheel drive to get out. He scampered off close to his mother, proud of his new adventure.

Another thrilling, but extremely dangerous grizzly bear encounter is locating a grizzly on a carcass. However, just as above, an encounter with a grizzly bear on a new kill or carrion is another major high-risk situation that deserves the highest degree of safety and utmost caution. Just as a female will defend her cubs to her death, so will a grizzly bear on, or nearby, protecting a carcass will aggressively defend its ground and a valuable high protein carcass, against any intruding human or other predators. The rule for a hiker, photographer, or any other person, is to never approach an "inactive" carcass, or of course, an actual bear on a carcass. To recklessly and in violation of established safety distance measures to do so, is to invite a near certain charge with a high risk of severe mauling or death. Furthermore, the bear itself, acting within its natural environment, may then be unnecessarily subjected to remedial removal actions, even euthanasia, by wildlife authorities. All in all, a tragic, losing proposition for both humans and bears. Every year, people recreating in grizzly country, especially in big game spring and fall hunting seasons, are mauled when encountering a grizzly bear on or near an elk carcass or gut pile. Gut piles left in the field are bear magnets for easy and important, high protein and caloric intake.

Consider the fact that an average adult Rocky Mountain bull will weigh approximately 700 lbs. A similar average adult cow weighs about 500 lbs. After field dressing, an elk will lose around 20-30 percent of body weight. Different factors affect these averages. However, the remaining field-dressed elk gut pile will weigh around 170 lbs. An absolute prize for a grizzly, raising the risk of human confrontation.

Grizzly bears feeding on, or guarding a carcass, has been one of the best activities for my grizzly bear encounters and photo opportunities. Yes, a minority of such sightings presented some safety concerns and risks, which I believed were well-self-managed, the more experienced I became. However, it is still a risky proposition and deserves the utmost good judgment and abandonment, if viewing cannot be safely attained, or if conditions/activities materially change.

Fortunately, through the years I've come across these viewing opportunities without any serious consequences, but in several situations, I unknowingly hiked into a most dangerous set of circumstances. Like most grizzly sightings, they occur by random chance and are culled out for safety and distance risk decision factors. When in the field, it's always a good policy to keep in mind that at any given time, a carcass can hold other unseen grizzlies or predators, in the immediate area, waiting their turn from the dominant feeding or guarding grizzly, before moving into feed. Additionally, ferocious grizzly bear battles may ensue when another bear (or wolf) moves in to challenge possession.

On one pleasant May mid-morning hike in the Canyon area of YNP, I ran into a very excited and animated young Asian tourist, who said that he had just seen a fox run across a nearby trail. On an intersecting trail, I had caught a glimpse of the "fox" he claimed to have seen, however, it wasn't a fox, it was a single grey wolf. I clearly understood his exhilaration and congratulated him on his sighting. He revealed this was his first walk into the woods. I cautioned him to perhaps prepare better if he intended to do any more hiking, as he only had a walking stick. He agreed and after a little more conversation, we went our own ways.

Hiking another mile or so, I turned off trail into a shallow draw to proceed uphill for a better view of the area. I heard some raucous ravens calling out some distance away, but never saw them. Twenty minutes later, in some high grass with the wind behind my back, I suddenly walked into a terrible obnoxious smell. Stopping in my tracks, I looked down and just ahead of me, saw two long coils of dark grey intestines in red matted-down grass. Removing the safety off my bear spray, I slowly proceeded another twenty-five or so steps. The awful smell increased as I turned to my right. My attention was drawn to a very bright red area in the grass. Lying there, was the dismembered half-body of an elk. Blood smears and puddles were on the ground and fresh red blood was still pooled inside the exposed rib cage.

I had just come upon an extremely dangerous and very active situation. Based upon what I saw, I'm near certain the elk was taken down, perhaps an hour or less earlier, and partially consumed by wolves. I saw bloodied wolf tracks around the carcass. I didn't see grizzly tracks, but in full appreciation that I was standing smack dab at a fresh kill, I was in a direct high-danger scenario. With the other half of the body gone, it is quite possible that a grizzly had been on the carcass and dragged away the upper torso, as a fresh matted bloodied dragline was very apparent in the tall grass leading away from the severed torso. For all I knew a grizzly bear could be on, or closely guarding the other half torso; within hundreds of feet, or less, from where I stood. If so, I couldn't see it ten feet away as the dense terrain all but obscured my visibility. One thing was certain; the predators will be back at any time on these now two separated fresh carcasses. I very nervously found myself alone at basically, a grizzly bear feeding station.

DANGER! Hour-old dismembered elk with pooled blood still in the rib cage. Upper torso severed, drag line toward the top. Entrails scattered behind.

My immediate attention was devoted to safely vacating the hour-old kill site, as well as the entire area. No doubt whatsoever, the wolves and grizzlies are already here, with others being drawn to the fresh carcass, by the smells of both the elk body and blood. I consider this situation to be one of the highest risks, I've encountered in all my Yellowstone backcountry experiences. Trust me, my nerves and adrenaline were being tested to the core, straining to effectively navigate my way back to safety. My thoughts drifted back earlier to the Asian tourist's "fox" sighting. In all probability, that wolf was on, or going to the kill site. I hate to think what might have happened to that young inexperienced tourist, if he, rather than myself, walked into this highest-risk situation.

I had another somewhat, but under different circumstances, high-risk carcass encounter, that still today, holds my attention and also reflects as a valuable experience for the uncertainties of hiking in grizzly country. On this once again, mid-spring occasion, I was hiking the Bighorn Pass trail on the northwest flank of YNP. After scrapping the heavy frost off my windshield and downing my second cup of hot coffee, I arrived at the trailhead shortly after the daybreak. Setting my GPS as I crossed over the Gallatin River log crossing, I had the sun in my eyes heading due east. A light east/northeast wind was in my face, as I crunched through the still-frozen ground. My plan was about a ten-mile roundtrip to check out the backcountry campsites. Most of the trees were partially snow-covered, as I hiked the mainly open flats, with small rolling hills or knolls and the swift spring Gallatin River flowing down from its rugged Gallatin Lake headwaters near Three Rivers Peak. This is all good grizzly country.

I had spotted a few elk out in the flats and wondered if the elk cows had, or were near, dropping their babies in the wide sage flats still dusted with snow and glistening frost. My best guess was it was still a bit early. In the open, with the sun rising, my trail began to thaw out the further east I traveled. Soon I approached a sharp turn in the trail with a high rock bluff to my left and a thickly forested patch to my right. I was especially vigilant for tracks of any source, especially grizzlies, in the remaining snow, but saw none.

All was quiet, as I then turned a blind corner with the rock ledge next to my left side. Looking down in astonishment, as my right boot was just about to come down, I froze my step-in midair above the ground.

The above photo is the blind curve. The grizzly was on the trail in the forested patch to the right of the rock ledge.

Directly below my boot was the largest pile of fresh grizzly scat I'd ever seen. Not only that but in the cold of the morning with the frozen, slushy ground, the scat was steaming as if someone had just poured a hot cup of coffee on the ground. Before I could even react, I knew this was an immediately dangerous situation. That steaming scat could not have been over one minute old if even that. Catching my breath, it immediately registered with me, that I had interrupted a grizzly bear on this very spot of the blind curve, likely less than a half minute ago. He either heard my boot breaking the trail or smelled my scent, even though I was downwind, and then bolted away in the thickly forested patch. All I could do in that millisecond was draw my bear spray and step back. I had no idea where he immediately was, or if he returns enraged. With my vision obscured, I very nervously held my ground on the trail until I was satisfied, the bear had hopefully moved on.

Not only was the fresh huge scat pile steaming, but upon closer inspection it was loaded with digested intestine, fur, bone and teeth fragments, etc.

Steaming seconds-old grizzly scat with carcass remains.

Unquestionably, the grizzly had been on a carcass remains somewhere close by this "near miss" encounter. Completely unknown or undetected by me, one minute more, or less, I would have walked right into a feeding grizzly without warning. The results would have been likely catastrophic, if the grizzly bear had not bolted away, mere seconds earlier before I turned the blind curve. While I never saw the grizzly that I almost ran into, a fellow hiker who had been in the area as I was passing through, later informed me that he saw a very large grizzly bear crash through the same forested thicket that I had just entered.

This "near miss" encounter happened earlier in my Yellowstone grizzly years. I was most fortunate, to say the least, and learned still today, from the chilling experience. Even though I saw no signs whatsoever, that a grizzly was around this area, on reflection, I recall sensing that I was entering a potentially dangerous portion of the trail with the blind curve and the constricted passage between the rock ledge and forested patch. In hindsight, I should have made abundant noise of my presence and had the bear spray already drawn and ready for immediate discharge before entering a blind curve, or other visually restricted situation. I'm grateful that I had an opportunity to learn that lesson and often have bear spray at the ready when entering a high-risk location.

In my judgment, the next two such encounters of massive grizzlies on a carcass, if not for the Yellowstone River between the bear and myself, would be examples of retreating and abandoning photo attempts. Also, the enormous size of the grizzlies involved would dictate leaving the area quickly and safely as possible.

Perhaps the following two sightings with grizzly bears on a carcass may have involved at least one, if not, the largest existing grizzlies in all of Yellowstone. Both situations occurred on the east banks of the Yellowstone River in the Hayden Valley area.

The first was on a fall visit to YNP. I was passing through Yellowstone heading to another location. Fortunately, I arrived just in time before the sun would set, diminishing my photo prospects. What I witnessed was incredible. As I took a position on the west bank of the Yellowstone, I soon spotted an enormous grizzly bear heading from the forest to the river bank. The distance separating us was the width of the river, which I'd estimate about one hundred yards, perhaps slightly less. With my binoculars focusing on the river bank, a set of large elk antlers appeared to be coming out of the river's edge as the massive grizzly arrived.

Large grizzly caches elk kill on Yellowstone River bank.

I learned from another source that this grizzly killed this 700 lb. bull elk. The elk was being chased by the grizzly above a small rise above the river bank. The elk ran into the Yellowstone River with the bear in closing pursuit. In around two feet of water, with some slightly deeper pockets, with amazing power and speed, the grizzly brought down the elk, killed it, and then dragged the body back to the east side of the river. There he commenced to open the carcass and began feeding. This was a prized and vital kill, as this event occurred in the fall, as bears were in the hyperphagia phase of putting on as many needed calories and protein to sustain themselves through the long winter before denning in hibernation.

The grizzly repositioned the carcass several times on the bank and aggressively defended the remains from a host of intruding coyotes, eagles, wolves, and other grizzlies' intent upon stealing his reward. He was victorious in several vicious fights with other scavenging bears. After a fair amount of the remains were devoured and the body began losing some volume, the bear proceeded to bury or cache the elk on the river bank. At times, only the antlers or a leg would appear from the ground. This was a perfect example of the extreme danger a human, or another predator, would face coming upon a bear on a carcass.

The second encounter occurred two years later, except in the spring, in the same general area of the Yellowstone River. However, this remarkable grizzly/carcass encounter involved what is believed to be one of the largest, if not the largest, grizzly in all of Yellowstone. I have no reason to believe otherwise. There was only one male grizzly bear that in his prime, may have challenged that assessment. More of that, in a later chapter.

Recall the adage of being in the right place at the right time. Well, this is exactly what took place on May 19, 2022. My youngest adult son Michael and I were on one of our father-son spring hiking/grizzly photography trips. Driving on our way to our designated hiking location, we came upon a stunning sight of an enormous grizzly bear near some rocks lining the east bank of the Yellowstone River. Near the same bank, we saw a large flesh-colored object with large open blood-red areas. We quickly descended or better stated, stumbled down a fairly steep wooded hill down to the west bank of the Yellowstone. We could now well see that object in the water, was a partially scavenged fairly fresh bison carcass with visible large areas of remaining red meat. Mike and I were at different vantage points as the steep hill was still snowy and quite slippery with deeper hillside snow patches. I had more difficulty traversing the hillside and had to settle about halfway down, propping myself up against some whitebark pine trees for support.

As always, youth prevailed as Michael safely made it down the slope near the Yellowstone River's west bank. While we maintained our positions for an extended period, we were transfixed with what our eyes were seeing across the river. The massive grizzly moved on many occasions, alternating feeding with chasing off the same suspects; ravens, eagles, and coyotes. I did not see any other bears or wolves approach the carcass while we were there. Suffice it to say, they made testing approaches.

Later we learned, unlike the previous elk caching I observed several years earlier near the same Yellowstone River bank, this grizzly bear did not kill this bison. Exactly what happened to the bison remained unknown. Perhaps it died of natural causes or drowned while fording the Yellowstone. In any event, the bison carcass was floating down the middle of the river when this massive boar crashed down from the east bank into the river and retrieved the carcass. Once again, a most valuable coveted spring, a post-hibernation source of badly needed protein. I don't know if any other grizzly bear would dare challenge a grizzly of his enormous size, weight, and stature.

Massive grizzly retrieves bison carcass from the Yellowstone River.

After we left this extraordinary viewing, we met a well-seasoned and senior YNP ranger who had arrived at the scene and also viewed the hulking grizzly. Like Mike and I, the ranger was in absolute awe of the grizzly bear he had just seen. He shared with us that in all of his many years in YNP, this was the largest grizzly he has ever seen and opined probably the largest ever. The ranger estimated his weight in the 700-750lb range. He further confirmed the bear was unknown to him and was not collared, nor tagged.

I listened as the ranger excitedly contacted other colleagues to describe the grizzly bear he just witnessed. I figured that if a senior YNP ranger was so amazed by the size and presence of this enormous male, indeed this bear could be the largest or contending largest grizzly bear alive in Yellowstone today.

Is this bear the largest living grizzly bear in all of Yellowstone?

Yes, Yellowstone is indeed a sprawling preserved wilderness with unrivaled beauty, as well as dangers within. If hiking in the field and running into a grizzly of this enormity, it would be a heart stopping encounter. I know that sense of dread from a personal experience. It happened to me. Again, more of that encounter in a later chapter.

I happened upon and witnessed both of these extraordinary river/carcass sightings while driving through Yellowstone en route to other distant planned hiking destinations. Both events perfectly exemplify the reality and randomness of exceptional wildlife sighting opportunities that may arise. However, the pure luck of viewing events of this type of activity and proximity are extraordinarily uncommon and few and far between.

However, you never know what just may be around the corner while in Yellowstone.

Another situation I've encountered is standing grizzly bears. I must readily admit, the first time I experienced one in close naked eyesight, my nerves and reactions were on high unsettled alert. Halfway through the meadow, with the wind swirling, but generally in a downwind direction, I spotted a grizzly on one of the meadow's tree lines. Instantly stopping I viewed him nervously peering into a thicket of brush and deadfall. The bear did not appear to be aware of my presence as I hiked through some thickets and forested patches. The meadow was starting to green up after a long winter buried deep in the snow.

Grizzly rears up and intently peers into a thicket.

The dead brush crunched slightly beneath his hind legs, as he slightly pivoted to his left. He was intently gazing (and listening) to something in the thicket as he stood erectly with his large front paws and long whiteish claws out in front for nearly a minute. I saw no other movement or presence of any other animal nearby, except for a few bison several hundred yards off in the distance. I have no idea what the grizzly was focusing on via eyesight, scent, or movement. Whatever it was, it had him spooked. He dropped back down to all fours and bounded away, thankfully in an opposite direction from my position still in the meadow. With the wind, could the grizzly have caught the scent of another larger bear, or a hiker? Whatever it was, in response, appears to have caused the grizzly to quickly vacate the area.

A "standing grizzly bear" on its hind legs, is related to generally several situations. With a standing position, a Yellowstone grizzly can reach heights up to eight feet. The bear may be standing to reach food in trees or shrubs. Other behaviors include; exhibiting a show of dominance, marking a territory, back-scratching, or gaining a better view of the landscape or object, with a grizzly's less than stellar eyesight. Whatever the reasons, when standing erect, it's sure to draw excitement from onlooking Yellowstone tourists and a sense of caution, perhaps fear, from hikers. My first solo sighting was more of a sense of fear.

Grizzly tree scrapes 7 ft high & hair embedded in tree sap.

Hiking several miles in the Shoshone National Forest outside of the east entrance to YNP, I heard limbs crack on a hillside to my left. Looking up for the source of the sound, it wasn't exactly what I wanted to see. It was a grizzly bear putting on the brakes as he was quickly coming downslope in my direction. The bear itself never made a sound or a warning by jaw popping or other verbalizations. He came to an abrupt standstill, glaring at me when I took this photo. I had already unholstered my bear spray. Much to my relief, as suddenly as he appeared, the bear turned and bounded back uphill into the forest. But for the cracking branches on the ground, I had no idea whatsoever there was a grizzly was in this vicinity. My actual photo is below.

As I've stated before, in my experience, most of the encounters and sightings are random events. Sometimes I'm aware that bears are, or have been in the vicinity that I'm hiking, based on signs such as grizzly digs, scat (fresh or old), or perhaps, familiarity with an area where I've seen bears or signs of bear activity. This chance encounter was unnerving but exemplified the need to know what and what not to do while doing your best to remain calm. This event also stressed the fact to keep your ears open to your surroundings.

While quietly hiking off trail through some deadfall in the northwest sector of YNP, at a distance I caught a glimpse of a dark object moving in the thicket. I thought at first it was a small bison. The animal was upwind from me as I remained still and my scent wouldn't be readily detected. Fifteen seconds later the animal continued moving through the brush and entered a less dense clearing area. It wasn't an elk, rather it was a grizzly bear. In very short order, a young, perhaps subadult followed what was now a sow. I always turn my camera settings so that there is no clicking sound when I depress the shoot button. Believe it or not, that sound can carry in the right conditions and alert an animal of your presence. I was photographing a grizzly bear that was visibly unaware of me. As I depressed the shoot button the "lens click" went off. The bear's head immediately raised and turned to sense what that unnatural noise was. Little things like that can mean the difference between a good photo and spooked wildlife.

Yearling cub follows Mom through deadfall.

Chapter 6

A Bison Funeral Service

Large boar feeding on the carcass while surrounded closely by bison.

My grizzly bear photography received a real gift with a photo opportunity, capturing a grizzly bear on a carcass, with six bison standing mere feet from the feeding bear. A sighting that rarely presents itself while in the wild.

I spotted this Yellowstone legendary grizzly following a carcass scent for well over a mile. He trekked over open terrain with a focused unbroken gait, only occasionally stopping to throw his nose into the air, in radar-like fashion, to home in on the irresistible source. Along the way, startled pronghorn gazed at the bear, ready to dash away with their incredible speed. The grizzly closed the final gap to the carcass by breaking into a rush and sending gathering ravens scattering away from the carcass he was about to claim.

What was so unique about this situation was the presence of six to eight bison standing within feet from the carcass. The bison was unflinching as the grizzly arrived and basically, "stood at attention" as the bear circled and sniffed, immediately starting to feed on the carcass. Several fool-hearty coyotes tried in vain to creep within the morsel snatching distance of the carcass. At no time, did I witness any aggressive or defensive behavior or posturing by the grizzly to the crowding bison. Incredibly, around eight adult bison, remained just a few feet away from the carcass as the large boar was actively feeding on and guarding the carcass. Some wildlife experts firmly believe that bison, similar to documented elephant behavior, will gather, defend and mourn a fallen bison, similar to a funeral. I think this little seen bison's behavior was exactly the reason I witnessed this drama playing out, without any aggressive behavior whatsoever, by the grizzly to the standing bison next to him. Yet again, perhaps the bison had no fear of the grizzly as it was content feeding on the bison and would not unnecessarily, exert valuable effort and energy to attack the live bison.

This amazing encounter just kept getting better as time passed. He would feed in intervals, often lifting and ripping off large portions of the still-bloody red torso. When he had his fill, he would scoop dirt with his four-inch straight claws surrounding the carcass to semi-cache the bonanza of remaining protein and calories. Bears often cache a large carcass to prevent the carcass scent from attracting other predators. Grizzlies can pick up a scent like these two to three miles away. With no apparent concerns, he would take prolonged naps on the carcass mound. After fifteen-to-thirty-minute naps, he would awaken, pan his surroundings, and when satisfied no threat was near, began feasting all over again.

Several years later, I witnessed "bison mourning behavior" which solidified this belief. I had been in the northeast corner of YNP and was returning west back to Gardiner, MT. Along the road, no more than a hundred feet from the shoulder, a bison carcass was lying in an open grassy area. One or two vehicles had stopped while a YNP ranger stood beside his truck. I stopped to speak with him. He informed me that late last night, a car heading west had struck and killed this bison that was on or crossing the road. The ranger along with two others were dispatched to the accident scene. After clearing the road and transporting the driver for medical attention, they had to return and move the carcass off the middle of the road. Unfortunately, they didn't have any four-wheeler or other heavy equipment to move the bison a safe distance away from the road and leave the bison remains for the benefit of wildlife and fowl scavenging. So, the three men by hand only had to drag the carcass as far as they could off the road, until wildlife management could later bring in the proper equipment to relocate it far out in the prairie grass. I knew by morning, this could turn into a prime, an intensely close opportunity for wolves and bears to locate and feed. I remained there for an hour or so and saw two very nervous coyotes cautiously move toward the bison. After half an hour, they arrived, smelled the carcass, and then left over a far hillcrest. They were too small to open the carcass. Magpies and a few ravens had located and perched on the body. I figured overnight, wolves and/or grizzlies would arrive to open and start the feeding process with their strong establishing domination.

Early the next morning I arrived back at the location. It was apparent some wolves had found the remains as the bison's head was nearly severed from the neck and the anal area opened and exposed. Both are typical wolf behavior. No signs yet that a grizzly was here, but no doubt that would happen at any time. What else I observed was amazing, sad, and very thought-provoking.

Agitated bison closely surround newly killed bison carcass, exhibiting bison mourning behavior.

Standing directly next to and around the fallen bison were several adult bison. They would lower their heads toward the body and grunt, as to provoke a response. Despite the reappearance of more coyotes, the herd maintained their guarding-like positions and attitude and would not leave his side. Suddenly, a giant one-ton bull bison running at full speed crossed the road not far from me and went straight for the fallen bison. It didn't slow or stop until it reached the remains. Observing his behavior very closely, the bull appeared very distressed and shifted his massive one-ton body, between the other guarding bison. He lowered his head and physically tried to raise the body from the ground. The head was raised slightly with repeated lifting efforts by the bull. He remained there for nearly an hour with the rest of the small herd. I could not help but feel or sense, these bison were paying their respects to a fallen member of the herd and had suffered the loss of life.

One-ton bull repeatedly attempts to raise the head of the fallen bison.

The bull very reluctantly moved away. Heading back in the direction he came from; he would occasionally turn around and look back down at the remains and the other herd members standing guard. After the bull departed, the remaining herd members moved in tighter and appearing as a group, nudged and prodded the body, as if in a final attempt to either revive or mourn, their fallen member.

After a long period of observation, I finally left knowing that I had just witnessed in very close proximity, a full rare "bison funeral." I too felt remorse and left the scene paying my respects and honoring the life of this bison. Viewing this incredible display of activity, strong bonds, and loss, I believed this was a genuine display of grief. After observing what I just witnessed, I didn't feel any desire to stay with the carcass any longer and record the predicable arrival of hungry predators. Yes, by leaving the carcass, I was certain that I was giving up a tremendous opportunity to observe and photograph the very first arrivals of large predators to claim the newly killed carcass. I guess that I simply had too much respect and reserved feelings for the bison herd and their fallen comrade. I left the area with competing feelings of sadness, astonishment, and empathy with strings of human feelings, watching this Yellowstone drama unfold.

Leaving the carcass so close to the road would invite all sorts of calamities with tourists and present a first-degree human danger zone. Before this inevitable situation had a chance to develop, on the following day wildlife officials removed the bison carcass from the entire area and hauled away.

Learning of this, some folks were quite upset, even mad, that the carcass wasn't just moved back several hundred yards to a safer distance away. This would allow nature itself, to provide a beneficial source of nutrition and value to other dependent wildlife. Nothing goes to waste in Yellowstone. Strangely, but respectfully thankful, I was comforted that no such event would occur here.

The Final Farewell. The last remaining bison guards over its fallen herd member.

Chapter 7

Tracking a Grizzly

Fresh Grizzly Tracks-Cutoff Trail Black Butte.

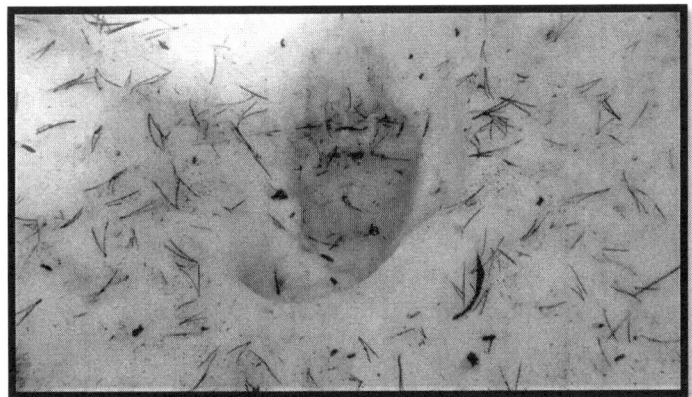

The Taylor Fork area is situated in the Gallatin National Forest outside and adjacent to YNP and is part of the Gallatin Mountain Range. This drainage also affords access to the Lee Metcalf Wilderness. It's a wilderness area with wide expanses to recreate. The Taylor Fork is also prime habitat for elk, wolves, and grizzly bears.

My son, Michael, and I had spent several late spring days hiking productive grizzly sections without any bear sightings. I decided to relocate our search back to YNP with a new, but familiar area I had hiked in years past. It would be a trail in an area that would be new ground for Mike. I knew he would like the terrain and wildlife potential.

The next day was seasonally cool and mostly sunny as we geared up at the Black Butte trailhead. There are many trails in that northwest section of YNP, all of which I have spent considerable time hiking. Not knowing what might be in store for us, we set out on the trail which borders a good portion of Black Butte Creek. The sound of the high-running spring creek was relaxing as we passed in and out of deep forested shadows. We took a little trail break after a few miles and refilled our filtration water containers with the clear cold water of Black Butte Creek. As we further proceeded, I was beginning to think our wildlife viewing opportunities were going to be difficult, as it was several days before with our Taylor Fork hikes. We had worked some of the areas persistently hard, but wildlife was elusive. Something ahead of me off the Black Butte trail caught my eye. My first distant impression was that of a large carcass.

What happened here, on the Black Butte Trail?

Scattered across the trail and downslope was tufted white and light tan/brown fur. On examination, I assume it came from an elk or mule deer which a predator nearby had taken down. Strangely, the fur appeared to have been plucked, or tufted from the animal. There was no skin or hide anywhere to be found. I wondered if this could have been the work of a mountain lion. I learned that bears will not eat fur/hair, but mountain lions will consume significant portions of it. Searching the area, we didn't find any evidence of carcass or skeletal remains, only this large section of animal fur. I've never seen a mountain lion in Yellowstone, but they do exist. Several years prior, in this same area on another trail, I came across a clear mountain lion track which I was able to easily verify by its very distinctive features from that of a wolf. What I understand is that mountain lions are more likely (though in low numbers) to be found in the northern half of Yellowstone where deer, their primary food, is perhaps more abundant, and the mountain terrain more suitable habitat.

Well, the bottom line was I couldn't be certain of exactly what took place here, or by what. Several other possible theories could have been involved, including extensive rubbing or scraping, perhaps involving an animal with severe mange. I'll leave this field mystery to the experts.

However, this finding rejuvenated my hopeful prospects of wildlife. I couldn't have imagined what later transpired. This is a good example of always paying attention to detail and signs while hiking the backcountry. It's also pleasurable to locate and read signs, and then determine with personal skillset and knowledge, what those signs reveal. Once accomplished, you may have then unraveled a storyline left behind by nature and actions. If you will, "reading the tea leaves" can be both an important and exciting rewarding field experience.

Continuing along the Black Butte Trail we reached a backcountry campsite. The continuation of our hike to this position was uncharacteristically void of wildlife, just as had occurred previously in the Taylor Fork. Given the lack of our success, I was beginning to question my selection, or judgment to continue working in this general area in and outside of YNP. Perhaps I needed to relocate from this area and move more to the interior of Yellowstone. Some trips are indeed just like this.

I discussed our options with Mike. We could stay here and move off in a different direction, or pull up stakes and relocate elsewhere to try and salvage what was left of our remaining daylight hiking hours. "Well Dad, you know things around here, you make the call," he diplomatically replied.

Pulling my crumpled seasoned map out of my jacket, I surveyed our situation. After some self-guessing, I decided to remain in place and go with my gut instinct. The Black Butte sector is a wonderfully scenic area, and despite a drought in wildlife spotting so far today, the entire area holds good prospects for many wildlife species. I also figured out a path that would take us over some new ground that I hadn't covered before. Less than an hour later, little did I know that I was about to embark on a new venture, and without a hiking partner, I'd find myself in deep trouble.

Strapping our backpacks back on, we climbed and headed northwest up a cutoff trail that would parallel King Butte to the north and eventually intersect with the Daily Creek Trail. At the base of the climb, the ground was mostly clear with sporadic lingering patches of snow below shaded areas. Michael took the point position while I was Tail End Charlie, bringing up the rear. About forty minutes into the climb at 7,780 ft elevation, Mike yelled down at me pointing at the ground, "Dad, come here, fresh grizzly scat!" Making my way up to him, sure enough, a little way off trail on open ground, was indeed very fresh grizzly scat. I excitedly replied, "Way to go, excellent find, that's what we are looking for." All signs indicated the scat was under an hour old, perhaps closer to under thirty minutes.

I remained with the grizzly scat, marking its GPS position, and closely examined my map to better visualize the cutoff trail, which was now entering a thickly forested area. We had reached a crest or small plateau section on the hill we climbed. Here the ground was mostly covered with lingering heavy spring-crusted snow. The sun was brightly shining, casting long shadows from the spruce and whitebark pine trees.

Mike, continued uphill as the trail became fainter and snow/ice patches became more dominant. Five minutes later, as I proceeded uphill, somewhere in the timber, I heard him once again call out. This time it was, "Hurry, I've found grizzly tracks." He was correct the tracks and the scat in the snow were extremely fresh.

Michael discovers fresh grizzly tracks.

The grizzly bear tracks were first located in a small patch of snow just off the cutoff trail. We decided to follow the tracks and hopefully catch up, to perhaps see the bear at a safe distance break out into an open meadow. Along the way up, we came across a large area of fresh grizzly digs on both sides of the trail. Both the digs and examination of the scat revealed the grizzly was feeding on early nutritious vegetation of glacier lilies and spring beauties. We also found an opened old cache of whitebark pine nuts under a tree that the bear just fed on. Once again, an opportunistic bear had robbed an industrious chattering squirrel of all his hard work by nipping the seed cones from the tops of the trees and then caching them below the tree for food stores.

No doubt, the grizzly we were tracking had very recently stopped and searched for food along the cutoff trail. Grizzlies are both carnivores and also omnivores, as they feed primarily on plant matter, which they can chew. While they have poor digestion of plant matter, that issue is offset by their long digestive tract and by feeding when the most nutritious part of the plant is present.

We follow grizzly tracks up into the thicker forest.

Continuing to closely follow the tracks with bear spray at the ready, we closely monitor for any sounds, motion, etc. The tracks now departed from the trail and went somewhere off the trail into a thicker forest. Noticeably, the remaining forest snow pack was more widespread and deeper as we continued. The tracks remained very visible and occasionally, I would spot the grizzly's belly fur leaving brush-like strokes on the snow. I may have misread this sign as exhibiting it was safe for us to continue, as the snow/ice cover was supporting the full weight of an adult grizzly bear. Therefore, it shouldn't be much of a problem to continue tracking.

As we continued to track, Mike had pulled ahead and disappeared into the deep snowy timber. With my hiking pole, my footing was going deeper through the crusty surface. It now dawned on me, the reason the much heavier grizzly tracks were far less deep than mine, was because the bear could evenly distribute his superior weight with a much wider center of gravity and balance than a human could. I had no more finished that thought when almost on cue near the base of a huge pine, my right leg crashed through the deep snow above my upper thigh. At the same time, I lost all balance as my hiking pole sank and my left leg, plunged through around three-quarters, painfully bending ninety degrees behind me. I rolled forward with my torso now embedded in the icy heavy snow as my chest pressed against the top layer. It's a miracle that I did not snap a leg or break a hip. My biggest concern turned to my already injured back. The jolt certainly didn't make matters better.

I could barely move an inch, almost entombed from the chest down with my left leg locked straight back at the knee. I immediately called Michael for help. I couldn't see him but heard his voice somewhere ahead of me in the forest. My expandable hiking pole has a fist-sized round cork top. Using that as sort of a shovel, in vain I tried to dig out in an attempt to relieve some of the pressure off my bent leg and back. It didn't do any good, in fact, the more I tried to move, the deeper and more stuck I became. Through the pines, I could hear Mike at a distance trying to work his way back to me. It was evident that he was also struggling. It was obvious we both underestimated the snow depth as the grizzly tracked away from the trail and deeper into the timber.

I could not free myself or move in this precarious position and increasingly painful position. It took about ten minutes before he made it back to me, it was tough going coming back. He didn't know what trouble I was in. By this time, I was getting very cold and worn out trying to free myself, all to no avail. Pulling me by the shoulders from behind, Mike said he lost the grizzly tracks ahead as the bear kept going deeper into the forest almost turning, or a flanking movement. Grizzlies have been known to widely circle back on following people or other wildlife. I could do little to help extract myself, as pulling efforts did not work. My bent left leg and back remained at risk in the frozen slushy deep hole I was in. With our hands freezing, we struggled to try digging me out. About fifteen minutes later I was able to partially free my left leg. With a final yank at full strength, Mike was finally able to get me up.

This incident was the most serious physical situation I've encountered in Yellowstone. If the same situation had happened if I had been solo, which is the vast majority of my time, this could have been a tragic situation. I literally could not move, nor extricate myself from that icy imprisonment. No telling how long I would have remained in that backcountry predicament before anyone knew I was in trouble or assistance could have arrived. Furthermore, there was a grizzly bear still close in the area.

This situation opened my eyes and serious attention to the numerous dangers of backcountry hiking, especially solo which is not recommended, but remains a reality for myself and many other Yellowstone hikers. I decided right then and there, I would not venture out alone again in grizzly country, without some reliable means of emergency rescue/medical contact. In reality, that decision should have been made long before this ever happened to me. You just never know when something unforeseen or seemingly low-risk, changes on a dime. I would always leave a handwritten note on my dashboard at a trailhead, or departure point, with the date, times, and other identity data points before venturing out. However, it is not a foolproof, nor a positive form of communication in all situations if an emergency should arise.

To remedy the situation, while somewhat pricey, I wisely invested in a reliable, quality registered Emergency Personal Locator Beacon, or PLB. In reality, as much time as I spent in YNP and the GYE, I should have done this years ago. That was clear mismanagement and oversight on my part. Now, when I go out with my PLB securely attached and accessible, I have peace of mind, wherever or whatever conditions exist, emergency SAR services may be immediately summoned with a push of a button. I do not endorse or recommend any brands or features, that is entirely up to the user, consistent with his or her preferences and own personal research. It is one of my most important pieces of hiking equipment, hopefully never to be used.

Chapter 8

There's No Bears Around Here

It's not often while I'm hiking in the backcountry, that I'll come across another solo hiker or several hikers, in or around an area I'm traveling through. Sometimes I'll only spot another party at a distance away or meet on the trail. In my experience, all human encounters occurred on the trail, rarely off trail. It's good to see some others out enjoying the beauty, intrigue, and adventure backcountry hiking in grizzly country offers. When our trails intersect, creating a passing personal meeting, it's a welcome opportunity to exchange pleasantries, exchange trail information, and offer or receive, well-intended advice or cautions. Most personal encounters take place passing through the front country trails where most tourists or hikers will pass. Regardless if the trail is within the front or backcountry, we must always be cognizant that this is all grizzly bear country, with associated risks and rewards of which we have voluntarily decided to enter.

As mentioned above and elsewhere in my book, I've used the terms "risk and rewards" to simply point out they exist, as well as co-exist for YNP visitors. I've recited those terms primarily with grizzly bear-visitor interactions and potential injury or harm by a grizzly. There is validating actual statistical data to support this rather perceptible risk. According to a recent Yellowstone NPS article; *Bear-Inflicted Human Injuries and Fatalities in Yellowstone;* since 1979 YNP has hosted over 118 million visits. Combining data for all park visitors with recreational location and activity; the overall

<u>chance of being injured by a grizzly is 1 in 2.7 million visits.</u> However, when the risk of grizzly bear harm is weighed against the type of recreational activity within YNP; distinct levels with risk of harm are materially altered from the combined 1 in 2.7 million visits.

If a YNP visitor remains in a developed area, roadside, or boardwalk, the risk of harm is the lowest at 1 in 59 million visits. Camping in roadside campgrounds increases the risk to 1 in 26.6 million overnight stays. Change that roadside camp to backcountry overnight stays, then risk dramatically increases to 1 in 1.7 million stays. According to the NPS, the <u>highest degree of risk of grizzly bear injury is hiking in the backcountry, with a 1-to-232,613-person travel day</u>. This level of risk just happens to be where I spend the majority of my hiking/grizzly photography. I'm rather unfazed by any of the other risk categories, but this one rather guardedly catches my attention. Little did the hikers, especially the man, and boy in my following personal experience, have any idea or grasp of what they were stepping into. That being said, I suggest that all categories of risk with injuries caused by grizzly bears, indicate how extremely unlikely such an event is……. except if it should happen to you.

Every hiker I have met has been friendly and pleasant. However, the majority have been far less properly prepared or educated for the possibility of a potential bear encounter. That is not to say, nor to infer for a moment, an individual should be dominated by the thoughts or fears of running into a grizzly. Several primary concerns lead to my conclusion.

Overall, in my experience, less than twenty-five percent of hikers carry bear spray. Of that very low percentage, less than half are properly carrying it or would be able to access and deploy, if quickly needed within seconds, which is very often the exact time bear spray is needed. Again, in my experience of years of hiking Yellowstone and familiarity with grizzlies, there are very few trailheads inside YNP, or surrounding state forest lands, that I would leave a trailhead without bear spray.

Most often when I've met others with varying degrees of experience hiking in grizzly country, from none to occasional, they will ask me questions about how I travel and the surroundings. I'm happy to share my ways, but I never impose or suggest my preparation as theirs. The only exception might be if I objectively see or learn of a glaring personal safety situation. On one occasion, I was on the Mary Mountain trail several miles well into the Hayden Valley. Off to the side of the trail, I was glassing an upslope tree line. I spotted what I believed was a bear slowly moving in and out of the tree line. At the same time, I heard some singing coming from the trail behind me. It was a young couple enjoying a mid-morning hike into the valley. Seeing me, they stopped. Both had on small fanny packs and earbuds draping around their necks. The young man asked me what was I seeing. I told him, likely a bear up near the tree and sage line. He responded, "Cool, we aren't worried, we have bear spray." Introducing myself, I didn't see any bear spray on either hiker and quickly determined they were very inexperienced. I used that opportunity to friendly ask him, what brand of bear spray did they carry? He turned to the young lady, fumbling through a small belt pack. "Here it is," she responded, waving a small several-ounce pink spray cylinder. It wasn't bear spray, but rather a small container of drug store personal mase.

Neither of them knew the difference between bear spray and dime store mace. Nonetheless, until now they felt comfortable that they had protection if a bear was encountered. I took the liberty of helping them, as they still wanted to do some more hiking on their first YNP visit. Taking a second backup canister of bear spray out of my backpack, I offered it to them and if needed, showed them how to use it. They were very nice kids, but they just didn't know any better. On our parting well wishes, I also smiled with them and cautioned them to leave the earbuds off and pocket them while hiking in bear country. That's a very bad, unsafe thing to do in grizzly bear country. They refused the bear spray I offered them. I did my best to try to help them.

Another similar occasion comes to mind. I started off hiking in the morning one early, somewhat foggy spring day in the general area of Central Canyon. The ground was very soft from melted snow. I first entered the area through a sizable stand of the forest before it opened up with many intersecting small creeks and rivulets. Ahead, I spotted a coyote slowly walking between the trees appearing ghostly like in the remaining ground fog.

After a messy crossing of somewhat flooded ground, I emerged into a large greening meadow. The sun continued to slowly rise, as my visibility increased. After ten minutes or so, I was able to locate and follow one of the trails that transected the large meadow. Watching the ground as I slowly continued, I came across recent elk, bison, and deer tracks and scat near the trail and numerous matted-down game trails in the still-wet grasses. A beautiful morning had evolved and my hopes were high that I might find a large moose or two, along the early budding willow streams. By all appearances, wildlife appeared to be on the move.

I went on for another mile or so, crossing or hopping over small streams and occasional deadfall bisecting my trail. Thereafter, I stood in near disbelief at the number of large and fresh grizzly digs spread out in the open meadow, on both sides of the trail. They were so prevalent, it looked like a John Deere tractor had been through here displacing the soft green earth into the likes of World War I trench warfare.

Grizzly bear homes in on the sound of a pocket gopher in digs.

My wildlife sighting expectations were rising, especially now for possible grizzly bears seeking nutrient emerging vegetation growth. I thought about locating a suitable vantage position to continually glass the large meadow for present or returning bears. Standing there on the trail pondering where to reposition myself, my eye drifted to the movement of two objects coming out of the forest above the south far end of the meadows. Focusing my 10x binoculars on the movement, it was an adult with a young child. I didn't know where they were heading, but I decided to move my vantage point for covering the meadows to the timberline on the far south side of the rich meadow. Without seeing any current active bears, I continued hiking on my trail to the south end. While hiking to my destination, I no longer spotted the two hikers. Around a quarter mile or less, south of my position, I could see what appeared to be an intersection of trails through the trees. I soon arrived and verified two trails are heading in opposite directions.

Dropping down to a little rise above the meadow, I eased my backpack off and started to set up my spotting scope tripod, when I heard a "hello there" from behind. Turning, I saw a middle-aged man with a ten-year-old or so, boy at his side. They were the two I had seen from the far side of the meadow near the start of the grizzly bear digs. I greeted them, introducing myself, and they did likewise. I'm terrible at this, but I would estimate the gentleman to be somewhere in his late thirties and only missed his cute son's ten years of age, by a year. We talked for a while and I explained to him what I was doing and where I had come from. They had not seen me but heard me moving about in the brush setting up my scope. In good nature, I jokingly said, "I hope I didn't scare you, by thinking I was a bear." He kind of snapped back replying, "Why, there's no bears anywhere around here, none!" Before responding directly to the point of his remark, I learned his family was here in Yellowstone for a second trip. He wasn't a hiker, but decided to just, "take a walk out in the woods with my son." Without a map, he had taken more than just a walk in the woods. He wore a jacket with very muddy tennis shoes, while his son had on a small school-like backpack. I congratulated the two on their choice and offered encouragement that they may have a nice chance to see some wildlife on their walk, as I have already seen good signs of movement this morning.

The young boy's eyes lit up, with an exclamation, "Oh boy, Dad!" when he heard what I just said. His Dad replied with words like, "Well I hope so, we'll just see as we continue on the trail." At this point, he shared that they were going to turn on and out, on the same trail I just came from. Asking the gentleman if he had bear spray with him, he replied, "No, what for? We've been here twice now and never seen a bear. Besides, I have my cell phone with me." I didn't want to scare his son, but I told the man the fact that you haven't seen a bear, doesn't mean "there are no bears anywhere around here," as he had stated. The fact was this area is bear habitat and bears indeed are in and foraging in this general area. I stated, "You or I may not see a grizzly here today, but they were in this large meadow very recently, evident by the numerous fresh grizzly digs I saw." He didn't seem to have any interest or accept my explanation of the presence of bears and their fresh ground digs. I explained what grizzly digs were. Perhaps he didn't care much or was just disgruntled about something. Well, that's his call. I was just trying to help out.

He congenially announced they were going to continue and head back out. I wished them good luck and to be safe as they said goodbye and started walking away on the meadow trail. I watched them hike away for three or four minutes and I just happened to look down on the ground where the three of us had been standing. My eyes just popped. Several feet to the left where the boy had just been standing, were huge fresh grizzly bear tracks, clear as day, in the muddy grass. It was one of the larger grizzly tracks I'd seen during my outing. I had no idea they were there.

Huge fresh grizzly bear track next to where the boy was standing.

I quickly got down and closely examined the huge track to be certain. No doubt, this was a classic, large grizzly track with claw prints extending far up from the toes. The pads are deep and wide. Moisture was still present in the toe and pad indents and the track ridges were firm. This track belonged to a very large grizzly, most probably a dominant male. In my estimation, the track was about two hours old, or less. Coupled with the fresh grizzly digs close by in the meadow, the presence of this bear all made sense. The question now was where is this large grizzly? He could have gone through the meadow, entered the forested area, or perhaps lingered somewhere out of sight on a nearby daybed.

With this disquieting discovery, I quickly stood up and yelled to draw the attention of the man and his son still moving away on the trail adjacent to the meadow and a tree line. Following several loud repeated attempts, I saw the young boy tug at his dad and point back in my direction. As he turned to me, I hollered for them to return here and repeatedly, waved my arm gesturing for them to come back. I was relieved when I saw him wave back at me and turned around, starting back. I positioned myself from where they first departed. Arriving, he asked with a somewhat annoyed tone, "What is it, something wrong?"

I gave his son a little high five. Smiling, he seemed to be liking all this. I asked the man, "Well sir, do you still believe that "there are no bears anywhere around here?" Remaining very confident in his statement he added, "Of course, I am, why should I believe any differently? Yea the country is pretty and with luck, we might see some bison, but certainly no bears. That's all a bunch of Yellowstone hype." Replying, in a thoughtful tone, I stated, "Well ok, I understand, but before you leave again, look down on the ground you're are standing to the left of your son." He replied, "I don't see anything, did we leave something here?" Taking a few steps over to them, I didn't say anything, rather with a branch stick in my hand, I circled on the ground the outline of the huge new grizzly bear track. He had no idea what he was looking at. After I explained the track and reiterated, indeed there are grizzly bears around here, he just stood speechless for a few moments. Next to me, the little boy got down on a muddy knee and traced the outer edges of the grizzly track with his index finger, and then placed his open hand inside the track. His mouth opened wide as his open hand was swallowed up by the bear track. His immediate response was, "Holy cow!" I just knew he had an adventure of a lifetime. I stood back up and further explained to his dad that I didn't want to frighten anyone, but this was real information he needed to know for both their and my safety.

My first thought was I could escort them out, as I had bear spray and know how to use it. The problem was, I was going in the opposite direction and still had much of the day to go. As we talked some more, his son was so excited with non-stop questions about bears. He was also a little afraid. I volunteered to keep an eye on them with my binoculars and scope until they were way out of distance beyond the grizzly bear digs and far meadow. He appreciated it and I felt it was simply the right thing to do.

Thanking me and expressing they would be careful hiking out, they set out once more on the trail. This time, knowing a huge grizzly stood exactly where they had hiked and had been standing, their step was quickened and he looked more attentive to his surroundings.

If I had a spare canister of bear spray with me, I would have given it to him. But it was his decision, consciously or otherwise, not to get bear spray. I can't help but recall at least three other individual YNP hikers who had been attacked and killed by grizzly bears several years earlier, around fifteen miles south of here. Failure to carry bear spray was the common denominator in those tragedies.

Shaking that thought from my mind, for half an hour, I kept a constant watch on them with my binoculars and spotting scope as they successfully hiked their way out, thankfully without incident. Who knows, this whole thing could have come out quite differently if the timing had been an hour, or so earlier. Whether the man ever ventures out again in grizzly country, I'm hopeful this was a learning moment. I entertain a much better hunch that perhaps someday, possibly his son, will recall this meeting in a grizzly bear meadow with a stranger; as he creates his adventures and safe travels, somewhere in the expanses of Yellowstone.

Chapter 9

My Tribute to Legendary Yellowstone Grizzly #211

I author this chapter with an enduring sense of adventure and respect with having three close personal encounters with #211, tempered by questionable killing activities that ended the storied life of this legendary 25-year-old male Yellowstone grizzly. He was fondly identified by Yellowstone visitors as "Scarface." His name was related to a maze of white scars crossing his face/muzzle and the loss of his right ear. All injuries were inflicted by fearsome fights with other grizzly bears. A few opine they were created by the bear pulling off numerous tracking collars. I don't share that view. I've observed collared grizzlies in the wild with white head scarring, albeit not as extensive as #211. Others have written about the life and death of #211. However, here in my book, beyond generic information, I'm restricting my writing and knowledge to my own close personal field experiences and factual knowledge relating to his killing from redacted official records disclosed in response to a FOIA request of same. Throughout this chapter, please keep in mind, that at all times, from birth to his death, this grizzly bear was afforded both federal and state protection under the Endangered Species Act.

"A Conflicted Truce" Scarface #211 on Carcass 2014.

Bear #211 was born in Yellowstone in 1990. Starting in his early life as a subadult, #211 would be no stranger to wildlife management trappings. As early as age three, he was first captured and collared. Over his next 22 years of life, he would be recaptured 16 more times with additional tagging and radio telemetry collars. In his prime, Scarface was one of the largest Yellowstone boar grizzly bears, weighing up to, and perhaps beyond 600 pounds. At the time of his killing on November 18, 2015, just a few miles north of Gardiner, MT, and the YNP border, given his advanced age his weight significantly declined to the mid-300-pound range, due to advanced old age and extensive loss of teeth with general dental deterioration. Collectively, these issues restricted his ability to feed. Before his later years of life, #211 was a dominating superb specimen of a large male grizzly. Rangers reported his presence and demeanor as having no fear and a roaming range, inside and outside YNP, of 579 sq miles, nearly twice that of other male Yellowstone grizzlies.

In my opinion, Yellowstone's East Entrance corridor to Lake Yellowstone is exceptional grizzly bear territory. While much of the territory is heavily forested and does not appear to have the vast areas of open and mixed habitat, favored by grizzly bears, as in the Gallatin Mountain Range, Hayden, and Lamar Valleys; it is nonetheless a very productive expanse for the bears. I might also add that I favor the mountains, forests, and meadows of the National Forests east of the YNP East Entrance (Shoshone, Absaroka, and others) as prime grizzly bear country. I often hike in some of these amazing areas.

During my early years of GYE hiking/photo grizzly bears, I had occasionally heard of an iconic, crowd-captivating YNP huge grizzly referred to as Scarface. I never expected that I would have an opportunity to encounter him in the field. Perhaps in years, I'd luck out and catch a glimpse of this intriguing YNP legacy bear somewhere in my backcountry hikes. The outlandish thought of a close encounter never entered my mind. Nonetheless, my emerging experience devoted to learning about, and locating Yellowstone grizzlies, kept that name in the back of my mind.

On a clear crisp early morning of September 29, 2011, I was solo hiking within YNP near the Cub Creek Drainage that eventually flows into Lake Yellowstone. I felt relatively confident that I might find signs, or even spot a grizzly bear still in the hyperphagia stage of pre-hibernation. The area I was concentrating on had large swaths of white pine bark intermingled with dying and dead trees from the culmination of prior fires, pine beetle infestation, and white pine blister rust. The presence of a few chattering red squirrels aided my hopes that I was in the right place and time, for seasonal sources of whitebark pine nuts and other late fall foods grizzly bears are now very dependent upon.

With the early morning sun from the east at my back I hiked along the shallow bubbling Cub Creek. While moving away from the creek, suddenly and silently emerging from out of nowhere, a massive deep brown, almost black grizzly bear slowly, but confidently emerged from a dense tree line walking in a determined gait straight toward me. I stood frozen, not blinking an eye, and with a swift flick of my thumb, removed the safety from my bear spray canister. I also stood in near disbelief, yet remained calm, at the enormous size of this bear as the rising sun shined directly on him as he approached me, around 30-40 ft away. The early low morning sun lit up his entire head and muzzle, as his massive paws with long straight claws, silently moved across the ground. I'll never forget that moment or this terrifying encounter. It was just way too incredibly close. His face was a crossing maze of pronounced white, highly visible scars, and all that remained of his right ear was a tiny stub.

Grizzly Bear #211 aka Scarface, walks past me 15 ft away along Cub Creek.

All I could do was try to remain calm and motionless. My side was perpendicular to him as he walked past me with a mere 15 ft separating us. His massive shoulder hump appeared to be nearly even with my field of view. As I now saw him so insanely close to me, I distinctly noticed he had a brand-new shiny right-red ear tag affixed to a tiny stub of an ear. He was also wearing a brand new, stiff shiny radio/telemetry collar. *This feature relates to a tragic hiker fatality that I previously shared and will come back to.

As I remained in position with eyes locked on him, he turned to his left and gazed at me as he passed directly next to me. Our eyes locked for a brief moment or two. He then turned his head around and kept walking past me. The grizzly's presence and proximity were simply overwhelming. The absolute truth was that at any moment if he had so desired, this mighty grizzly bear could have taken me out in the blink of an eye. No doubt whatsoever, and I knew that fear from the very moment I saw him.

However, by the Grace of God, this bear whom I then knew for certain, was the Yellowstone legendary Scarface, had no interest or desire, in harming or instantly killing me. While standing there, just one ill movement, bad decision, or reaction on my part, could have altered my encounter into a Yellowstone fatality. Somebody was watching over me, years later I know that to this very day. In total silence, Scarface appeared, and in total silence, he left. Slightly trembling, trying to collect my wits about me, I watched #211 disappear into the colorful autumn forest.

After passing me seconds ago, #211 continues up Cub Creek.

Days later I shared my encounter and photos with a YNP Ranger stationed at the East Entrance. He indeed confirmed, this was Scarface and informed me that he was seen several days prior in the forest around Sylvan Lake east of here.

Please refer back to Part I, Chapter Five, Page 23, Death in the Hayden Valley/John Wallace. There you will specifically see a reference to "Bear #211 being captured in the Hayden Valley area three times. He was released after being cleared in the August 25, 2011, grizzly bear death of hiker, Mr. John Wallace. An excerpt from that chapter by investigating wildlife officials follows:

Grizzly bear #211 during this period was captured three times. On September 15th then 21-year-old, 453 lb. male was first captured at the Grebe Pit site. He was released as physical and DNA testing also cleared him of involvement. On September 16th one day later, "Scarface" was recaptured at the Otter Creek trap site and released. Three days later, on September 19th, *he was captured a third time at the Crater Hills trap site and released without handling on-site.*

There was a ten-day difference between Scarface's multiple trappings in different locations in the Hayden Valley fatality location and my encounter on September 29[th.] Based upon the investigative research, ranger information, and now my close encounter, I highly suspect Grizzly Bear #211 had been recently relocated from the ongoing bear trapping in the wide expanse of Hayden Valley to some undisclosed distant location deep inside eastern YNP. Sometime during that period, a new shiny red ear tag and radio/telemetry collar were placed. That would identically match what I viewed a meager 15 feet away. I concluded that Scarface was making his way back west/northeast to familiar habitation territory with the quickly approaching hibernation period. These very recent events led to the early morning harrowing intersection of both our paths at Cub Creek. To this very day, I remain quite unsettled with the very realization, at any moment, our extremely close unforeseen encounter could have exploded with terrifying results. Despite my handling of the situation, I give all credit to #211. He was in absolute full control of whatever outcome would come to be. Fortunately, I believe his nonaggressive demeanor and long history of avoiding serious conflict with humans, ruled the morning on Cub Creek. Also, at the time of this event, I was amazed to be within just a few years of initiating my journey with Yellowstone grizzlies, to not only witness but become a focal part of such an uncertain close encounter with Yellowstone's iconic legendary grizzly.

A few years had passed since the Cub Creek-Scarface encounters. You can bet your bottom dollar, that experience remained etched in my psyche as I continued my passion for hiking/photographing GYE grizzly bears. I never expected to see, nor planned backcountry hikes to locate #211 again. If not, I had experienced a never to be forgotten, incredible personal encounter. Well, if you remain steadfast with Yellowstone, expect the unexpected.

While glassing the distant confluence of Slough Creek and the Lamar River, I sighted a grizzly bear moving and lying down on the river bank. To better gain light on the shaded area and get a better view of the bear, I moved to a closer vantage point to continue glassing. Now I could see the large bear. What I first thought was a bear napping on, or near a daybed close to the banks, was a resting grizzly lying on top of a carcass at the water's edge. Upon closer inspection with my spotting scope, it was not just a large grizzly, it was #211 Scarface. Through my scope, I readily visualized his web of white scars and that missing right ear. I recall seeing a collar, but not the shiny red tag he was sporting a couple of years ago at Cub Creek. I celebrated the gift of seeing him again, this time without drama or risk from a high vantage point. During the period I observed him, #211 appeared more interested in napping than feasting on a partially cached elk. Smiling as I hiked on, Scarface was undoubtedly enjoying his sunny mid-day slumber atop breakfast, lunch, and dinner. This was a fitting conclusion to my interactions with #211. Or, was it my final lucky observation?

During the early morning of May 20, 2014, I spent several hours hiking off trail in the Swan Lake Flats area to see if I could locate nearby elk and hoped to see if any grizzlies were out in the sage flats, on the hunt for new elk calves. During my time there, I didn't see any elk or bears. I wasn't sure if the elk calves had yet been born, due to weather conditions. I decided to recheck the area several days later. I then decided to head east out to the Lamar Valley and hike some new ground. Arriving in the Lamar an hour or so later, I again geared up and started hiking off trail in some open expanses in the Valley's rolling hills. Bison and pronghorn were plentiful, as I made my way eastward. Still, I didn't see what I was searching for and was very close to pulling up stakes and heading elsewhere.

Stopping on a small rise, I pulled my Nat Geo map out for reference of another fairly close section of interest. No sooner after unfolding the map, I glanced up and my eye shifted to a large dark brown, almost black single animal exiting the edge of a small pond with a small feeder creek. Raising my binoculars, I focused on this large animal, which at first, I was thinking it was likely a bison. Well, it wasn't. Rather, it was exactly what I had been searching for, a grizzly bear. But this grizzly didn't present itself quite like the many others I have spotted. It was exceptionally large and as it slowly walked away, its massive body rippled. He appeared to be focused on something other than a small herd of pronghorns that alertly stood in attention as the bear approached and passed them. I was quite a distance away as I too, headed eastward for over a mile and somewhat parallel to his moving direction. Continuing to hike his line of travel, I closed the gap between us. Now, closer to this bear on a focused gait to whatever was holding his attention, I again paused and glassed the moving grizzly. As he turned broadside, with focused 10X magnification I knew this was no ordinary (if there is even such a thing) grizzly bear. Now I could visualize what appeared to be white lines on his face and one ear larger than the other. It then dawned on me, could I have been tracking Scarface, for now, a third time?

He occasionally briefly stopped and appeared to be chewing as if something was impeding his jaw motion. As the bear got closer to some cottonwoods with bison standing about, his gait quickly sped up to a trot. Whatever was going on, he was approaching with determination. A flock of boisterous ravens scattered as the grizzly arrived. At once, the bear without hesitation tore into what appeared to be an elk carcass as four or five adult bison stood motionless, within feet of the grizzly. After establishing a safe and well-positioned vantage point, I could now clearly see all the grizzly's characteristics. Indeed, this was Bear #211 aka Scarface. What was even more astounding was the calm, uninterested presence of large bison standing next to the aggressively feeding grizzly. I wondered if this was another exhibit of a "bison mourning or a funeral" or did the bison realize that as long as it fed on the carcass, the grizzly would not exert further energy to attack them and posed no risk to them while feeding? In any event, I couldn't believe I was so lucky to stumble upon the legendary #211 yet another time. This developing experience was another example of staying the course in GYE by following seasonal food sources and behavioral patterns.

Remaining for hours, I observed Scarface as he would eat, chase away pesky ravens and timid approaching coyotes, take naps on top of the carcass, and otherwise, enjoy the bounty of the carcass from which the scent trail drew him in from miles away. While the Junction Wolf Pack (perhaps they took down the elk) were present in the valley, they made no move whatsoever, to push this king off his feast.

#211 emerges from a pond on a carcass scent trail, miles off to the east.

Having observed him for hours of alternating feeding, protecting the carcass, and napping; by all appearances, it appeared he would remain in a long nap. I left my vantage point with yet another, tremendous third extended observation. I hiked away with a great sense of gratitude, good fortune, and achievement that I had doubted I'd ever see. Despite his advancing age, in the back of my mind, I wondered if our paths would ever cross again.

Any hope for a chance to encounter #211 again, was disturbingly destroyed, upon learning of a strange delayed public Press Release on April 25, 2016, by Montana FWP announcing that grizzly bear #211 was killed in the Little Trail Creek drainage, north of Gardiner, MT. The event was under investigation by USFWS. Little did I know, that my May 20, 2014, third encounter, would be the last time I would see #211 alive. According to the Press Release, the last known radio-telemetry location of bear #211 was near YNP's Sour Creek on September 30, 2015, located in the eastern sector of the Hayden Valley. The Press Release Talking Points only stated generic information about the grizzly, lacking the detail of the shooting and killing event itself. Social media, domestic and abroad, was abuzz with broad reactions and even more so, saturated with questions and emotions about the killing, along with rumors, tributes, etc. to #211. This sad announcement drew passionate national and international attention. The five-month delay of public reporting by responsible wildlife officials in announcing the death of #211, also fueled a great deal of skepticism.

It was now apparent that sometime after his last verified location inside YNP on September 15, 2015, to the north Scarface fatally crossed the invisible boundary line between YNP and Montana, as he had likely done hundreds of times during his long-storied life. Undoubtedly, a common natural trait of nearly all YNP grizzly bears is crossing in and out of the Park's sanctuary borders. Federal and state ESA legal protections follows the grizzly bears wherever they roam, Scarface was no exception. On November 18, 2015, with hibernation shortly occurring within a matter of weeks to days, radio/tele collared bear #211, was unceremoniously shot and killed by an elk hunter in the Gallatin National Forest. His carcass was then dumped down a hillside, into the freezing Little Trail Creek.

Having three vested personal encounters with bear #211, including one at Cub Creek with direct contact at 15 ft, where he simply passed by and we glanced at each other, without incident or exhibiting any threatening behavior, I was both sad and upset, upon learning of the long-delayed public news announcement that he was shot and killed by a hunter. The same feelings and more were exhibited by several decades of Yellowstone visitors who had the privilege of viewing Scarface or following his legendary Yellowstone life. Coupled with my many years of hiking with GYE grizzlies in the wild, I along with a host of other grizzly bear advocates and followers, had a public right and need to know, what happened that fateful night and beyond.

Given the lack of transparency and disclosure of follow-up events by investigating authorities, the public remained completely in the dark about what transpired for nearly several years. To many, the killing of bear #211 wasn't just the killing of any grizzly bear (there is no such thing.) He represented to millions, the visible symbol and legacy of Yellowstone wilderness and the beneficiary of conservation and preservation efforts under ESA protection.

Finally, on March 21, 2017, a Freedom of Information Act (FOIA) request to the United States Department of the Interior, Fish, and Wildlife Service was filed by grizzly bear advocates and preservationists, requesting copies of public records relating to the shooting death of bear #211 by researchers.

I was provided with a copy of investigative redacted official records provided by the United States Department of the Interior, Fish, and Wildlife in reply and response to a FOIA (Freedom of Information Act) Request filed on March 21, 2017. Having thoroughly reviewed the heavily redacted provided copies, they revealed some factual and some contradicting information, within the investigative reports. However, the FOIA records did shine some light, absent from public knowledge for nearly two years, on events that occurred that night on the Little Trail Creek.

....

Investigation of the November 18, 2015 shooting/killing of grizzly bear #211, who at the time of his killing, was afforded full ESA protection by law, of both federal and Montana governments.

....

My review of FOIA-produced USFWS and MFG&P investigative reports, provided partial factual and investigative information about the incident, well beyond that of an early Press Release by the Montana FG&P wildlife authority. The records reveal in part, the following:

The shooter (redacted) on November 18, 2015, was hunting elk out of a hunting camp located at the trailhead of the Little Creek trail, northwest of Gardiner, MT. The hunter held a valid MT elk license, but no bear license (black bear.) He claimed that he hunted in this area since 2000. He was not carrying bear spray, because he had never seen a bear up there. At the time the hunter shot and killed the collared grizzly bear, he was carrying a bolt action Weatherby Accumark rifle with shoulder sling, 30-378 caliber, with a 6-18 Redfield scope. The bullet used was a Combined Technology 150gr Ballistic Silver Tip.

According to (redacted), on November 18, 2015, he was coming home alone on the trail at 6:20 pm, deep in the dark with a good headlamp. While just walking down the trail when all of a sudden, not knowing if he heard her, or just looked, or somehow, she was there, close enough to growl. Seeing her well enough and "that's time to sling lead" didn't take too long to figure out what the hell was going on. When he first saw her, she was motionless. He just walked out from a tree and a big deadfall, almost like walking around a brick wall, and all of a sudden boom there she was. He claimed the bear was 10 ft away when he took his rifle off his shoulder, pointing it from the hip, "It was boom." It was close enough to time to start slinging lead and claiming, he would seriously do it all over again. He shot three times, not knowing where he shot the bear. "The bear was angling, not knowing if she was coming his way, or not, but was damn well sure pointing towards him."

After shooting at the bear three times, he sat there and trembled a little, ran down the mountain a way, hit the creek crossing, turned around to look, and restacked his gun. When he hit the creek crossing, he was pretty sure it wasn't coming, "I was like good she's dead." After the shooting, he returned to the hunting camp. Sometime, later that night (doesn't recall what time) he returned to the killing site. When asked why he went back up in the dark, (redacted) said, "Make sure." When further asked why they did not come in from the trail (to get the bear) (redacted) said it was his idea because they did not want to disturb it. (Redacted) stated, "Don't ever disturb the crime scene." When confronted that they did disturb the crime scene when they picked up the bear, (redacted) stated, "I just wanted to identify it." SA (redacted) asked him how the bear got down into the creek bed? (Redacted) stated, "That's where he fell after I shot him." When confronted that is not what he stated earlier, (redacted) stated, "Well no, because we stood him up on the log, I stood him up and he fell back." SA (redacted) remarked that it does not add up how the bear got into the creek bed.

According to a report sent on 11/20/15 by a local Montana Game Warden, the (redacted) stated to dispatch, "*he located a dead grizzly that had been shot*." The Warden, upon later calling him back, "*he stated he was the one that shot the bear*." He further stated, "*It happened that morning*." Another official down from

Billings also interviewed the hunter who stated, *"It happened the night before on his way out from hunting."* He further stated that he waited to call Tip Mont because he didn't think we were open. The local Warden also reported, "We have some issues with the (redacted) story of events that happened after the bear was killed."

On November 19, 2015, USFWS conducted a voluntary interview at the hunting camp located at the trailhead of the Little Trail Creek. According to investigating authorities, (redacted) on his initial recorded call-in report to TIPMONT stated, "*he found a grizzly bear that had been shot*." However, when confronted on his initial report, he responded," Yeah, that's because I didn't want to get, there's supposedly, there's even a bunch of buffalo hippies running around down here telling everybody not to shoot buffalo. I was just hoping to avoid, get as little of attention here, that is all that was. As soon as (redacted) called me back, *I said yeah actually I'm the one who shot him.*" The report states that while reviewing license documents, (redacted) remarked, "*Doubt I get to keep my bear*." The agent responded that definitely he would not be able to if it is a grizzly bear, and would not even if it was a black bear because he doesn't have a black bear license. Investigating agencies, along with (redacted) returned to the grizzly bear killing site for further investigation, including a field necropsy of the dead bear found on its right side in the running, partially frozen, Little Trail Creek. (Redacted) was asked what he thought should happen to someone who mistakenly shoots a bear when it is not self-defense, (redacted) responded, *"This was self-defense."*

The necropsy located entry gunshot wounds forward of the left front shoulder and a second entry wound, forward of the right shoulder. Two bullets were also retrieved. The killing bullets were sent out for private ballistic testing. Upon receipt of the ballistic findings, the investigating authorities concluded, the bullets recovered from the bear were very likely fired from a very close range. Before leaving the dead body of bear #211, the investigating agents removed the GPS collar and severed all four paws and the head. They also scarred the hide to deter anyone from taking trophies. Eventually, on July 6, 2016, records reveal the head and paws of bear #211 were transferred by USFWS to a Grizzly Bear Specialist with MFWP. The parts from the bear will be used for science and educational purposes within the Yellowstone Ecosystem. The remaining decomposing body of Scarface was left at the kill site.

The FOIA produced records included the investigative photo on the following page. The photo document includes the author's amended descriptions of items one and two.

Sadly, and of great concern, the photo graphically illustrates the fact that far too many ESA federally protected grizzly bears have been killed by the very same means as legendary Scarface and many more will suffer the identical fate; absent timely and thorough investigations, strict law enforcement, mandatory hunter education, process accountability and transparency.

I suggest to think about it this way. Whether the accurate and unbiased population of Yellowstone grizzly bears is 700 or 1,000, or some other estimate; the advantage of the law of large numbers, do not come into play with such a small population of bears or for that matter, anything else. In fact, just the opposite occurs. Removal of just a very small number or percentage of bears, greatly and adversely affects the proportionate number of a smaller group or population, than that of a larger body or group. Thus, killing "small numbers" of grizzlies, relates to higher population loss.

Investigation Photo /FOIA Produced Document

Top: bear #211 body lying in frozen Little Trail Creek.

(Note GPS collar and extensive hide scarring)

Bottom: One of the killing bullets.

The preceding photo from the provided FOIA records revealed original photos were taken by investigating authorities. The top 11/19/2015 photo reveals the position of bear #211 lying in the partially frozen Little Trail Creek. Note the tracking neck collar. The bottom is one of the two killing bullets removed from the grizzly bear.

According to the Report of Investigation

LAWS VIOLATED:

On November 18, 2015, within the District of Montana, (redacted) did knowingly take an endangered species; to wit, a Grizzly Bear (Ursus arctos horribilis), in violation of Title 16 United States Code Section 1538 (a)(1)(B).

However:

In spite of Endangered Species Act (ESA) federal laws protecting the Grizzly Bear;

On July 5, 2016, an attorney for the U.S. Department of Justice declined to prosecute this case.

RESULT

All that remains of the shot and killed iconic, legendary Yellowstone Grizzly Bear #211 aka Scarface?

His severed head and severed four paws. Left behind, his decomposed mutilated hide and body in the Little Trail Creek.

RIP Bear #211

You deserved better; rather than that which failed you.

I, nor anyone else, not present during this incident, has any right to judge the facts and circumstances of this event, or subsequent actions by the U.S. Department of Justice. However, the findings of investigating state and federal authorities, concluding that Laws were Violated under the ESA, may or may not, give rise to personal opinions or questions, that may be of use for educational purposes to possibly assist the general public with ESA and future grizzly bear preservation and recreating in grizzly bear country.

In my personal opinion, based upon the FIOWA-produced documents and beyond the investigation records revealing material inconsistencies in reporting the shooting and subsequent handling of the bear, my attention is curiously drawn, to the actual shooting itself. I do not consider myself by any means, to be an encompassing firearms expert, though many years ago I achieved the Expert Marksman designation from the U.S. Air Force before my deployment to Korea.

In that capacity, I'm somewhat perplexed with the reported facts that at the precise time of the grizzly bear shooting. The hunter was carrying a heavy caliber, bolt action rifle, fitted with a scope and slung over his shoulder and yet, was able to remove it from the shoulder sling and without aiming, fire three times from the hip in the dark, with only a headlamp, at close range and deliver two zonal shoulder killing shots, near to both the left and right front shoulder areas of a motionless bear. Add in an adrenaline factor while this is all going on and it appears to be a near-miraculous effort. Perhaps it was, but there was no investigation reference whatsoever, except a printed diagram of a bear indicating the entry/exit bullet wounds, in the FOIA-produced documents.

As a corollary, I was also drawn to the attention that the hunter was not carrying bear spray. According to the investigation, the bear was shot and killed at close range, while motionless. In my opinion, but for a once in a lifetime most improbable shot; deploying a large 45-degree cone blast of bear spray (orange/red hell in a pressurized canister) to a stationary, non-charging bear may have been the best possible outcome, for human and bear alike. Furthermore, if the miraculous two unaimed shots from the hip in the dark, missed or just wounded the bear (which the majority of all grizzly bear shootings do), in all probability the hunter would have been seriously mauled or killed, by a then enraged grizzly bear. Proper deployment of bear spray may have greatly reduced or eliminated, the high risk of a missed shot, resulting in all but a certain, high degree of morbidity or mortality probabilities. Successful use of bear spray may also have aided the shooter, by eliminating the resulting stressful federal investigation and a federal charge of Laws Violation under the Endangered Species Act. Bullets only bring about finality. In this case, the death of Bear #211, with the use of bear spray rather than lethal deadly force, the potential or an opportunity, for a win-win outcome was eliminated; with the possibility that the hunter walked away unscathed, and the grizzly bear while temporarily incapacitated, would be free to roam and prepare for hibernation.

Not only is my above opinion for the use of bear spray but it is also reported on and expanded by various studies and publications, including the *U.S. Fish and Wildlife Services, Living with Grizzlies, Fact Sheet No. 8*. That report, includes in part; "When it comes to self-defense against grizzly bears…experienced hunters are surprised to find that despite the use of firearms against a charging bear, they were attacked and badly hurt. Evidence of human-bear encounters suggests that shooting a bear can escalate the seriousness of an attack, while encounters, where firearms are not used, are less likely to result in injury or death of the human or the bear." The report goes on to state, "The question is not one of marksmanship or clear thinking in the case of a ***growling bear***, for even a skilled marksman with steady nerves may have a slim chance of deterring a bear attack with a gun. Law enforcement agents for USFWS have the experience that supports this reality based on their investigations of human-bear encounters since 1992, persons encountering grizzlies and defending themselves with firearms suffer injury about 50% of the time. During the same period, defending with pepper spray escaped injury most of the time, and those that were injured experienced shorter duration of attacks and less severe injuries." According to the USFWS report, Stephen Herrero, Professor of Biology and Environmental Science at the University of Calgary in Alberta, Canada and recognized throughout the world as a leading authority on bear ecology, behavior, and attacks; "Reached similar conclusions based on his research…a person's chance of incurring serious injury from a charging grizzly double when bullets are fired versus when bear spray is used."

The USFWS report concludes; "Like seatbelts, bear spray saves lives. No deterrent is 100% effective, but when compared to all others, including firearms, proper use of bear spray has proven to be the best method for fending off threatening and attacking bears and for preventing injury to the person and animal involved."

A further study by Tom Smith, a wildlife professor at BYU, along with colleagues from the National Park Service and U.S. Minerals Management Service researchers, studied more than 20 years of Alaska bear spray incidents, finding that, "98% of persons carrying bear spray were uninjured after a close encounter with bears."

I would argue and draw a parallel that the killing of collared male Bear #211 known to throngs of YNP visitors, was to Yellowstone; as would be to the GYE, if now famous female Bear #399 and/or her cubs in the Grand Teton National Park, were shot and killed by elk or black bear hunters. The public outcry would be enormous, not to mention the incredible damage to already precarious grizzly bear reproduction and mortality statistics.

Well, you may think that can't possibly happen. It's impossible, or highly improbable that hunters could shoot and kill bear #399 or her cubs as they age, or for that matter, other GYE grizzly bears as well, outside of the national park boundaries, could never happen. Think again. Incredibly, renewed wildlife management and special interest group efforts to do just exactly that; are again alive and well, with their advancing sustained efforts to remove Yellowstone grizzly bears from existing protection under the Endangered Species Act. More about this exceedingly serious and very real threat in a later chapter.

Many years later, to this very day, I'm still bothered by the factual manner of death and final disposition of this most memorable GYE grizzly bear. The dichotomy pairing my encounter with Bear #211 silently emerging from a tree line next to me, trading glances at each other a meager 15 feet away, without any threatening bear behavior; compared to his bullet-riddled, dismembered, and scarred body wasting away after being dumped into a freezing creek bed, as his final resting place; remains very difficult for me to reconcile.

Chapter 10

Grizzly Bear Characteristics

This is a good opportunity to take a break from my field experiences and briefly discuss, some of the important physical attributes of the Yellowstone grizzly bear, to better understand this iconic apex predator. I found this information to be very helpful with my good fortune in locating Yellowstone Grizzlies. It was important for me to know some vital attributes and physical characteristics of the mighty bear, to better prepare and plan for locating, and photographing while weighing both the risks and advantages, they may play while hiking in grizzly country. Above everything else, it's imperative at all times to never forget or minimize, the fact that every grizzly bear, regardless of location or circumstances, is a wild and very dangerous animal. Never assume for a moment that a collared or tagged research grizzly bear is somehow less wild or less dangerous than an uncollared bear. Some would argue that just the opposite, a collared grizzly may be of greater concern as it has been handled by humans, often numerous times.

As humans trying to relate to bears or other animals, we often attach a human name or word to impart human characteristics to wild animals and their behaviors. This seemingly good feeling practice is known as "anthropomorphism." We all do this with nothing but the best of intentions and goodwill. However, caution must be exercised extending this human behavior toward grizzly bears, or for that matter all predators. Why...what's the harm? By doing so, it tends to modify or sustain the animal as less dangerous and more approachable, without potentially unpleasant results. At its extreme, labeling bears with human name identifications, could be misleading and potentially foster improper or unsafe human attitudes and conduct around grizzly bears. If a certain grizzly is encountered that is recognizable with a cute identity or human name, this factor alone may entice viewers to use less than better and safe judgment in approaching or interacting with a wild and dangerous grizzly bear. Other than that possibility, I do not find much, if any harm in identifying a bear with a common human name/identity. I might counter-argue that doing so might be a good thing, in the sense of promoting or sustaining positive public sentiment and encouraging grizzly bear acceptability and conservation measures. My bottom line on this topic is just don't ever let your guard down. A collared, tagged, and/or a "human named" grizzly is not any less wild or unpredictable.

I've shared a number of my actual encounters and sightings of the Yellowstone grizzly bear, and while doing so, I've witnessed many behavioral patterns while others, reacted with no discernable predictability. But, what about some of the physical characteristics that make the grizzly bear the top apex predator in all of North America? There are extensive and varied disciplined reports and studies, that could fill a library with abundant grizzly bear facts and data basis. As reasonably expected, some of the information may reveal variances in conclusions or findings, but in general, appear to be quite complimentary. I leave that all to the experts. However, I've drawn upon and condensed, some of the commonly accepted grizzly bear natural physical characteristic findings of interest. I find the study of Yellowstone's top apex predator characteristics to be influential with my evolving knowledge and an indispensable benefit while in the field. Beyond their incredible strength, speed, and aggressive nature, grizzlies are quite intelligent and often very curious. It appears to me, that often their curiosity above their intelligence, gets them in troublesome situations with humans.

The Yellowstone grizzly bear is more or less, an inland subspecies of the coastal dwelling brown bear, or Ursus Arctos. Their color ranges from blonde to black. It is common for many to have a brown/blonde shaded girth extending around behind their shoulder hump. It was named Ursus arctos horribilis and also referred to in history the past two hundred years as "grisly bears" and later evolved into the grizzly bear, as we refer to today, as well as "Silvertips." How did this name evolution come to be? Naturalist George Ord, in 1815 classified the bear as Ursus "horribilus." While color variations of the bear exist, the added classification of the North American grizzly as horribilus or "terrifying bear" was based upon its fearsome reputation and encounters with the Lewis and Clark expeditions as they explored westward through Montana. The "grisly" and later grizzly denotation, was also influenced by its pale white/silver hair tips. Literature indicates that prior explorers and fur trappers of the 1840s often used the term, "white, or white bear" to refer to a grizzly bear.

Consider the following when fortunate enough to see a grizzly bear in the wild. An adult male stands three and a half feet at the shoulder and weighs 200 to 790 pounds, while the smaller females range from 200 to 400 pounds. With all that weight, they can run short distances, from a dead stop to 35 /40 mph, and are very nimble. They cover 100 yards in less than seven seconds, that's as fast as a quarter horse. This is another reason, beyond triggering the bear's predator/ prey instinct, why a human cannot and should never attempt to flee from, or attempt to outrun a grizzly. Grizzlies require very large tracts of mixed terrain for suitable habitat. Within the lower forty-eight states, both males and females have impressive home ranges. Observed home ranges by the U.S. Fish & Wildlife Services reveal a female range of up to 138 sq. miles with males ranging from 183 sq. miles to 835 sq. miles. These large ranges are important factors to promote healthy genetic diversity with mating grizzlies. It's interesting to note, despite home ranges, grizzlies are not territorial, often overlapping with other adults. Despite this large home range, another telemetry finding by the agency discovered that generally, grizzly bears remain in a home range area fairly close to that of their mother's home range. Females roam up to 8.9 miles from the center of their mother's range. As males roam more than females, they averaged 18 to 26 miles from the center of their mother's home range. Both sexes also exhibit long-distance range travel up to 56 miles, with males most often doing so. The maximum male range detected in the GYE was 109 miles.

  Bears are solitary, except for females with cubs and mating adults in the late spring/early summer. Another scenario of clustering feeding bears in GYE is the late summer presence of army cutworm moths in the high-elevation alpine talus slopes. Of course, there are always exceptions to general characteristics. I witnessed this myself outside of YNP. At first, I could not believe my eyes. In the early evening dwindling daylight, glassing a far distant meadow, I began seeing individual grizzlies from different locations, emerging from the adjacent woods, and working their way to the middle of the meadow. Here they uncommonly gathered digging up roots or other vegetation. As they moved about in the high grass, I identified a total of nine different grizzly bears, all collectively foraging in several square acres of a field. They ranged from large males, females, sub-adults and I believe a yearling. Incredible, to the naked eye at a distance they looked like a herd of cattle. Obviously, as in this amazing sighting, grizzlies may feed in groups when the food source is highly abundant. However, they disperse to their solitary nature, when the food source diminishes.

According to a consensus of wildlife biology experts, the grizzly bear's primary senses reveal characteristics that are vital to their overall well-being and survivability, enabling them to live up to thirty years or some, longer. Their average life expectancy in the wild is about 22 to 25 years of age. In captivity, they may live to the upper 30 years of age. Their acute sense of hearing develops rapidly, and may well be their first line of defense. The rounded ears grow quickly and to full size before any other part of their body. Unlike the sense of smell, which is directionally located, a grizzly can hear high frequencies all around, especially in dense timber, and is more than twice that of a human. I like to think of it as a "surround sound" auditory platform.

Their sense of smell is excellent and dominating. Their level of scent is the greatest of all land animals. Smell plays a dominating all-around role in a grizzly bear's environment. It is believed the sense of smell evolved to compensate for less-than-superior vision. No wonder that a nine-inch-long nose, lined with millions of scent receptors and an olfactory bulb five times that of a human, governs the grizzly's presence, reactions, and defenses in the wild. A bloodhound has 300 times the scent of a human. The grizzly has an astonishing 7 times the smell of a bloodhound. The scent of a carcass or a campground can be detected as far as 18 to 20 miles away. As far as hiking in bear country, a grizzly is very likely to smell the scent of a hiker, far earlier than hearing or seeing you, and is more likely to run away without being detected. Predominantly grizzlies try to avoid humans. This is one reason it is important while recreating in grizzly country, to be aware of wind direction. Their sophisticated sensory organ is a driver for detecting danger, locating food, finding a mate, protecting their young, and just about every daily activity. The vast majority of times I see grizzlies in the wild, their noses are either on the ground or testing the wind, and always testing their environment.

According to the experts, vision appears to be of lesser importance than its superior and unmatched sense of smell and hearing. A grizzly has the same eyesight as humans, with variations humans experience with age, disease, injury, etc. Some bears may have very good eyesight, others much less. Within the eye structure, the rods gather available light while cones differentiate color. The retina is like a screen where the light gathers. Grizzlies have color vision. They also have ten times the number of human rods and a specialized doubling feature, allowing the doubling of the collected amount of light. Unlike a round human pupil (which regulates the amount of light in the eye), bears have a slit, which opens slower but opens twice as wide. This affords a collection of greater light in dark or low-light areas. This and several other factors explain why a bear's night vision is superior with their eyes gathering fifty times the light of a human. With their color vision, a grizzly can discern among colors. They excel with colors in the blue spectrum but do not see reds or oranges very well. An interesting theory explains a long-held perception that a bear has very poor vision. This is simply not the case. It was thought that bears do not exercise, or use their vision as a primary sensory feature, as their sense of smell and hearing are far superior to detect and help determine their environment. Others may propose a perception that bears see very poorly by judging it to that of a deer's ability to instantly pick up or focus on, even the slightest amount of movement. Bears' eyes have a different focus band that registers differently from that of a deer. It's a matter of nature and survival. A bear's eyes (predator) are designed to help locate food along with their other senses, while a deer's (prey) instinct is to avoid becoming food. Thus, a predator-prey differential exists for survival.

Grizzly in sage, closely monitoring the nearby Hayden Valley trail.

In the above photo, a grizzly is bedded down about 75 feet while facing and watching the Mary Mountain trail. I came across this unusual sighting while hiking off-trail in the Hayden. While hiking through the sage and over a very small rise, with the wind in my face, I came up behind this grizzly and immediately stopped in my tracks. He had not sensed me but was utilizing his senses of vision, smell, and hearing intent on the trail in front of him. While never turning back toward me, he would raise his nose and test the wind every so often, then flatten out nearly undetectable in the sagebrush as if in a daybed. I guess the gusty wind direction and the near-constant sounds of the wavering brush, along with the intensity of whatever he was focusing on, helped to evade my detection. I was quite uncomfortable with the position I found myself in and the presence of this grizzly so close and yet hidden from the trail. Certain any abrupt wind change would have spurred his immediate attention in my direction, I quietly and carefully retreated away from the area. I suspect this bear may have been searching the sagebrush in search of elk calves and became cautious and undecided about the trail in front of him. It would have been an interesting experience to view what would have happened, had a hiker approached from either direction on the trail. Would a hiker be in immediate danger, or would the grizzly run off when human presence was detected? Or, would the bear maintain his ground position and stay put, undetected as a hiker passed him by? Both of the foregoing are possibilities, however, one important thing I validated from my unique vantage point was the realization while hiking in grizzly country, I had undoubtedly passed closely by grizzly bears that I never saw, but they unquestionably watched me. I believe this is another valuable piece of information for hikers to consider and perhaps, slow down rather than risk provoking a prey-like response from a nearby concealed bear. I admire trail runners' ability and enjoyment of their recreation. I've had both small groups and lone runners come by me mostly while I was passing through front country trails. My foregoing grizzly bear "trail watching" observation in the Hayden Valley had gained my full cautious risk attention.

That's a little unsettling feeling, but that's a part of venturing out. Despite my experience and the safety measures I follow, I'm not the least hesitant to reveal that on several occasions while alone far out in the silence of Yellowstone backcountry, I've stopped and questioned myself, "What in the world am I doing out here, especially alone." So far, I quickly shrug it off by reinforcing my alertness, attention, and risk tolerance as I pursue what I love doing.

A few more major grizzly bear characteristics that I find both fascinating and helpful for my educational and field experiences related to the following. Hibernation itself is an amazing process of both survival and reproduction.

From my viewpoint, the hibernation process itself, coupled with the grizzlies' pre- and post-hibernation activities are very unique. Unlike their coastal cousins, inland or Rocky Mountain grizzlies spend nearly one-half of their lives, five to seven months, hibernating in the den. That is a long time. Before hibernation, grizzlies enter a critically important period for their long winter survival, called "hyperphagia." This process lasts several months before hibernation, from August through November, when they must create an extraordinary intake of proteins and carbohydrates to build fat reserves needed to survive through post-hibernation when they are finally able to search for, and secure winter kill and early emerging vegetation. During hyperphagia, they gain 3.5 lbs. per day, amounting to hundreds of pounds of fat for pre-hibernation.

Yellowstone grizzlies typically seek out dens in two configurations. They may visit existing rock shelters, or most often with their signature muscular hump and four-inch straight claws, dig out a den at a dense thicket base of a tree on a steep 60-degree north slope at 6,000 to 8,000 feet in the GYE. The ground den itself is not simply a hole in the ground. Rather, it's an excavation of nearly a ton of dirt, debris, rocks, etc., and the formation of a three-chamber dirt dwelling, large enough to accommodate an animal weighing up to 700 pounds. The typical layout is a very small entrance, a short tunnel, and the resting chamber itself. For insulation against months of brutal subzero degree temps, the bear will bring in spruce boughs or other material to create air pockets and line the floor. A bear cannot use a previously ground den, but on occasion, may reenter a prior natural rock cavity. However, grizzlies may use the same general denning areas repeatedly. They start entering dens in late November through December, with the males hibernating later than the females. Denning is normally solo, except for some females with subadults who may den together. Denning is not a haphazard retreat for shelter, or birthing new cubs. The bears secure steep north slope locations, as the Yellowstone winds are predominately from the southwest, thus gathering and piling up, the most snow accumulation for insulation of the den below. Even more instinctively, after a den has been dug out, the grizzly often defers from entering the den, until the passage of a heavy prolonged snowfall. This practice may add additional den security by reducing the risk that another bear or other animal will locate their safe place for the long winter.

Once secure in the den, the grizzlies embark on their biological path to hibernating. They will not eat, drink, urinate, or defecate in the den. While in hibernation, their metabolic rate drops up to 60% as they slowly lose body heat, Respirations significantly decline to 1 bpm every 45 seconds from normal of up to 10 bpm. Their heart rate drops to 8-19 bpm from normal up to 50 bpm out of the den. Uniquely, with these biophysical factors in play, their body temp while in hibernation only drops 12%. This too is important, for if an emergency or outside danger occurs while in the den, the bear can awaken faster than having to heat up first.

Recall all those hundreds of pounds of fat stores the grizzlies pack on during hyperphagia. Well, now those very same fat reserves provide energy and sustain them for the long months ahead. Fat metabolism produces urea when broken down resulting in nitrogen formation. That nitrogen is converted by the bear into protein to maintain muscle mass and other organs. Ironically, the bears may lose up to 30% of their full body weight while in hibernation but increase lean healthy body mass over an extended period.

As temperatures begin to warm and post-hibernation sources of food (winter kill ungulates and the earliest suitable emerging vegetation) the males usually leave the den first in early February. Females, especially those with new cubs, follow within a couple of months after the males have departed. Clearing their dens is also subject to variances in weather, temperatures, and food availability. These new mother bears then tend to remain within two miles of their denning area through the month of May. This behavior is likely related to the need of females with cubs, to avoid proximity to large males on the roam, who will often attack and kill their new cubs in an attempt to promote mating. Normally by early May, the majority of bears have left their subterranean shelters after of upwards five to six months of residency.

What happens to pregnant females hibernating in the den? Please recall that mating season for Yellowstone grizzlies occurs within a period of late May to early summer. The female grizzly has a unique characteristic known as "delayed implantation." Other Yellowstone mammals, from the smallest (mice) to the largest (black bears) also have this attribute. The process itself first commences with breeding season, when a female will mate with one, or more males. Once pregnant, for several months, the development of the embryo temporarily stops. However, upon entering hibernation in late fall, the embryo then first implants into the uterus, thus the beginning of gestation. Her cub(s) are then born in the den in late January and begin nursing for several months, slowly weaning off with an introduction to foods, after emerging from the den with their mother.

Recall that "hyperphagia" or pre-hibernation feeding frenzy grizzlies employ to create fat reserves and pack on the weight. Well, now that critical stage is of utmost importance to both mom and cub. If the female failed for whatever reason, to achieve sufficient fat stores, that may even prevent her from having cubs. If the levels are sub-sufficient, they may adversely affect the cub's birth date and growth rates. Both of those results may harm the new cub's health and growth. Furthermore, failure to successfully give birth to new cubs has a negative influence on reproduction rates and population growth. More about these two concerning issues later.

Finally, let's turn to diet and seasonal characteristics. Perhaps these two independent, but connecting factors are the top factors I employ to assist my search of inland Yellowstone grizzlies.

Contrary to some common belief, plants/vegetation (80-90%) comprise the greatest caloric intake, not meat (10-20%). Grizzlies are opportunist omnivores (consume both plant and animal) with consumption heavily influenced by seasonal, annual, geographical location, and food availability variations. I'll restrict my findings to the GYE/Yellowstone grizzly bear. It is reported that Yellowstone grizzlies consume greater than 260 different food species, with high adaptation to available foods at fluctuating seasonal levels. Consider the grizzly's teeth and jaws. They have an enormous 1,000 pounds psi (pounds per square inch) bite with the strength and ability to easily snap the neck or spine of any large ungulate, second only to the polar bear with 1,200 psi. Their molars allow them to grind or chew plant life, while the four sharp long incisors provide all that is needed to pierce and take down prey as well as help to tear meat. The cubs are also beneficiaries, as adult teeth are used to carry them about. Tooth loss through decay and feeding patterns is of concern, especially as they age. The grinding of plant life, grasses, etc., takes a toll and affects their feeding ability. I've witnessed that several times, with older adults visibly chewing gingerly or guardedly while foraging, but displaying no hesitation or difficulty tearing flesh, cracking bones, or separating a torso of a carcass. Similarly, some bison winter near thermals, for warmth and better ground access to grasses, chew a great deal of silica-laden grass, prematurely eroding their teeth and contributing to undernutrition and reduced life expectancy from other bison avoiding the thermals.

In addition to feeding on a host of natural plant and animal food sources, Yellowstone grizzlies also engage feeding on carelessly placed garbage or available human-conditioned foods i.e., dog food, birdseed, chickens, birds, eggs, etc. In addition to carrion, they will occasionally prey on available large mammals i.e., moose, elk, bison, and bighorn sheep, and have been known to consume black bears. However, they will restrict their prey to either calves or injured larger prey and mostly avoid large adult healthy prey. Grizzlies are often the beneficiaries of wolf kills, by taking over a wolf-killed carcass and then fending off the defending wolves. In spring, both elk and moose calves are actively hunted. As the thick ice of Yellowstone Lake thaws and feeding spawning creeks flow in, cutthroat trout are on the menu. However, with the improper introduction and proliferation of large non-native lake trout, ferocious predators of cutthroat, the amount of native cutthroat trout as a food source, has appreciably lessened. Grizzlies also feed on smaller mammals like marmots, ground squirrels, insects, ants, and moths.

In the Yellowstone mountains, there are two extremely vital sources of food for the grizzly, one by ground, the other by air. Respectively, they are army cutworm moths and whitebark pine cones/nuts.

In the first instance (by air), is an out-of-state horde of summer visitors, the army cutworm moths, aka "Miller Moths" so named, because of dusty wing scales that easily rub off, imitating a fine dusty flour-like substance that covers a miller's clothing. Grizzlies will congregate and feast on these highly nutritious three-inch moths. They originate in the Great Plains and in June, migrate westward to some of the highest and inaccessible alpine regions in the Yellowstone Rockies. As larvae, they consume vegetation/grass in the ground (cutworm designation) and seek out new food sources in a vast ground search (army designation.) With their great numbers and crop destruction, farmers and ranchers consider them to be costly pests. Eventually, as temperatures rise to hot in the plains, they start a three hundred mile or so, winged migration to the high mountain talus to escape the life-threatening heat and to aggressively feed at night, on the nectar of the high alpine wildflowers. The consumed nectar contributes to the moth's high caloric and protein levels. During the day, they seek refuge in the cool jumbled formation of rocks on talus slopes up to 10,000 ft elevation. From here, during the next couple of months, army cutworm moths and grizzly bears' paths intersect.

Gathering in gigantic numbers under the talus, the sluggish moths become a major daylight food source for hungry bears, old and young. It is believed that the grizzly's intense sense of smell is utilized to locate the moths resting in the dark cool cavities of talus slopes. Research indicates a grizzly will consume up to 40,000 fat-concentrated moths per day, providing 20,000 calories per day of just moths. This intake may provide a grizzly, with up to one-third of its nutritional needs. By mid-summer, the moths begin to migrate back down below the high alpine. Consequentially, by following the food source principle, the now well-fed grizzly bears, disperse to lower elevations. This gorging feeding pattern occurs in advance and may coincide with the grizzlies' rapidly forthcoming hyperphagia phase.

Grizzly resting in high talus tree/search for army cutworm moths.

      The above photo is one of my favorite interesting encounters. Looking closely, you will see a grizzly gazing out of a downed gigantic hollowed-out tree and remaining stump. This enormous dead tree was the only structure to be found on this talus/scree field. Apparently, at some far past distant time, lightning brought it crashing downslope. After decades of decay, this was all that remained.

      As I was glassing the talus-strewn slope, this grizzly bear appeared from another slope. As he slowly meandered on, I watched him continually turn over rocks and quickly dip his muzzle into the talus/scree. He was feeding on something holding his attention, as rock after rock was rolled over with effortless dexterity with his front paws and long sharp claws. Although I saw no other grizzly, I'm pretty sure he had located and was feeding on army cutworm moths or other insects. This was the time of year and area in Yellowstone for this type of abundant feeding opportunity. When I first spotted him, I was unaware of this downed massive tree, or any other trees or structures on the high slope. I followed his wandering path as he continued to actively search and feed.

The grizzly stopped turning over rocks and lifted his nose off the talus. Suddenly, he broke off into a slow trot, heading east on the downslope. Following his movement, I then spotted a single distinctive brown patch of something, lying on the boulder-strewn ground. Slowing to a cautious walk, the bear pulled up and began testing, what was now this massive downed tree, with his super keen nose. What had been the stump of this tree, was now a massive tower-like structure, with a long semi-open area behind it, appearing as if a dugout canoe. Like the beginning of an entertaining sideshow, the grizzly went inside the hollowed-out area and laid down to rest or sleep for twenty minutes. In his slumber, I could see him turn from side to side. After a while, he rose his head up from the hollow and laid it on top of the very large stump. He remained in this position for quite a while, as if he was a sentry, gazing out in all directions from his castle.

To give perspective to this photo and the size of the tree the grizzly claimed as his temporary hotel room, this was an adult grizzly bear, absolutely dwarfed by the uprooted tree stump. After awakening from another mid/late day nap, he rolled out to the side of the hollowed tree trunk and continued his eastward path across the slope. It's those unforeseen, "you never know" amazing wildlife events like this in Yellowstone that make venturing out into grizzly country so very rewarding and unpredictable. This was just one small, but very memorable example of those, "you had to be here to believe it" or "you should have been here an hour ago" moments, that hiking in Yellowstone grizzly country often rewards. Unquestionably in my experience, not all bear encounters are tense, challenging, or accompanied by fear or danger. Events here happen unannounced and often, very quickly. They then flash by or dissipate, just as quickly as they arose. While in Yellowstone, my frame of mind has grown to prepare for the moment, which is just as important as enjoying the moment. For without preparation, those moments, encounters, or events, may never be realized to their potential.

The second (by ground), pre-hibernation source of high fat and protein critically important for grizzlies, is the cone/seeds produced by the whitebark pine trees. This is an amazing tree for its ability to grow and thrive in the harshest alpine climate, along with the all-important function to provide a stable and highly nutritious food source with its cone and seed production. In a sustained healthy environment, the whitebark pine can live past 1,000 years old. Unfortunately, the trees are no longer and far from thriving. In reality, just the opposite is the case. This is a staple pre-hibernation food source for a majority of GYE grizzly bears. The whitebark pine grows up to thirty to fifty ft tall and five ft diameter. The trees grow extremely slowly, taking approximately up to thirty years to produce the cones with the valued seeds. Cone production itself is a slow process, taking two years to reach maturity with a maximum production of up to eight decades. The needles grow in clusters of five on the upper tree branch tips. Both grizzly bears and black bears feast on the bounty when plentiful.

The whitebark pine has two sustainers if you will. Both the Clarke's Nutcracker bird and the mountain red squirrels help disperse the seeds from the cones, thus assisting with tree reproduction. The Nutcrackers feed on the seeds and can store up to ninety seeds in a pouch under their tongue. Importantly, they also distribute the seeds up to 14 miles away and cache up to 98,000 seeds annually. The squirrels do the hard labor by cutting the pine cones from the high branches and then caching the seeds. Raiding bears then sniff out the caches and feast on the squirrel's hard labor. While hiking in higher elevations in autumn, I've often been loudly scolded by red squirrels when passing under trees with the ground below, holding their cached stores of pine seeds. Why are the small seeds so highly sought after by grizzlies? Remember the "hyperphagia phase" which begins in late summer/fall when the bears variously eat to establish fat stores to sustain them while in hibernation? Well, by the time other various food sources dwindle as fall approaches, they must still turn to other limited food sources to pack on the fat/weight while in the den.

The white pine bark trees grow at high elevations, which also happens to be where the bears will eventually den up for winter. The whitebark pine seeds provide that vital function. The seeds themselves are highly energy productive and nutritious, comprised of 52% fat, 21% carbohydrates, and 21% protein. These seeds are a major fall source of protein and are highly favored by Yellowstone grizzlies. However, not all GYE grizzlies have a habitat where the whitebark pine is present. Consider the reported fact that of 19,305 sq miles of GYE occupied bear territory, only 14%, or 2,702 sq miles, has concentrated forested whitebark pine. These bears, being highly adaptive, seek out alternative food sources and may account for research observations that Yellowstone grizzlies, compared to other Rocky Mountain grizzly populations, are more carnivorous with ungulates and insects, providing up to fifty percent of the annual diet.

The alarming loss of forested whitebark pine is an ongoing major threat not only to the grizzly bear but is also a negative factor contributing to alpine erosion. This very vital tree, once it establishes itself in harsh growing terrain, promotes other tree and ground growth, thus aiding subalpine stability. However, in recent decades, the introduction of two extremely damaging species, the mountain pine beetle and white pine blister rust have literally, destroyed expansive stands of forested whitebark pine. What was once a vital slow-growing conifer, aiding both animals and the subalpine environment, is now reduced to a skeletal-looking, grey lifeless expanse in the GYE. With the advent of warm temperatures and periods of less severe subzero days, these destructive stressors flourished. One destroys quickly, the other over a longer period. The small black mountain pine beetle wreaks havoc hurriedly, by infesting the tree and deeply burrowing through the bark. In doing so, orange/brown pitch tubes are created on the surface of the bark, like raised blisters, as the beetles bore deep within the tree, pushing out sap and wood dust. This also causes the loss of water and nutrients to the tree. After one year after the attack, the needles will turn from green to red, signifying the tree is dying or dead. Four years after the beetle attack, the tree is now a skeletal grey.

    The somewhat slower-killing culprit, the white pine blister rust, is a non-native fungus introduced into North America in the early 1900s. Its destructive path is escalated as it seriously damages saplings and seedlings, in addition to trees of all ages. The killing process starts in summer when the fungus spores are blown to and infect host plants. These spores are then dispersed by the wind to the whitebark pines where they attach to the moist five-needle configuration and infect the tree. Here, the fungus grows slowly and creates localized cankers on the tree. The cankers eventually rupture, revealing the yellow/bright orange spores. Once the tree stem is encircled all growth above is killed.

    When observing enormous areas of both red needles and grey ghost-like white pines, I'm very distressed and alarmed every year to witness the ever-advancing blight brought about by the intersection of these pathogens aided by locally changing climate conditions. Forestry Management estimates that within the GYE, up to 80% of whitebark pine has been affected. I don't know where or when, if at all, this destruction abates or stops, furthermore from what I read and research, I'm not confident the experts have the answers or solutions. According to the U.S. Fish and Wildlife Service, 88% of white pine bark habitat is owned by the federal government. While hiking within the forested GYE, your own eyes do not lie or deceive, with visible extensive loss of this much-needed valuable tree. It is further reported that more than 50% of standing whitebark pine are dead. Time will tell, but the grizzly bear, with all the expanding adverse natural and human influences, may not have that time. If this all ends badly, the only guardedly ray of hope I see for both grizzly and black bears alike is their ability to adapt to generalize or find alternate food resources. However, my hopes for an alternation of food sources, are dampened by the sheer weight of overwhelming significance and reliance on the potential loss of the perfect food (fat and protein) for hibernation survival, the whitebark pine nut.

    Positively, a ray of long overdue hope and action to address the critical loss of whitebark pine and the ominous threat to the grizzly bear population has now materialized. At the time of my writing, the USFWS has belatedly, announced federal protection is forthcoming and has designated the whitebark pine is threatened with potential extinction, requiring officials to enact both recovery and restoration plans. Some early concerns or criticism has evolved, by those critical of the fact that officials failed to designate which of the whitebark pine forest habitats in the West are most critical to reverse the risk of extinction. However, despite this environmental priority habitat concern, researchers along with private groups, are collaborating with federal officials to address restoration remedies. Some are already in place; however future efforts are necessary to reseed one-third of the enormous habitat.

    Wrapping up GYE grizzly bear seasonal food sources, the following generalizations offer some mainstays. In my search for Yellowstone grizzlies, I concentrate on these food/plant groups, along with the fluctuating conditions and elevations the bears are searching for. I also diligently scan the ground for signs of grizzly tracks, scat (revealing what they are feeding on), and grizzly digs (searching for vegetation or pocket gophers, voles, etc.) No guarantees, but merging these two disciplines, enhances my odds of locating grizzly bears, by seasonally reducing or eliminating areas outside the main food sources. Keep in mind though, bears roam a great deal and can be found passing through or to other productive food regions. They may be romping about in meadows during the late spring/early summer mating season. I strive to reinforce myself when often finding a grizzly is elusive; to be patient, stay on a pattern, or adjust tactics, if search efforts are unproductive. Remember, that being in the right spot, at the right time, isn't always the result of a successful strategy, but sometimes is created by sheer luck, perhaps aided by knowledge. Also, an opposing reality is getting skunked without a grizzly bear sighting. In my own field experience, as hard as I may press, I often fail to locate a bear. However, while hiking in grizzly country with the beauty and bounty of Yellowstone ever present, there is no disappointment, only learning experiences, for the next day or the next trails.

Springtime: For backcountry hiking, I consider springtime to be mid-May through the first week of June. The food sources coming out of hibernation are primarily winter-killed elk, bison, or other ungulates failing to survive the harsh winter. This is closely followed by or coincides with grizzly digs for pocket gophers or voles. I have watched with amusement, many grizzlies expending considerable effort and energy, tearing up the ground for a meager several-ounce reward. Later in this period, elk calves in the sagebrush are a delicacy for searching bears. This period also provides the valuable emergence of early nutritious plants, grasses, and insects. Two of my favorite flowers, white spring beauties, and yellow glacier lily bulbs, are actively sought out by the grizzlies creating large and numerous grizzly digs. When fresh digs are located, you can reasonably assume grizzlies are somewhere in the vicinity. Other plant life will include emerging dandelions, clover, horsetail, and other grasses and sedges. In the event of a prior heavy fall harvest of whitebark pine nuts, bears will feed on leftover caches. With a quick swipe of a paw with four-inch claws, grizzlies will level large active ant hills and expose thousands of frantic ants. Their long tongues make quick work of ant hills and decaying logs.

Summer: Heavy snows are no longer a barrier to backcountry hiking in the June-August period. Grizzly food consumption expands to include; elk thistle, biscuit root, brilliant purple fireweed (so named, as the first flower to appear in the charred ground of a forest fire), leftover fall whitebark pine nuts, and army cutworm moths in the high talus slopes. Native spawning cutthroat trout are a food source, though perhaps less common, as cutthroat populations suffer from non-native lake trout. As the short summer season progresses toward fall, berries become an important food source with vital sugars for energy and weight uptake. Berries include; buffaloberry, huckleberry, wild strawberry, and whortleberry. During late summer, grasses and other plants are diminishing. Yampa and bistort become food sources. Grizzlies will consume carrion for the entire spring through fall seasons.

Fall: Consumption remains about the same for late-season surviving plants with the all-important diet escalation of whitebark pine nuts for the hibernating grizzlies to maintain energy during the long months before emerging from the den.

There are a lot of plants and flowers to identify in the GYE, both nutritional and poisonous. So, it's important to identify their presence. Consider purchasing GYE lightweight waterproof placards of vegetation and animal tracks/scats to carry in your backpack. Or have fun creating your own "field guides" with your photos.

Chapter 11

Hiking with Yellowstone History

In addition to the importance of acquiring all-around knowledge relating to my Yellowstone journey, equally significant was my interest and desire to learn about the historical composition, personal accounts, developments, and adventures of the land and its inhabitants. After all, as a new venture, I would soon embark on exploring the all-new wild territory and part of the country that I had minimal knowledge or familiarity with. All of which was exciting and perhaps, quite intimidating. I soon discovered there was a wealth of informative entertaining books, journals, periodicals, etc., written about every natural and scientific component of Yellowstone's makeup. Truly, a considerable reservoir of valuable, and enlightening information awaited me to read and complement my advancing relationship with the GYE. The purpose of this chapter is to simply offer my insight, thoughts, and relativity of Yellowstone's developing history which often co-occupies my mind before, during, and after excursions and visits anywhere I traveled by road or hiked within her borders. In other words, I'd be traveling with a knowledgeable silent companion.

If you have ever had, or will in the future hike Yellowstone, whether for wildlife viewing, awe-inspiring landscapes, or just a short pleasurable outing, in some form or fashion; you are walking with undisturbed history. Think about it for a moment. Especially in the backcountry, say you are following a named or unnamed creek. Your very own footprints and paths of direction may be following those of fur trappers from the 1840s era of mountain men, or Native Americans, patrolling soldiers from Fort Yellowstone, explorers, and others navigating and viewing exactly what you are now seeing. Or, your footsteps are the very first to imprint the ground you may be now walking in this rich vast wilderness. I find these experiences to be thought-provoking and respectful to those who ventured here before us. What stories might remain and are silently hidden on the very ground we are standing? Imagination, coupled with historical facts, are great partners that I enjoy hiking with.

Through the years, I've accumulated a respectable-sized library of books relating to all things Yellowstone and grizzly bears. The majority are centered upon grizzly bears, however, with my sense of Yellowstone history, a fair number are devoted to the period of YNP's early discovery, explorations/tales, and intriguing facts about the area. There are several outstanding authoritative books in my collection relating to Yellowstone's history that hold my great interest. I also suggest that either a Yellowstone newcomer or a well-versed experienced reader would find them to be very informative and entertaining. In my mind, the history of Yellowstone from the days before early discovery to the present day entails an expansive range of often evolving and perhaps conflicting records of hardships, struggles, successes, failures, injustices, conflict, explorations, politics, and so forth.

While I am not a Yellowstone book critic in the least respect, concerning the overall history, personalities, and events concerning Yellowstone's early beginnings from the early 1800s to the late 1870s; I find *Empire of Shadows*, authored by George Black, to be an excellent read in all captivating realms of detailed historical context. Both the extensive scope and detail of the book bring history and development into light. In my eyes, this scholarly epic story of Yellowstone brought familiarity to me with Yellowstone personalities, places, and events the more experience and travels I obtained in my search for grizzlies. When entering or crossing certain areas in YNP, I could draw upon the knowledge imparted from the book, to make my journeys more meaningful and connect with the heritage of those who proceeded me in both time and place.

Many modern-day visits to Yellowstone originate with flights in and out of Bozeman, MT. Today, three miles to the east of what was a tiny frontier town of less than a hundred residents, a simple placard sits on the ground where once a vital army post stood. In 1867 Fort Ellis was established to patrol three mountain passes located in the rich, fertile Gallatin Valley. While little attention was paid to the fort's closing in 1886 and the often-contentious relationship with the nearby residents, its presence played an important role in the creation, expansion, and safety of the fledging town and frontier settlers.

The fort was also integral in providing vital resources and escorts for early explorations 95 miles to the south, into what would become several years later, Yellowstone National Park. Colorful officers and enlisted personnel of the Army and the Second Calvary also provided regional safety for Gallatin Valley against the "hostile" Sioux and more lenient relations with the Crow tribe. The fort also provided security for the advancing Northern Pacific Railroad. No Indian tribes were established in the Gallatin Valley, rather the area became an intersection of various traveling tribes to their hunting grounds around the Yellowstone River.

Another favorite book of mine, *LOST Fort Ellis, a Frontier History of Bozeman*, authored by Thomas C. Rust, Ph.D., in my opinion, is a superb intricately detailed account of Fort Ellis's creation, staffing, operations, and relationships with settlers and Native Americans. The book itself contains many restored photographs and fort diagrams, bringing alive its time and place in Yellowstone's history. Some context itself lends its accounts to my hiking travels in YNP and places along the way south through the Paradise Valley to the North Entrance into YNP.

I suspect, that a good degree of my self-interest in Fort Ellis relates to my great-grandfather on my mother's side. To my knowledge, he did not directly serve at Fort Ellis. However, he was stationed at various forts or outposts in the general area. His history was that of a trooper with the U.S. Seventh Calvary in the Northern Plains Indian Wars, in a regiment known as "Custer's Avengers" after the Battle of the Little Big Horn. He was directly involved at Wounded Knee, with accounts describing both his personal memoirs and period news articles. He was transferred to the Second Cavalry at various outposts, including Fort Grant in Arizona where he served in the Apache Wars. As mounted cavalry he was known for his special skills with the Sabre and as a teacher. After he retired from the Second Cavalry, he later served as a captain in the First U.S. Volunteer Cavalry, better known as the legendary Teddy Roosevelt's "Rough Riders." Accepted volunteers had to be skilled horsemen with combat experience, or a strong desire to so serve. As a captain, he raised a troop to serve at San Juan Hill.

His memoirs and history in the Northern Plains draw my attention to calvary life and my deep respect for Native Americans. After his retirement and advanced age, he often remarked through his first-hand experience and knowledge, that, "The Indians were very mistreated by the U.S. government." His efforts to express his strongly held sentiments and experience were rejected by the government.

So, where does that take me concerning hiking in Yellowstone history? Through the years, I often hike and explore the sprawling Hayden Valley in search of bears and other wildlife. In addition to abundant wildlife, The Hayden itself also harbors a rich tradition of history. I enjoy immersion into that history with a committed study of YNP history and the aid of both high-detail and vintage maps. The Hayden Valley was prime buffalo hunting grounds with the Yellowstone River bisecting its wide expanses. Seasonal passage and historical connections to Yellowstone were 27 indigenous tribes including, the Crow, Cayuse, Coeur d' Alene, Blackfeet, Shoshone, Nez Perce, Tukutuku, or Sheepeaters, Kiowa, Sioux, Comanche, and others. The Sheepeaters were the only permanent tribe. Beyond being a vital area for food and shelter resources by indigenous peoples, shortly after March 1, 1872, when Yellowstone was established as the First National Park; positioned in the valley were army encampments, horse corrals, and Park Ranger outposts. Hunters and poachers also hunted here, slaughtering wildlife at will.

On the western flank of the Mary Mountain Trail in the Hayden Valley, another historical area exists. The valley is a maze of game trails, primarily from bison that have roamed this area for eons. This valley was well known and traveled by the indigenous tribes in pursuit of the bison and other natural resources. Historically, another element in the Hayden was in pursuit of one of those tribes, the Nez Perce. The U.S. Army was in close pursuit under the command of one-armed, Brig. Gen. Oliver Otis Howard. He lost his right arm during the civil war battle of Fair Oaks.

In 1877 under the tribal leadership of Chief Joseph, the Nez Perce left their native home range in Oregon after they refused relocation of hastily prepared government edicts to relocate them to a much smaller reservation. Gold had been found on Indian ground, triggering the deterioration of what was formerly amicable relations. The Army pursued the 800 men, women, and children along with 2,000 horses eastward. Several notable skirmishes and battles occurred during their trek until the Nez Perce entered YNP on August 23, 1877. They were on their trek to seek safety in Canada. The Nez Perce made their way into the park near the present-day West Entrance at West Yellowstone. After fleeing 13 days through the park, General Howard's 600 troops remained in pursuit as the Nez Perce made their way out of the Hayden Valley and the park itself. Historical places of interest in the Hayden, include the Nez Perce Creek, Otter Creek, and the Nez Perce Ford across the Yellowstone River. These are areas of historical interest to hike and explore, bringing into perspective, Yellowstone's witness to history.

Yet, while the hostile pursuit was going on through the Hayden Valley, another element was also in the park, namely tourists. At this point, Yellowstone was still underdeveloped since becoming the first national park five years earlier. At least 8 groups or 35 park visitors were present. On what was to be an exciting foray into "Wonderland" to view the thrill of spewing geysers, boiling mud pots, and hissing ground; some found themselves in the middle of harm's way. Yellowstone history reveals one such party of nine members from Radersburg, MT. Thirty-five-year-old attorney, George Cowan and his twenty-four-year-old wife, Emma, accompanied by family members and others were camped for eight days in the Lower Geyser Basin, along Tangle Creek (near present-day Firehole Lake Drive.) On August 24, 1877, a band of Nez Perce scouts entered their camp to obtain their provisions by force or handout. An angry defiant George Cowan would have no part of that and forced the Nez Perce away from their camp.

Following this event, the Cowan party packed up and headed north on horseback with their two wagons pulled by a four-horse team. But now, what had been a pleasant, exciting venture, dramatically turned for the worse. Cowan and company found themselves directly involved in the growing contentious hostilities with increasing loss of life from the months-long escape, now entering Yellowstone. As the Cowans made their way north (presumably to leave the park via the Madison River), awaiting them at the Nez Perce Creek, was Chief Joseph himself along with 75 warriors. The Indians refused them passage. Rather, the Cowan party with the threat of harm, was forced eastward with the Nez Perce on the present-day Mary Mountain Trail. About a mile in, deadfall prevented further wagon travel. Here at the intriguing thermals at Morning Mist Springs, the wagons were disabled and ransacked.

The captives headed eastward on the Mary Mountain trail through the Hayden Valley, towards the Nez Perce camp near the Yellowstone River. Arriving at the camp, by a vote of the Nez Perce tribal council, they were released to return west through the Hayden; provided they surrendered their supplies and horses. Begrudgingly, they complied and headed back west on the Mary Mountain trail. A band of disagreeing Nez Perce would intercept the released Cowan party. The tourists were intercepted by a following band referred to as the "Bad Boys." These twenty or so, warriors wanted to retake them as hostages and return them to their chiefs.

This event sparked, yet another Yellowstone incredible story of survival. Gunfire ensued. Some of the tourist party escaped into the woods as the clash continued. Emma Cowan remained at George's side as he was mounted. He was shot in the right thigh. As he saw another warrior aim at him, he fell to the ground unable to move. Another approached him on the ground with a pistol to shoot him in the head. With her 13-year sister at her side, Emma then fell on her husband's body to protect him. All Nez Perce guns were pointed at the three. As another warrior tried to pull her off George, another shot him in the head near point blank. Another Cowan party member was shot in the face and survived by hiding in the brush.

The" Bad Boys" element of the Nez Perce took Emma, her sister, and her brother as hostages. They left George Cowan for dead. The two women were released on worn-out Indian horses, her brother on foot, the next day at the present-day Nez Perce Ford on the Yellowstone River. George Cowan's incredible plight wasn't over. He was shot twice, once in the head, and later regained consciousness. While trying to stand up, he was shot again, in the hip with the bullet exiting his stomach. Incredibly, with a loss of feeling in his legs, he would crawl for three days over nine miles, to where their wagon was overturned. Here he met his dog. The Cowan party was later met by Army Scouts and taken in the safety and care of the pursuing U.S. Army. An Army surgeon removed the bullet in George Cowan's head and presented it to him. Later he would create a watch fob with the bullet removed from his head. The Cowans were reunited 21 days after George was found alive. Twenty-four years later in 1901, the Cowans' along with others returned to the exact site of their capture. A creek flowing off the north flank of Mary Mountain in a westerly direction intersecting the Mary Mountain trail was named Cowan Creek after this historical event.

Historical events within YNP are far too varied and numerous for many volumes of books and journals to mention here. Suffice it to say, whenever hiking in either the front or backcountry, you are highly likely to be treading with history. One final broad area of hiking with history I enjoy in my travels is that of early Yellowstone exploration. Beyond what was considered at the time, "unbelievable" individual stories and accounts by mountain men, explorers, and others, there were three major expeditions whose contributions led to the formation of Yellowstone National Park.

In September 1869, three prominent Montana gentlemen conducted the privately funded, Folsom, Cook, and Petersen expedition. Their journals entailing 36 days of exploration, ending on October 11, 1869, were of much value for the benefit of forthcoming and better organized, funded, and extensive expeditions.

History and modern times have concluded that in 1871, the third and final Yellowstone expedition by the Hayden Geological Survey, led by geologist Ferdinand Vandeveer Hayden was the catalyst for the creation of Yellowstone National Park. This was the first federally funded expedition with $40,000 approved by Congress in March 1871 to fund the survey. The extensive survey team was comprised of 32 members, including multiple scientific and artistic experts, who arrived from many destinations in Utah, where on July 4, 1971, they reached Fort Ellis, MT to resupply and coordinate with the Army, their further expedition. On July 21, 1871, the Hayden Expedition entered Yellowstone at Mammoth Hot Springs. The survey team conducted extensive exploration and documentation of Yellowstone's wonders that many formerly dismissed as nonsense. On August 26, 1871, the party left Yellowstone and rendezvoused at the Bottler Ranch located at Emigrant Gulch, along the Yellowstone River and north of what would later become the North Entrance into YNP. From there they returned to Fort Ellis to prepare for departure six days later. After boarding a Union Pacific railroad train, the Hayden Survey officially concluded on October 2, 1871, at Fort Bridger. The

Bottler Ranch (also referred to as "Boteler") with three German immigrant brothers (Frederick, Philip, and Henry) running the small ranch, was an important hunting/supply shanty and shelter at the time. It is often mentioned in other accounts as being a stopping place for expeditions and others alike, entering or exiting Yellowstone. Of note in my research and memory, I came across information that at the time of the Hayden expedition, as a guide, Frederick Bottler was still recovering after being mauled by a grizzly bear.

The Hayden Survey was rightfully so, the most eminent scientific and artistic expedition into what would later become YNP. With national backing and a strong public showcase of its findings, photographs, and stunning paintings, this survey not only verified prior accounts and explorations but provided the push necessary to transform unbounded beauty, into the nation's first national park. Its productive influence on the railroad expansion was also a positive catalyst. But what about, its predecessor, the second of the three major expeditions leading to the creation of YNP? I haven't forgotten about that. I find it to be the most fascinating and adventurous exploration with far fewer resources; harboring a central colorful, highly educated, productive, complicated, and controversial U.S. Army personality; enter, Lt. Gustavus Cheyney Doane.

The 1870 privately funded expedition known as the Washburn, Langford Doane Expedition was formed on the heels of the lesser-known accounts and journals a year earlier by its predecessor, the Folsom, Cook, and Petersen expeditions. Henry Washburn would lead its 16-member party, while U.S. Army Second Calvary, Lt. Gustavus C. Doane with his hand-selected five soldier contingents, would provide military escort, departing from Fort Ellis. After four days of travel, the expedition entered Yellowstone, staking camp at the mouth of the Gardiner River.

The Washburn expedition held one member destined through fate, to become one of, if not the most incredible stories of Yellowstone survival: Truman C. Everts, tax assessor of Montana Territory. On September 9, 1970, Everts was discovered as being lost by the party somewhere along Yellowstone Lake's southernmost rugged terrain. Repeated concentrated efforts to locate him were in vain. On September 19th the expedition was forced to leave Yellowstone, due to dwindling rations and advancing bad weather, leaving Everts missing. What then ensued is a truly harrowing, remarkable story of his 37 days of survival alone in the wilds of Yellowstone. Left utterly unaided without any provisions, firearms, or his lost horse, he somehow barely survived with only an opera-glass and eating elk thistle. Almost miraculously, he was found near death, a skeletal remnant of himself, by two trackers far to the north on the flanks of Crescent Hill. The trackers, George Prickett and "Yellowstone Jack" Baronett spotted him on the hillside appearing as "a skinny small black bear." Nursing Everts back to some semblance of health, he was returned safely back to Helena, MT. A $600 reward for his return was offered by Judge Lawrence, a law partner of Cornelius Hedges, a principal in the Washburn party. Not a penny was ever paid to his rescuers! The Everts account, in my opinion, is a must-read for Yellowstone followers. Several detailed, descriptive books and journals bring full life and appreciation to the facts and circumstances of this dreadful early Yellowstone event.

Back to Lt. Gustavus C. Doane, who disliked his name Gustavus and preferred to be addressed by his middle name "Cheyney." When reading or studying early Yellowstone's history and conflicting intersections of conflict and development, Lt. Doane's presence is unmistakable. Many of his talented educational skills and accomplishments draw applause, while other parts of his military career duties, responsibilities, and actions, may draw criticism. I suggest the entire body of his history and Yellowstone's relevancy must be viewed through the period of the lens of time, as all history should dictate. The Washburn expedition was exceptionally important, especially with Lt. Doane's presence and leadership. He created the most thorough map of the territory with his combined excellence in navigation, geology, and spirit of exploration. Combined with his most enthusiastic relationship with the land itself, his contributions to the further understanding of Yellowstone and the means to accomplish and transmit that understanding were paramount to becoming the national park we enjoy today.

However, Doane felt his role was undervalued, denying himself both earned recognition and position with the advancement of Yellowstone. Perhaps his sentiments were partially derived when on January 19, 1871, expedition principal Nathaniel Langford, who had ties to Jay Cooke of the Northern Pacific Railroad and funded his speeches about the expedition; presented a speech in Washington, D.C. Attending the speech was none other than, geologist Ferdinand Vandeveer Hayden. A year later, the next expedition would be Hayden's. Despite prior expedition escort achievements and his many notable discovery accomplishments accompanied by finely detailed journals; Doane was destined to be a passing footnote to Yellowstone history.

In my library, a book authored by Kim Allen Scott, *Yellowstone Denied* is one of my favorite fascinating reads of the complex life and times of Lt. Doane, especially his post-expedition Yellowstone disappointments. There seem to be very few locations in

YNP or the GYE, where his presence or reference is absent. I submit, after studying his history, rather than being denied, his overall presence looms large as a central figure in the creation of YNP.

I've hiked (respectfully to the edges) of the remaining stagecoach wagon wheel ruts from Yellowstone's first public transportation in 1886, fourteen years after YNP was established. How did these historic wagon tracks get here, with some remaining today? After YNP became a railroad destination, throngs of excited visitors would arrive by rail north of YNP. Mass transportation was needed to convey them from the rails to the park. The Yellowstone Park Transportation Company had the vision and execution to address that need, with the creation of bright yellow "Yellowstone Coaches." Gardiner, MT was a departure point to Yellowstone. "Tally-Ho" six horse-drawn stagecoaches, carrying up to 36 passengers would depart Gardiner, traveling five miles to the Mammoth Hot Springs Hotel. Those "heavy hauler" coaches were far too big and inefficient to safely navigate the terrain in the park. Guests would then climb into a smaller Yellowstone Observation Wagon. From Mammoth Hot Springs, ten passengers would embark on a five-day viewing trip, pulled by a four-horse team, following the Grand Loop, basically the same loop as today.

The above are all but a tiny segment of Hiking with History in Yellowstone. Everywhere we travel or view here, is immersed in history. While I'm hiking in search of Yellowstone grizzlies, whether I recognize it or not, the history or a specific historical event or view along the path I'm traveling offers dividends to my experiences. Many events which take place today in or about Yellowstone will become part of its future history. Just how those overall events are properly and wisely protected, managed, and funded will determine the health of this irreplaceable land, wildlife inhabitants, and history. The discovery expeditions are long ago finished, but Yellowstone's history is not.

One day while exploring new off-trail ground well outside of YNP, looking down to retie a bootlace, a flash of black stood out on the ground. Picking the object up between sagebrush, I quickly identified it as a small piece of obsidian. Holding it in my hand, it had the beginning semblance of the shape of a small arrowhead, or perhaps a small spear tip. Examining it further, chipping and striations marks were etched around its sharp black smokey translucent edges. I'm certain it was indeed the makings of an unfinished arrowhead or a tool for sharp cutting. It had an intended purpose. Was it dropped or discarded and if so, by whom and when? The numerous possibilities are not important, its presence at that precise location and the discovering glint from the angle of the sun is all that mattered to me.

Chapter 12

My Hiking Equipment

      The constant field packing conflict between weight and necessity goes on with each of my long-day ventures into the backcountry. The adage "every ounce matters" could not be more on point with me, especially given my advancing age and several handicaps. I kind of laugh at myself at times as I often pack, then repack several more times in preparation for a departing hike. However, it's not self-amusing, for what you have, or more importantly, what you don't have with you when you're alone in the field. Concerning advance packing in preparation for travel departure to Yellowstone; I won't even go there! Suffice it to say, with me, it's like a battle between War and Peace. Trying to dismiss in my mind and speech, are my ever-present packing self-questionings, "I might need this, or if I don't take this?" Regardless of how many times I have done this and my trip packing experiences with many prior trips, I still wind up in the twilight zone fog of packing, with a floor littered from wall to wall with competing traveling items and clothes, etc. My decision-making ability is tested to the limit, as indecision always seems to stubbornly hold out. After many hours or disgustingly, even split days of negotiating with myself, a treaty is reached between myself and the final selected inventory. I must readily admit that nearly every time I overpack. Vowing not to do so again and "go light" never seems to materialize.

      I offer my personal field packing and items that I normally carry for most of my Yellowstone hiking/photography ventures. I'm well aware, that others with their specific purposes, length of travel, etc., may vastly differ from mine. However, I suggest most, of my critical items, should find their way into your pack or on your person. Please keep in mind, the personal equipment I carry today was created as an evolving process of experience, trial and error, comfort and struggles, etc. I purposely avoid identifying retail brands and do not endorse one over another. It's a matter of individual preference. Regardless of the individual use or purpose, in my experience, the most critical factor to consider is selecting based on quality and reputation for your intended purpose. Quality is closely followed by weight, function, durability, and longevity. An imperative factor to always keep in mind; while in YNP or the GYE, you are traveling through grizzly bear country. In addition to other risks of wilderness hiking, that fact alone warrants careful consideration and attention.

The following is a grouping of my Yellowstone hiking items. The list is not all-inclusive to other items I may have or consider taking, but touches upon the major categories.

BOOTS:

IMO, perhaps this is the most important item of gear for Yellowstone hiking. If your feet are not comfortable and well-protected, you aren't going to be comfortable. If you intend to do much hiking, on or off trail, it is essential that you have quality hiking boots and inserts and know how to properly care for them. I learned this lesson the hard way. Again, as I acquired early experience journeying around Yellowstone, I upgraded to a more suitable supporting mid-high hiking boot. For several years other boots performed as ok to so-so, but I soon discovered deficiencies in my hiking. They nearly ruined a significant GYE trip and season. I had not experienced any foot trouble for years, until one day while extensively hiking outside YNP. While traversing downhill from a long and semi-steep grade, my left foot became extremely painful. My laces were tight and I wore quality Merino wool hiking socks. By the time I hobbled downhill, I could no longer place my left foot on the ground. The foot pain was so bad that I feared there was no way I could remain in YNP and complete my trip.

After I reached my vehicle, I could not even rest or place my left foot on the floorboard. I then decided to see if medical attention might better my situation. As I made my way back into YNP, heading to the Mammoth Clinic, I wasn't the least bit confident about salvaging my remaining trip. With my left leg tiring from having to uselessly lift my foot, I arrived at the clinic upset with my situation, or how would I even make it back to travel home. With my hiking pole, I gingerly entered the clinic. It didn't take very long for the doctor to diagnose that I was suffering from a severe level of plantar fasciitis, something I never experienced before. The doctor advised that oral medication would not help much, if any. Wanting to try to salvage my remaining days in Yellowstone, she offered to inject the heel of my pulsating foot. I agreed without hesitation, "Anything Doc, anything!" The good doctor cautioned me that this injection would be very painful and she, "Didn't want to get kicked like a mule." Sharing some unpleasant bad patient experiences in the past, I replied to her; "I'll do my best to prevent that, I don't care, tie me down, let's just do it!" Well, I wasn't tied down, but secured with my stomach down on the table, like one of my wife's fantastic rib roasts. The injection was most unpleasant, equally important, the doctor avoided any bucking patient reaction. Resting for five minutes, I cautiously put my left boot back on and laced it. Now the acid test. Anticipating some major discomfort, I ever so slowly took a step forward on the clinic's hard floor. I couldn't believe it! What had been incapacitating pain, was now 100% gone. Walking around the office for another five minutes, I began to wonder what was I even doing there. As the doctor returned and opened the door of my treatment room, before she even had a chance to ask a single question; I spiritedly exclaimed, "Doc, you are an absolute angel, the pain is entirely gone! You are my angel!" Smiling, she replied this was the first time a patient had ever called her that. As I jittered about her office, she advised this shot would only last around three hours or so, but then a second round of longer-acting steroids would kick in and take over. Informing me that I should be good to go for the remainder of my trip, I left the front door rejuvenated with immediate impromptu plans to head straight for the Specimen Ridge Trail. Time to get back on the trail was all I thought. As I climbed up a fairly steep hill, nearing the trail at the top, my vigor quickly diminished as the same foot pain was gradually returning. I didn't expect to be 100% once the first medication faded, but I kept on moving with the doctor's advice that the second steroid component of the shot would take over and I should be good to go for days more. Well, that second long-term medication seemed to take a holiday. Making matters even worse, I now had to unpleasantly retreat and retrace my path back down the high trail on now again, a bum foot. In the end, the plantar fasciitis won out and I had to cut short the remainder of my trip.

The Clinic doctor, after all this? She's still an angel in my mind, perhaps with her halo tilted just a tad, but still a miracle worker that early morning. The real culprits were my hiking boots. They were not stable enough, exerting displaced torque on my foot to cause an acute case of severe plantar fasciitis. Following a period of medical attention and the purchase of a much better-suited pair of advanced hiking boots and inserts, this annoying malady has been kept at bay. Lesson learned I could have avoided this nagging problem by buying top-quality supportive boots to fit my needs, not boot advertisements.

HIKING CLOTHES:

Very simple; I layer, layer, layer with comfortable, light, and breathable inner and outer apparel. Yellowstone weather conditions often change unexpectedly, and so must we. Always in my backpack are; a spare pair of quality hiking socks, a lightweight waterproof (not water resistant) rain jacket with hood, wool cap, whisking long sleeve shirt, gloves, reflective high visibility work vest, lightweight vest, and neck gator/ buff. A pair of knee-high gators are indispensable. Spare sunglasses are a must.

MAPS:

I don't rely entirely upon my dedicated GPS unit with the GYE-specific loaded map. Problems can and do occur. Being in the backcountry without reliable means to identify my position and navigation is not a wise risk to take. Inside YNP I carry two quality topo Nat Geo maps. One, a higher topo detailed map of the YNP quadrant I'm venturing in. The second, is a full map of the entirety of YNP and its boundaries, to discern if needed, where a trail, creek, or off-trail area I'm concentrating on, runs short within my primary quadrant map. Outside of YNP while hiking in the GYE, I'll consult either USGS or USDA Forest Service maps. I don't wait to study my maps until I arrive at the destination that I plan to hike. I do so well before arrival, often weeks or months earlier. Doing so allows me to search the area I'm planning to explore on Google Earth or other visual mapping services. Through this process, one of which I enjoy, I've discovered discrepancies between the visuals and map references i.e., streams that no longer exist, forested areas that are now blackened by forest fires, trails that have been altered or no longer exist, etc.

A little firsthand advice, be sure to have your map secured while hiking. Stuffing the map into a pocket after repeatedly referring to it as you travel, leads to a lost map. I know that's not a good feeling, especially in the GYE backcountry which may not hold as much familiarity as inside the park. This happened to me for failing to follow my own advice. I carelessly failed to secure my map while looking for bears in an area of new ground I was exploring in the GYE. After hiking for two hours after last consulting my map, I reached into my jacket pocket for the map. I needed it, but it was gone. I dropped it somewhere in the tall grass, sagebrush, and forest I had been hiking. My immediate reaction was that I would never find it after extended time and distance since I last viewed it. Then a thought flashed in my mind. Reaching for my GPS, I was fortunate to be able to pick up a signal. I proceeded to backtrack my exact path via the GPS track manager. It was a long haul, but I was amazed. By zooming in and following all the twists and turns I had taken, I arrived back in the area I last knew I had the map. But the grass near an unnamed small creek was dense, three feet high, and the ground was marshy. A needle in the haystack, I reckoned. Ten minutes later, crawling on my knees, nearly buried in the ground, there was my lost map. I had competing senses of an unforced error, versus a sense of a small victory/accomplishment in finding what was much needed.

OTHER ITEMS: *These are items that I carry and/or consider.*

In my pack back I include many other personal and hiking necessities. I may adjust the items to have on my person, consistent with the type and length of my outing. This includes medications, first aid articles, spare AA batteries (lithium, they are longest lasting and lightest), titanium whistle, emergency foil blanket, spare sunglasses, and strap retainers (I've misplaced too many), sunscreen, lip sunscreen (high SPF), compass, toilet paper, windproof matches and/or lighter, flint, multi-function Swiss Army knife, heavy duty zip lock bags for trail mix, coffee, and soup packets, energy bars, etc. Depending on the length, time, and weight management of various hikes, I will either pack or leave behind at my departure location, my Jet Boil Flash 1Liter with one small canister of fuel. In the field or back at my vehicle, I enjoy the ability to boil up hot coffee, Ramen noodles, or a freeze-dried meal pouch. I always pack a water filtration device to secure clean safe drinking water from trail creeks, ponds, etc. I favor the lightweight easy-to-use Sawyer squeeze filtration system. Regardless of the water filter type or brand, they all help avoid carrying heavier bottles and eliminate the potential for Giardia intestinal tract parasites.

I always include mosquito and tick repellant as necessities. As a Southerner, I'm well aware of ticks in our neck of the woods. I didn't realize that ticks may be prevalent in the GYE before spring arrives and snow is still an issue.

With a chest strap, I carry high-quality prime-coated water/fog proof 10X42 binoculars. I also carry smaller, less-weight quality 10x8 binoculars, a great alternative for longer hikes or in less open territory.

PERSONAL BEACON LOCATOR (PLB):

Following several near misses of serious injury in the field, I firmly decided it was long overdue for me to have a 24/7 means of emergency communication to reach a SAR (Search & Rescue) Team with a simple press of a button. The vast majority of wilderness in Yellowstone backcountry, has very little, to no means of communication. Though pricey, I purchased and carry at all times a PLB or Personal Locator Beacon to meet my need. Secured on my shoulder strap within easy access, is my personal choice of a PLB, an ACR ResQLink View 425. For my style of mainly solo travel along with the backcountry locations I explore, after much research, I found this PLB best fits my needs. IMO, a PLB is not a luxury gadget or toy but rather may be the single item to save your life. The PLB itself is small, less than 4 inches in size, and 4.6 oz weight. It must be certified and registered with NOAA SARSAT. In case of a life-threatening emergency without other means of rescue; with the push of a button, the unit is activated with a network of satellites and immediately notifies the nearest SAR unit to your precise emergency location. The system coverage is worldwide, on land, or at sea. This unit does not require any subscription or usage fees. Ironically, the PLB itself is the one item a hiker, explorer, or traveler never wants to activate. Closely followed by the #2 item, bear spray.

I suggest that an interested person research the narrow PLB market to locate a unit that meets their individual preference and budget. Some models offer an additional specialized texting feature. Model features, unit prices, and annual subscription costs vary from non to monthly or annual fees.

My only caution with a PLB is not to carry or overly rely on it. What I mean is; don't unreasonably push the envelope by taking safety risks that you would not normally consider.

CAMERA:

First and foremost, I am not a professional photographer. As an experienced wildlife amateur, I exclusively use a Nikon B500 digital camera for all my photo/hiking. In my situation, given the type of hiking and the territory I'm usually in, I need a camera blend of features primarily consisting of low weight, compact design, ease of operation, reliable optic zoom, and easy access to capture quality photographs. While in the field, I need instant uncomplicated performance to get the shot of a grizzly before it disappears into a tree line or over a ridgeline. Some hard-earned bear, or other wildlife sightings, can appear and be gone in a matter of seconds, especially those at close range. In my experience, weather conditions also play an important factor. While sacrificing some limited picture quality, I do not use a DSLR camera with long-range lenses in the field for several reasons. Having to carry additional weight, time and effort to change lenses, extended setup time in a fast-moving encounter, and simplicity of operation while under pressure; all influence my choice for the digital camera. A Go Pro Camera is a nice compliment for video.

The camera type that I carry while not perfect, provides the right comfortable balance that I prefer for what I do. In a side pocket, don't forget to carry a cleaning pocket lens pen, (also used for binoculars) and a lens cloth. That prized awaiting grizzly bear photograph of yours will thank you.

BEAR SPRAY:

I made a vow that I've never broken. I fully vowed that I would never step off any trailhead in YNP or the GYE, without bear spray. Based on my specific hiking venture, I often carry two canisters of bear spray. One for the ready, and the other for backup. In my experience, I realized that I might encounter a bear within 100 yards or less, of a trailhead or from a roadside departure point; as easily as encountering a bear many miles away in the backcountry. You just never know while being in grizzly bear country. If you are going into grizzly bear country, in my opinion, this is the most important safety item to not only have but also how to properly use it. In previous chapters, I've referenced the use of bear spray including my personal use. Being such a critical safety product, for the benefit of first-time users, as well as a reminder for experienced users including myself, I offer additional information. Similar to my take with a PLB device, bear spray is another hiking item that you hope you will never have to use. However, the possible use of bear spray is far more likely to materialize, rather than deploying a Personal Beacon Locator in a serious personal injury life-threatening emergency.

Above all else, whenever purchasing or using bear spray, it is imperative for the user to carefully read and comply with all manufacturers' product information, labeling, usage, and warnings. Bear spray and "pepper spray" are not the same thing, far from it. Only bear spray should be used for its intended purpose. Different manufacturers now produce bear spray for retail sale. The canister of spray should contain 2% capsaicin and related capsaicinoids with a registration number on the can from the U.S. EPA. Canisters are produced in either 7.9 or 10.2 ounces. I prefer the 10-ounce size as it affords seconds more of deployment. This size provides up to ten seconds of discharge.

One of the surprising facts encountered by first-time users is the very short duration of the spray itself. Keep in mind that bear spray is not intended as a preventive or repulsing spray, rather it is a next-to-last alternative to stop an advancing or charging bear at close range. I recall during one of my YNP hikes my path merged into another trail where a young man and woman were day hiking. Instantly I knew before exchanging a single word they were way out of their element and inexperienced. As we stopped to greet one another, the young man pulled his earbuds out of both ears, apparently enjoying whatever music he was listening to. Hiking in grizzly country deserves the utmost attention to your surroundings, movements, and sounds. None of which were being recklessly exercised. He wasn't paying the least bit of attention to his surroundings or being cognizant of potential risks in the area they were hiking.

After a little friendly conversation, much to my surprise, I discovered he had bear spray for the two of them. Of course, it was packed away, totally inaccessible in a zippered pouch with sandwiches. Well, it turns out he might as well have a jar of pickles in the sandwich pouch rather than bear spray. Seeing my bear spray secured on my chest strap, he asked me, "Have you ever had to spray yourself with it?" Knowing he didn't know enough to only be joking and appeared sincere with his question, I responded, "Are you kidding, no and why would I want to do that?" His reply was, "Well that's what you do if you see a bear. If we saw a bear, I'd spray our clothes and the ground around us to keep it away." Between the earbuds and his absolute lack of knowledge of bear spray and how to properly use it, I offered to help them out with some gentle how-to information. For all I knew, it seemed to have some intended impact. Bidding adieu the couple left with their bear spray on his belt. Unplugged earbuds down the trail, or the Rolling Stones blasting away…. who knows? At best, I'd give the Stones a better than 70 to 30 odds.

Bear spray is never to be used as a protectant or repellent. Never spray it on a person or anywhere on your person, property, campgrounds, or surroundings. Experts report that spraying the highly pressurized red/orange oily mist on the ground or surfaces can draw the attention of a grizzly bear to the irritating oily residue, they like the taste. For further information on how and when to discharge it, please closely refer to and follow the manufacturer's precise instructions.

In my experience around Yellowstone, I'm disappointed to see that the majority of people I meet in the field or visualize their hiking, are not carrying bear spray or do not have it properly placed for immediate accessibility. In my personal opinion, I suggest this observation may be due to the price of bear spray and the manner of transportation to and from Yellowstone. For many, there is resistance to paying the $40-$60 range for one canister of bear spray, especially with perceiving little risk of running into a bear, much less having to discharge the can. For others regardless of price, the mere knowledge that wild bears inhabit the area is all they need to purchase and carry. I've made my position of having bear spray, abundantly clear without reservation. For the annual millions of visitors, hikers, and photographers who travel to/from Yellowstone by airplane and need bear spray, a large number will return multiple times to YNP. As you most likely know, transporting bear spray by air is strictly prohibited by the TSA. This rule applies to both carry-on and checked baggage. Purchase and repurchase of bear spray for air travelers, such as myself, is simply an unavoidable travel cost factor. The product is readily available from multiple retailers at your destination. Rental bear spray is now being offered at various airport baggage claim areas. While there is a minimal cost differential, the rental hassles of registering and returning the spray versus private purchase, deserve personal evaluation. For those travelers departing from home to Yellowstone by automobile, bear spray surrender is not an economic issue. Nevertheless, you need to check the storage shelf life which varies by manufacturer. Depending upon storage conditions, the general period is three to four years.

While simply having a can of bear spray while in grizzly country is better than nothing; if needed, it has little value unless you know how to use it. After fully reading the instructions, following the first time I purchased bear spray, I decided that I needed to test using the product. This was a very useful exercise to appreciate the fluid mechanics of quickly drawing the spray, flipping the safety off, properly aiming, sensing the report of pressurized discharge, and then actually seeing the cone impact and range of the bear-stopping spray. Trust me, unintentionally I also caught the slightest whiff of the suspended oily mist. It was not at all pleasant. It was not until 20 minutes later that it partially cleared up. This was only an extremely limited peripheral exposure. I could only imagine the incapacitating impact of a full couple of seconds of blast. I might also add that most people do not know, or question if bear spray works with different animals. According to the experts, the answer is yes. It is also highly effective with other predators and ungulates as well. This includes: threatening wolves, mountain lions, coyotes, moose, elk, and other mammals. Some bear spray brands also sell at a deeply discounted cost, testing canisters without any of the active ingredients. New or experienced users may find this to be a cost-effective and no-harm training option.

    According to the National Park Service, bear spray is also effective against bison. I've had my share of concerns in the field with large single bull bison approaching me, or otherwise blocking my trail. I found other means to de-escalate what could have become a very troubling and dangerous situation. I would have used bear spray, if necessary, but quite honestly would feel very unnerving and perhaps less confident out in the open, with the consequence it may have on one ton, six feet tall bison not at all happy with my presence.

    Regarding my final disposition of bear spray at the end of my hiking when I cannot transport it home via airplane, I make it a personal habit of freely donating the canister(s) by several means. I rather see recycling of my unused spray go back, without compensation to another person or organization. Again, to me, it's simply a matter of travel costs. After my trips, I've often donated to strangers without bear spray, I've met nearing the trailhead I'm departing. Other times at my accommodation checkout I'll leave the spray with the front desk. Some places will provide such donations to their other guests inquiring about hiking etc.

One final personal observation and experience with bear spray. A couple of years prior, my son and I needed to get bear spray after we arrived at GYE. I never experienced this before, but this was the first time my preferred brands of bear spray were sold out, or otherwise unavailable. Uncertain if I could secure them going into Yellowstone, I decided on a last-chance stop at a local retailer. Well, discovering the same unavailability issue there, I purchased two packages/cans of another brand of bear spray. I was unfamiliar with this brand. Closely reading the product (unnamed) literature, I was comfortable purchasing the bear spray with the contents, manufacturer date, expiration, etc.

After completing our last hike, rather than donating the new cans to someone else, we decided to test them out as this brand was new to us. Good thing we did. I was first to go, fully expecting normal performance at a target 30 feet away. Upon discharging the canister, I was perplexed. There was barely a blast, more like a fizzle sound as a low can of paint spray. Rather than the 45-degree cone discharge, the cone was sizably constricted and fell far short of the 30-foot target. Closely observing my test, he asked, "What did you do wrong?" Nothing was my reply, can you believe this? We both closely again examined the canister data. Nothing appeared out of order, such as an expired usage date, etc. There was no outward appearance of damage to the can or nozzle. Prior use wasn't plausible as the can was tightly packed with undisturbed tough clear plastic. While not a comforting explanation, perhaps somehow, I just wound up with a can that did not meet my prior use of bear spray. In my mind, if needed, this canister would have been far less effective, if at all, than my trusted bear spray expectations.

  Michael then proceeded with the very same test I had just completed. Before deploying it, we both examined his can and imprinted information. Like mine, nothing appeared to be out of the ordinary. The results were almost, if not identical, to my test discharge. Beyond being stunned, our first reaction was what could have happened if either one of us had to use this bear spray during our week-long in the field. I have no explanation other than it failed to produce to the extent of other brands I use and trust. I would not have been confident if I had to use that brand with an angry grizzly. Maybe it could have been somehow internally damaged or compromised in handling or transport. I'll never know. I'll stop short of opining that these two canisters were defective. Strangely both failed to meet my confident experiences with bear spray. In absolutely no manner did our self-tests that day, dimmish my faith, trust, and full reliance on bear spray. My takeaway from that day? Suffice it to say, I'll stick with the major brands I've used and trusted.

Chapter Thirteen

The Shoshone Lodge Captive Grizzly

After a successful spring 2019 trip, fall was just around the corner. During my summer planning, I meticulously planned an ambitious fall GYE hiking/photo grizzly trip with my son Michael. Our itinerary started in the Tetons. From there we would head north to YNP and out past the East Entrance to the Absaroka Wilderness and Shoshone National Forest. Along with breathtaking scenery, this was an area where I hiked with success in finding many signs of grizzly and black bear presence. This would be a new area for Mike and I wanted to share my favorable experiences here with him. From Shoshone, we would head back into YNP and West Yellowstone for more hiking before departing back to TN.

Departing Nashville on September 27, 2019, before we knew it, we were anxiously landing at Jackson Hole to launch our venture. Awaiting baggage claim, I expressed my confidence that I would find us grizzly bears. It was late fall in the Northern Rockies. The grizzlies were well into hyperphagia, eagerly feeding on dwindling food resources with hibernation soon on the horizon. However, in my wildest dreams could I imagine what lay ahead for us.

The weather was good on our arrival, but as we began our hiking, it turned quite cold, and gloomy with periodic heavy rain mixed with snow. Just as fluctuating the mountain weather is in the spring, so it is during late fall. In any event, we were prepared. Trying to locate Yellowstone bears my philosophy is always to push on, regardless of weather conditions. That's not to say I always enjoy doing it, but my reality is, "You got to dance with the one who brung you." Of course, in adverse weather conditions, rational discretion and safety are always top priorities.

Compared to YNP, I've spent little time hiking in and around the Tetons and therefore, I don't have the same high degree of knowledge and experience as that of Yellowstone. Nevertheless, the handful of hikes I had taken were superb. Admittedly, my experience with grizzlies in the Tetons was very limited compared to the YNP and surrounding forests. As a result, my ability to find the presence of grizzlies was very challenged, with limited success. One of my favorite short hikes is the Two Ocean Trail. It holds abundant wildlife including bears, beautifully accented by the ever-present striking views of the Tetons.

After a couple of hikes in the Tetons, on our departing day from Jackson Hole, we agreed to hike up Pilgrim Creek located in the north section of the Grand Teton Park past Moran Junction. We were a little concerned about the water flow of Pilgrim Creek, but this was a fall trip with greatly reduced flow, so that shouldn't be much of a direct concern. In reality, at the time, it wasn't. However, the dropping temperatures accompanied by heavy rains resulted in very difficult hiking conditions. The ground was heavily saturated and difficult to navigate. Deep pools of muddy rainwater filled in ruts, depressions, etc. The extent of runoff made it nearly impossible for us to locate or follow tracks. Due to deteriorating ground conditions coupled with my unfamiliarity with this area, we often found ourselves wandering off trail. As we kept hiking north and outside of park boundaries, we came upon an uninhabited extremely large hunting camp. The camp held a horse corral, hay supplies, and several large group tents with multiple wall tents. The camp appeared to be bear-proofed, encircled with electrical wire, along with batteries. Cautiously approaching outside the wire and announcing our presence, we found the camp to be void of people, horses, or signs of activity. After several minutes we left the area undisturbed, as we continued hiking out.

Shortly thereafter, with the cold rain continuing to fall, something just dawned on me. If we came across a grizzly under these conditions, how in the world could we ever get a decent photo? Many of my bear pictures in the field were taken under bad conditions, but not to this extent. Well, first we have to locate one to even worry about getting a photo. I reasoned, perhaps this could be just one of those times when you're forced to settle for a "mental memory picture" rather than a camera shot. When it comes to grizzly bears, they both leave an indelible memory that can be relived repeatedly in your mind, regardless of the passage of time.

After proceeding for many miles, at some point in time, we both agreed it was best to turn around and head back to the trailhead. A major fall cold front was dropping down from the north and I needed to get back on the road north to Yellowstone where weather conditions were more likely to harbor advancing snow, rather than this miserable cold rain/snow mix. During our return at some point a couple of miles away from the trailhead, Mike and I got separated in a patch of dense forest. You know the old expression, "A horse always runs faster the closer it gets to the barn." Well, while running is next to impossible for me, I sure felt like the horse's urgency to get to the barn, post haste. I knew I was off trail, but was assured that I was now near Pilgrim Creek. The rain/snow continued to pelt down when I spotted a very small opening ahead in the direction I needed to be heading. The opening was small and bordered on both sides by near impassable thickets and trees. I made an executive decision not to try slugging through that impenetrable labyrinth.

Spotting what appeared to be a muddy, submerged rut or channel in the opening, I decided to advance by carefully walking out between the ruts. The entire area was covered with muddy water, but this looked like a good way out. After a couple of minutes of cautiously walking, I felt comfortable about my decision. Not so fast. My trailing left boot got snagged somewhere on a submerged root. I had no time to react. I plunged forward taking a header into the deeper channel. I was now miserably face down submerged in the dirty rain water. Trying to clear my airway, I was blowing muddy bubbles as I grabbed for some thicket to pull myself up. Calling out for my son, I heard his distant voice, "Over here." Slowly making my way through the deep thickets, we reunited near the wide Pilgrim Creek. Not able to hide a reserved snicker on his face, he exclaimed, "Jesus Dad, what happened to you?" I too would have been laughing, emerging from the thicket I must have looked like some sort of Wyoming swamp creature.

Arriving back at the trailhead I shed my soaked clothing and changed with the car heater on full blast. Fortunately, after its baptism, my camera was spared any water damage. Now I had a pressing issue. The wind was picking up as snow, rather than rain was gradually taking over. We needed to get up to Yellowstone with the weather deteriorating. My major concern was the roads to get out past the East Entrance to our Shoshone Lodge destination. To do so meant crossing the Sylvan Pass in the Absaroka Mountain range. The 8,524 ft mountain pass is situated in a saddle between Hoyt and Top-Notch Peaks and is named after Sylvan Lake, a small lake west of the Pass. During the winter months, its steep mountainsides create avalanche risks. On short notice, the Pass is often sporadically closed due to accumulating ice and snow before it can be plowed or deiced. While the views from Sylvan Pass are breathtaking, so is the sheer drop-off on its southside.

It is not my favorite stretch of mountain road, even in the best of weather. And for good cause. After a clear fall day of taking my elderly mother and my brother-in-law on their first Yellowstone trip tour, I was returning to our lodge and had to cross Sylvan Pass westward and downhill. After cresting the top of the pass, I started my descent down the long twisting road. Going the speed limit, less than midway down, and while we were talking about the grandeur of YNP, I heard a shrill screeching sound behind my vehicle. My eyes shot up to my rear-view mirror. All I saw just feet off my rear bumper was a huge cloud of blue/white smoke and a speeding, out-of-control swerving Bronco-like vehicle. There was no place for me to go. To my left was a towering mountain rock wall. To my immediate right was a two-foot stone wall, with nothing but air plunging a thousand feet below. If that spinning vehicle behind me had just tapped our car, it would have launched us to our deaths over into the abyss. All I could do was maintain control and speed up to try and separate us from the nightmare behind us. As I did, I could now see the still-swerving vehicle trying to gain control. I didn't think there was a chance, but an angel must have been his passenger as almost miraculously, it straightened out. I couldn't believe my eyes when the driver then came speeding past me in the opposite lane still on a sharp descent. Collecting my breath and nerves, I watched him continue racing downhill and out of sight. My first thought was perhaps this guy lost his brakes and cars further down could be in danger, but likely not as he locked up his brakes feet behind me. Inattention, distraction, drinking, or pure stupidity were all suspects.

I think I had my answer. As I made my way out past the East Entrance, I passed the same vehicle that nearly killed us. Obviously, its brakes didn't go out. It was parked unattended in front of a lodge that serves alcohol. With time to reflect and adrenaline down, I was now quite upset. But for my mother still, in the car, I would have gone in and searched out the driver. After that terrible ordeal, perhaps his angel jumped into my car as I drove on. Days later while driving back up Sylvan Pass, I viewed his skid marks all over the two-lane road and a foot away from the drop-off ledge.

Back to our trip out to Shoshone from the Pilgrim Creek ordeal. I wanted to relay the above experience for a couple of reasons. First, as a friendly reminder to all YNP visitors, traffic accidents are the number one killer in Yellowstone. Also, years later, our brush with death remains a stark reminder whenever I need to cross the Sylvan Pass. As I thawed and dried out, my concern was focused on the weather. With current traveling conditions, would the Pass have temporary but time-consuming, closure possibilities? I wanted to get over the Pass and to the Shoshone Lodge before snowy or icy roads could set in. As expected, after entering the South Entrance the temps were dropping with mainly heavy snow bursts. Without stopping we made our way east from Fishing Bridge and soon started to climb the west side of the mountain. It was looking quite dicey as we neared the summit, but as of now the Pass and road were open. As we started our descent down Sylvan Pass on the east slope, I wasn't comfortable with the road and was concerned ice could form. Little, if any traffic was seen. I incrementally eased up with each completed section as I neared the bottom. Ten minutes or so later, I exited YNP through the East Entrance. The snow was gone with no accumulation at the lower altitude as I passed by Pahaska Teepee. Five minutes later we arrived at the Shoshone Lodge. We planned a couple of days to hike the Absaroka Wilderness and search for grizzlies.

I stayed at this wonderful Lodge several times before and always enjoyed my visits. I would use my cabin lodging as my base camp while hiking the Shoshone National Forest and the North Absaroka Wilderness. The Lodge is tucked in between two towering mountains with the rugged bubbling Grinnell Creek racing downhill to join the South Fork across the highway from the Lodge. The scenery around this entire area is nothing less than spectacular. In the past, I've viewed grizzly bears in the Shoshone N.F. From my experience, it appeared that a number of the trails in this area appeared to be quite underused, perhaps due to their more primitive location and outside of YNP boundaries. It's good bear country. My main goal on this leg of the trip was to introduce Michael to the east section of Yellowstone and areas of the Absaroka I've hiked. From my map studies and past experiences, I felt our chances of hiking to photograph bears, especially now as they were in hyperphagia, were good.

Several years earlier, I took family members to the Shoshone Lodge for an extended early fall stay. This was their first visit to Yellowstone and my week to serve as a tour guide in the Tetons and YNP. I was prepared as this would be a no-hiking trip for me. Of course, I was yearning to do so, but I stayed true to my pledge and enjoyed my role. They would see and learn more of Yellowstone in one full day than most new folks would experience in a short week. My sister, her husband, and I did get in some great mountain trail riding with our guide from the Lodge.

One morning we left our large cabin after a great breakfast and headed back into YNP. It would be a long touring day soaking in the vastness of Yellowstone as I narrated where we were and the features along the way. As all tourists desire, they too wanted to see a bear. I was very hopeful I could deliver. After all, I had quite a bear reputation to live up to. As we finished a long day, the stops and sights were fantastic. However, as I pulled into the Lodge after all the hundreds of miles and hours I drove, we didn't see a single bear. I wasn't even buying into my own excuses. Some days or multiple days are indeed like that. To make matters even worse, ten minutes later my unsuccessful bear spotting hurt a tad bit more. As we were getting out of our rented van at our cabin, a gentleman was sitting on his small cabin porch across from us on the gravel drive. Exchanging greetings, he lowered his book. Excitedly he said, "You should have been here ten minutes ago." Well, with just those three words "you should have" out of his mouth, my spirits immediately sunk as I knew the proverbial outcome before he even finished. Those three words are universally understood as Yellowstone code; admonishing you that you just missed something awesome by not being there. He was reading a book on his cabin porch and for no particular reason, just happened to lower it. In the middle of the gravel drive between our cabins, a grizzly bear was standing up twenty feet away looking straight at him as he read. Rather stunned as their eyes met, he dashed in the front door as the bear dropped down and scampered off behind Grinnell Creek flowing next to our cabins. That's the eventual balanced Yellowstone spontaneity of how good or bad timing, joined by luck, produces one person's treasured sighting and another's frustrated, "Oh no, you got to be kidding me!"

Now begins the Mystery Death of the Shoshone Lodge Grizzly.

Exiting the Tetons and bushed from our Pilgrim Creek hike and long drive, on Sunday afternoon Sept 29, 2019, we arrived to check into the Shoshone Lodge. The comfortable lodge is nestled in between the towering peaks of Crow Peak and Sleeping Giant Mountain. With our planned hiking in mind, I clearly noticed the lodge grounds were all very muddy, but clear of snow. Some light snow was visible on the higher mountain elevations. Entering the front desk, I was once again greeted by an inviting crackling warm fireplace in the adjoining dining room.

Sipping a cup of warm coffee, I checked with the front desk manager. I immediately recognized the friendly person (name withheld) from prior visits. The wrangler tack shack was still open for trail rides with horses in the corrals. Soon the majority would be relocated for the upcoming winter. Mike made arrangements to take an early morning trail ride. He needed to return to the main lodge early the next morning to get signed in. From my earlier trail rides in this beautiful rugged land, I knew he would truly enjoy the mountain ride and stunning views. I passed on taking the trail, reserving my senior citizen aches and pains for our next day's planned hike into the North Absaroka Wilderness. My early morning baptism at Pilgrim Creek certainly sealed my decision.

Appropriately, we checked in to Camp Grizz Cabin located on the far end of the gravel road near Grinnell Creek and the horse corrals. Pausing to leave the lodge front door, the manager very casually informed me," Be somewhat careful out there. There's a trap somewhere for a grizzly bear coming in at night near the lodge and cabins." Rather astounded, I asked a few questions. They had taken down an outdoor BBQ or grill near the lodge. I asked if the bear had caused any damage or confronted anyone? The manager replied, "No, it hadn't caused any damage and had not threatened or approached people. Very interestingly, the manager then said to me, "***This bear had been relocated once before.***" I don't know how, when, or where this information was obtained.

If that statement was true and acted upon by others, it would be a statistical death sentence for this grizzly bear. Why? According to an article published on February 16, 2021, by the *Cowboy State Daily Newsletter,* the 2020 Wyoming Game & Fish Annual Report reveals they captured 26 grizzly bears and euthanized 18 of them throughout 2020. Of the captures, 15 were from Park County, more than half the total captured. Notably, the report references one bear that was captured twice. In July a grizzly was captured first in Teton and relocated to Park County. In August, the grizzly was trapped again (now twice) and was then euthanized. It is rather stunning and disturbing to learn by WG&F's report and statistics, that 70% of grizzly bears they captured just that one year alone, were put to death! Every single grizzly bear killed was federally protected under the provisions of the ESA. Therefore, if indeed true that the Shoshone Lodge grizzly had been relocated once before, it would now be a second capture and was bound to suffer the same fate by WG&F, as the Teton euthanized prior relocated bear.

Much later, the statement that this bear had been relocated before, was proven to be false. Months later, according to WG&F, ***this grizzly bear had never been relocated.*** Could this be an important relocation discrepancy that was acted upon, in what was yet to disturbingly follow in less than 24 hours?

Leaving the lodge door, I inquisitively asked, if it was ok for us to look at the trap. Replying, "Sure that's fine, but I don't know where it is." I drove over to Camp Grizz Cabin to unpack, and even joked with Mike, "See, I told you the east section of Yellowstone was good for grizzlies, but I wasn't expecting a grizzly at check-in." Unpacking our stuff, we left the cabin. I wanted to show him the lodge premises. On the far eastern edge of the property, Grinnell Creek was tumbling down over boulders and under the North Fork Highway, emptying into the North Fork of the Shoshone River. We then turned back toward the horse corrals. We spent some time visiting the horses as Michael would be riding early the next morning. The tack and wrangler shacks were next to the corrals and only a few hundred feet below our cabin facing toward the highway. As we passed the shacks on our way back to our cabin, to our left was a very muddy partially loop-like, gravel drive.

Along this drive, I saw an unattended, flatbed white truck parked off to the side, near the horse corrals. Away from this truck, I saw what looked like a small green-colored trailer or piece of ground equipment close to a wide muddy gravel intersection. Through the mud and large puddles, we walked over to see what it was. As we got closer, sure enough, it was a green box bear trap. It had a mud-covered WY license plate.

This had to be the trap the front desk mentioned. It was parked close to the middle of this gravel intersection near some other lodge buildings or structures. This active baited trap was also very close to the row of lodge guest cabins on an adjoining gravel drive. There were no other people around the area, nor any vehicle attached to the trap.

Unmarked, unattended baited bear trap on Shoshone Lodge premises.

Note: No snow on the ground.

The photo was taken by the author on Sun. 9-29-2019, at 4:45 pm

Walking around the trap, we closely looked for signs of grizzly bear tracks. We spotted none in the area. If tracks were present, it would have been fairly easy to see them on the soft muddy ground. At that time, we didn't know the owner of the trap, or even who, and when it was set and baited. The rear steel trap gate was open and a deer hind quarter was hanging as bear bait on the front open wired panel. There were no ownership signs and absolutely no safety warnings anywhere on the active open trap, nor anywhere around the lodge grounds or the trap perimeter. There weren't any bear trap notices/warnings on or within the cabins. We saw no requisite posted notices and warnings. None whatsoever. Most bear traps I've seen are round cylinder culvert traps and all active traps and trapping areas were posted with strict danger warnings to stay away, along with other very important safety warnings.

At this time, we even wondered if the trap was privately owned.

On later reflection, after I learned of much more official detail, this all amounted to a very dangerous setting for lodge guests, or visitors coming or going to the lodge, cabins, etc. Even the pedestrian public, on or near the very close by highway could be at risk. Not only do you have a baited open unmarked bear trap, but you have an active grizzly bear near and, on the premises, coming in at night.

Position of the baited trap at the gravel intersection. Facing south, the North Fork Hwy is just below the tree line.

It was now late afternoon as we returned to our cabin after locating the bear trap. The skies were slowly starting to clear as the temperature was starting to dip down. Finishing unpacking our hiking gear for the next morning, it was just incredible that we just checked in the lodge, with an active grizzly bear roaming around the guest cabins and a set, baited bear trap only several hundred feet away from our cabin door. Kind of hard to just make up something like this. However, this was just the beginning of what would soon develop into a very troubling and mysterious set of circumstances that still exist today.

Mike and I settled in our cabin for the night around 10 pm. We finished reviewing our maps and organizing our gear for our hike the next morning. The cabin was very warm with the room heater. My bunk was positioned by the front porch window. I cracked the window a tad as temps during the clear night was to drop into the twenties. After an unbelievable day, soon we were both sound asleep. I'm a very light sleeper. Throughout the night I never heard anything, nor was I awakened by the head of my bunk below the cracked opened window. Early the next morning, I was awakened by Michael as he was dressing and leaving the cabin to walk over to the main lodge for his trail ride sign-up. About 15 minutes later, I got up and decided to go over to the lodge for some coffee and a hearty breakfast in preparation for a long day of hiking after he returned from the trail ride.

Walking over to the lodge, the morning air was crisp and the ground remained snow free. It felt like a good day to hike. Arriving at the lodge I entered through the front desk. The same front desk manager was there. Out of curiosity, I asked if there was any news about the grizzly bear trap. Evasively, with a slight smile, the reply was, "Yes, we got him!" I was quite surprised to learn this as I (we) didn't hear anything the entire night from 10 pm on with our cabin around a one-minute walk from the trap. I didn't hear anything; no gunfire, no unusual sounds, nor the slamming of a tripped large heavy steel trap door slamming shut. I would certainly expect to hear something with my light sleeping pattern, my window cracked, and the clarity of sound traveling in the cold still night air. I naturally asked a few follow-up questions. The manager replied, "The bear was trapped at 1:00 am, lodge personnel (unnamed) were drawn to the trap when they heard something and went to the trap to find the grizzly." It was very apparent to me that the desk manager didn't want to discuss this situation anymore. Turning away from me, I further asked if I could walk over and see the trapped grizzly bear. The reply was, "Well, there's nothing to see. They came out early this morning and removed the trap and the bear. It had really long claws." Moving away from me somewhere behind the desk into another area, was the desk manager's final statement.

I then went to the adjoining dining room and took a table seat next to the windows of the extended front porch. As my kind waitress poured a second cup of coffee, I was both amazed at the events and thankful that no one was hurt. At that time, I had no reason not to believe or fully assume, the grizzly was safely live-trapped and was on its way to be processed and relocated to a distant relocation. I could easily understand how drifting grilled food smells from the lodge's outdoor BBQ grill, would be an enticing invitation for grizzlies' great sense of smell, to seek out the source of this alluring food scent. This would be especially true during the late fall period, when the grizzlies are in the peak of hyperphagia packing on all the calories and proteins needed before hibernation.

After finishing breakfast, I started walking back to my cabin to get geared up for our hike, as soon as Michael returned. On the way there I decided I'd just go over to where the bear trap was positioned last night and check if anything was remaining to see. As I approached the area, indeed the bear trap was gone. However, there was something to see.

Fresh tire tracks and grizzly bear tracks left a message in the muddy ground in the area the bear trap was positioned last night at 10:00 pm. Examining the ground, it was obvious that a grizzly bear walked there sometime last night. It was also apparent that a vehicle pulled away eastward in the direction of the main lodge. Neither the tire tracks nor the grizzly bear tracks were present there at around 5:45 pm, late the prior afternoon, when I last, viewed the baited trap site. Muddy water remained in some of the grizzly paw imprints.

Top Photo: Grizzly tracks to the right of tire tracks leading out

Bottom Photo: Author's photographs 9-30-2019 10:49 am. Discovered fresh front and rear grizzly tracks near the intersection with the baited bear trap.

Just what happened here last night? How, when, or with whom, I don't know. While I never personally saw the Shoshone

Lodge grizzly, I certainly located and examined his fresh sizeable tracks that morning.

With these developments, I had certainly wished I could have been here when it was first trapped, or in the morning before the trap and grizzly bear were hauled away. I wanted to speak with anyone that had direct knowledge or participated in any capacity during the entire trapping event. This included those that responded and removed the trap. I returned to my cabin still perplexed why the bear trap wasn't identified and the complete lack of any posted area warnings of a live active bear trapping in progress within extreme proximity of a mere few hundred feet at night of a returning grizzly. Also, I wasn't sure just who "they" were, as referred to by the desk manager. But

Left hind grizzly track next to tire tracks near trap site.

again, at the time, I thought all was well, that ends well. Nobody was mauled and the live-trapped grizzly was on his way to be relocated.

Returning to the cabin, Mike soon arrived back from the trail ride. As expected, he had a great time. In no time, he geared up with his hiking items. We did a final departure check and headed out. A couple of miles back to the east, we would depart into the North Absaroka Wilderness near Pahaska

Teepee. On our initial climb out, we talked about the unreal events that took place at Shoshone Lodge with the trap and the grizzly bear. I joked with him that I didn't want him to think that I had staged this all out just for him on his first arrival in east Yellowstone. But in seriousness, we did discuss the potential gravity of the situation. Together we had more questions than ever, just what had transpired here. One of the lodge employees had told us that the dining room would be closed early so the lodge staff would have time to prepare for a season-ending night party. The next morning most seasonal employees would be leaving to return to their homes. If I correctly understood, a few cabins would remain open for arriving hunting parties, that's why many horses remained corralled.

On the trail, we continued to hike up to higher elevations on our way to Sam Berry Meadows or east to Jones Pass. Around three miles in, I heard Michael behind me call out he thought a wolf or coyote just ran by him in the hilly brush to our right. I immediately turned and then we both saw it was a large brown dog with an antenna tracking collar racing by us. We kind of laughed saying we had enough drama yesterday. We continued our hike out and wondered what happened to the dog that raced by. Well, ten minutes later we got our answer. Coming up behind us at a fast trot was an extended mounted column of horses and Reese mules. We quickly climbed off the trail to the low side, as you're supposed to do when passed by stock. Well, it was a sight to see as they passed us. We waved hello, but received no return greeting. They looked and sounded like the U.S. 7th Calvary racing to the Little Bighorn. There were more rifles and sidearms than I have seen on a firing range. Other mules not carrying a rider were packed with provisions, stoves, wall tents, and panniers. Passing by, the inexperienced or panicky riders were easy to spot, bouncing around with wide eyes holding on to the saddle horn with both hands and boots flopping out of their stirrups. Wherever they were headed, anything with four legs was in deep trouble. As far as our hike to photograph bears was concerned, I feared the thundering herd pretty well ruined that. Nonetheless, we continued and would adjust by moving off trail when possible.

While we strive to be quiet while hiking grizzly country and keep our eyes focused on our surroundings, I sensed something might be wrong or bothering my son. He hadn't said a word for a while. While trailing behind me, he called out, "Dad stop, I just have to tell you something that has bothered me since we left. I know it's going to disturb you a lot." Turning around and walking back to him, I had no idea what the problem was, but by looking at his face I knew something was wrong. He then stated to me that the trapped grizzly bear at the lodge wasn't relocated, it was dead inside the bear trap. At first, I thought he was mistaken because earlier this morning, the desk manager told me "They got the bear" and hauled the trap and bear away. That person never said a word to me about the grizzly bear being dead in the trap and appeared to be quite reluctant to talk about it. In my viewpoint, while I asked about the bear trap last night, not informing me that the bear was dead, but only had "really long claws," was a significant omission or misleading statement for some other unknown reason. On that trail, at this time was my first inclination or suspicion something doesn't sound right about the trapping and disposition of the grizzly bear.

I was stunned and taken aback by this news. Michael replied, "That's why I didn't want to tell you now, but I just had to let you know before we went on much further. I know how much grizzly bears mean to you and the time and effort you put into their preservation and photography." I sincerely appreciated his comments and more so, empathized with him for carrying that burden all alone for the past number of hours during our hike out. I could easily see a mixture of sadness, concern, questions, and reserved disgust on his face. These and more were my initial internal responses. This new unanticipated information was a kick in the gut for me. That was the last thing in the world I was expecting. In one sense, I was very relieved and thankful that the sudden stop to tell me something important wasn't related to any personal or family matter.

I asked him how and when did he know the bear was dead in the trap. He related to me that when he went to the main lodge earlier this morning for sign-up and while sitting in the lodge dining room he was waited on by a young waitress. Asking the waitress if there was any news about the bear last night, she brought out her smartphone and laid it on the table. On the screen was a gruesome photograph of the dead grizzly bear laying on its side with gore all over the trap floor. She wouldn't say or didn't know anything more about any details. He asked if she would email him the photograph. They unsuccessfully tried, but could not get a signal. Michael then asked her permission if it was ok for him to photograph her phone with the bear picture displayed. She responded sure and permitted him. He then left the lodge to go over to the wrangler shack for the scheduled trail ride.

On the trail, I asked to see the cell phone picture. He didn't show it to me then because as he put it, "It's really bad and would only make matters worse for now." Respecting his position, I agreed this was enough for now, but I want to see it. After receiving this bad news and discussing the situation, we both agreed to continue with our hike into the backcountry. Due to time constraints, we somewhat cut the hike short. I was right about one thing. The "thundering herd" had spooked whatever wildlife was in our vicinity. We failed to spot any bears or wildlife whatsoever. Of trail on our way back to the trailhead near Pahaska, we did run across fresh wolf tracks.

Below is a copy of the actual photograph my son took of the Shoshone Lodge waitress's cell phone that she laid down on the dining table in the lodge and permitted him to take.

9-30-2019 am photo taken by Michael Nevens of the lodge employee's cell phone.

The picture on her cell phone reveals a dead grizzly bear in the green box trap, covered in gore and regurgitated chokecherries and other stomach contents. The bear suffered a terrible agonal death evidenced by visible claw marks and thrashing on the trap floor. One would highly suspect a significant amount of noise and clamor from a large grizzly bear during its death throes, emitting from the trap. The hindquarter used as bait on the back screen, is either missing or perhaps lying on the floor between the bear's leg. Also noted is a semicircular rub on the floor, suggesting a drag mark or a large paw swipe toward the rear trap door. Note the abundant sunlight shining through the front trap screen. According to Google Earth for weather data on Mon. September 30, 2019, reports area sunrise at 7:11 am or 1711 hours. Given the brilliant sunshine, it appears the original picture may have been taken, well after sunrise. The weather data was reported as clear. It remains unknown who took the original photo of this grizzly, or when and precisely the location of the picture displayed on the waitress's phone.

In hindsight, but for the chance discovery of this photograph by my son Michael of the trapped dead grizzly, we would have left the Shoshone Lodge the next day thinking all was well. The lodge was rid of a safety risk of a visiting grizzly and the bear would be safely relocated to help preserve an Endangered Species. But regrettably, all was far from being well.

The next morning, we would be leaving the Shoshone Lodge and heading back into YNP to West Yellowstone for the remainder of our trip. We would spend our remaining time in the Gallatin Range before heading back to Jackson Hole for our departure flight.

The next morning dawned as we packed our car to leave for Yellowstone. Mike was still working on his stuff as I went over to the main lodge to check out and grab some breakfast. The dining room was next to empty, as I took my seat at the window table facing the lodge porch. During my second cup of excellent coffee, I looked out the window as a few people were gathering next to the porch, pointing and looking up over the lodge roof above. What is that all about, I asked myself.

Well, just when I thought there couldn't be any more drama here than we encountered the past couple of days, I was about to see something I could not believe was happening, especially after the strange circumstances this same morning with a dead trapped grizzly. Grabbing my coffee cup, I went outside and asked what were they looking at. Someone said there was a bear on a small hill right behind the lodge. I thought to myself, are you kidding me, this can't be happening, especially after the strange unexplained night before with a grizzly bear dead in a bear trap only a few hundred feet away. I quickly left to retrieve my camera from my packed bag and returned in a few minutes. Standing on the drive, several people were still gazing over the roof. A couple of folks left, whether they saw a bear or not, I didn't know.

I scanned above the roof line on a small hill with a flat bench-like ground surface with a few scattered trees and rock outcroppings. On this flat space approximately 50 yards away, with the naked eye, I saw a brown hump slowly move between a few trees. After a minute or so, it moved into an unobstructed view. Sure enough, it was another grizzly bear.

Author's 10-1-2019 am photo of a grizzly bear on a hill behind Shoshone Lodge at our morning checkout.

But hold on, a short while later a second grizzly appeared and joined the first bear digging up food sources on the hill. All of this is directly over the main lodge, with a trapped dead grizzly bear removed nearby a few hours earlier. Was I entering or leaving the Shoshone Twilight Zone? The mystery was just beginning.

The two grizzlies on the hill above the lodge, turn to look down at me.

<u>The First "Never Before" Shoe Drops-Wyoming Game & Fish</u>

After finishing the West Yellowstone leg of the trip and returning home from Jackson Hole, I took time for several days to unpack and decompress from the remarkable Teton/Shoshone/Yellowstone trip. For days I didn't devote much if any time to recounting what I inexplicably experienced at the Shoshone Lodge. I still had many questions surrounding all events of the baited trap very close to the front of our cabin and the crushing news a grizzly suffered a terrible death in the trap on the Lodge premises. As a paying guest of the lodge and as a partial fact witness to the death of an ESA-protected grizzly, I was at a loss to explain or understand what happened there in the middle of the night. I was still confused by the total lack of posted warnings and identification of an open trap with an active grizzly coming in at night on the premises. The more I thought about things, the more uncomfortable I felt about what lodge management directly communicated, or perhaps better stated, failed to communicate to me about the disposition of the trapped grizzly bear. I had a growing feeling something might not be quite right, though I hoped it was. I was unsettled with the death of a trapped grizzly and whatever happened there that night and morning. As I relayed earlier, I always enjoyed my stays at the lodge and the nice people there. Those were the primary factors in my return booking.

After waiting over a week, I thought it was best to call Wyoming Fish & Game in Cody, WY to see if they were aware or had a record, of the trapping death of a grizzly at the Shoshone Lodge. On October 11, 2019, I called WG&F. Introducing myself, I asked the friendly lady answering if a dead grizzly bear at SL had been reported. She couldn't comment and the supervisor in charge was out of the office. She would have the supervisor return my call. Later that day, I received a return call from the Regional Supervisor (named withheld, hereafter designated as *F&G*.)

Later the same day *F&G* returned my call. Advising that my son and I were guests at the Shoshone Lodge and potentially partial fact witnesses, I inquired if WG&F was aware of the September 30th trapping and death of an ESA grizzly at the lodge. It was acknowledged they were aware as we continued with a very cordial conversation. The decades experienced *F&G* confirmed this was their bear trap and "*F&G* never had heard of an event like this." I explained we both saw the open baited trap without any identifying signage on it, no warning signs, and the absence of area-posted warnings that trapping was in progress. I received no response. *F&G* advised an investigation was continuing and, "This was the first time he had heard of a dead bear in their traps. There were no signs of gunfire and they had no history with this untagged or uncollared bear, this was their first contact." *F&G* went on to state, **"This bear wasn't a prior relocate."** This confirmation was in direct opposition to the lodge manager's check-in statement to me, **"This bear had**

been relocated once before." I thought to myself, relocation history appears to be a very important deciding factor given WG&F's excessively high rate of euthanizing bears. Why the discrepancy with now, a dead grizzly in the trap?

Continuing, I was further advised they automatically check all traps early am, and remains unknown what, and why the grizzly died. The bear may have had a food reward at the lodge. Importantly, *F&G* stated, "The grizzly was in poor condition and was emaciated, they were waiting for toxicology/lab reports. But then, we may never know what or why the bear was dead."

Asking if the US Fish & Wildlife Service was involved, *F&G* responded they had informed USF&W, but they were not investigating, pending results of the WG&F report. Our pleasant conversation ended with *F&G's* statement, "If anyone did anything wrong regarding the dead grizzly, we will prosecute to the full extent of the law." I felt that I did the right thing by following up with by contacting Wyoming wildlife authorities and would assist if my information was needed.

Several weeks later, on November 14th I followed up with a status call to *F&G*. The report might still be open, but they had no information to indicate any foul play. It was unknown if lab reports were back, however *F&G*, suggested they were back, but if without indications of poisoning, etc., *F&G* would not be notified.

Continuing, it was expressed to me this was extremely rare, if ever, in 20 years of experience, they never had a bear die inside WG&F traps. I then asked if their agency had investigated the entire event. Astoundingly, *F&G* replied, "There were no interviews of lodge people or anyone else, as there were no initial signs of foul play and no apparent reason for the death." Privately, well after our continuing pleasant conversation, I was perplexed by this and other forthcoming information. Again, I only contacted WG&F in the first place to inquire if they were aware of the dead grizzly bear at the

Shoshone Lodge. But now, my view was shifting to what was going on. My private thoughts focused on what was now, an alarming reportable event without any witness questions or investigation. Why wouldn't the responsible wildlife agency, want to know some basic information about the capture event from people on the scene? This made no sense whatsoever. It's not like this was a bear trapping somewhere in uninhabited backcountry. It occurred at a public lodge with some present personnel and lodge guests.

Proceeding to discuss matters, I was informed that the dead grizzly was taken to WG&F's laboratory in Laramie, WY. Asking what did they find, responding *F&G*, "would have to check with their "large carnivore biologist, expressing a single first name only (name withheld.) This person (overseeing this case?) conducted an external exam of the grizzly and saw no bullet holes or damage to the bear. There was no reason to believe human harm or death was involved, so no interviews were taken. "I've been involved in thousands of bear relocations and have never heard of a bear dying in a trap," stated *F&G*.

I replied that right now, I'm looking at a picture of an agonized trapped dead bear with open daylight at the front gate and inside the trap, claw marks scrapping the gore-covered floor as if thrashing around in agony. The bright daylight shining through the front trap screen could suggest the picture was taken sometime after sunrise, not very early am as sunrise on September 30th was at, or about 7:11 am. As we wrapped up our discussion, *F&G* asked me why the questions and if I had concerns. My only concern was yet another Wyoming dead grizzly bear, this time a never happened before event. I was further concerned that they had no information about who first, or later contacted or visited the trap with the bear inside and if so, what was the condition of the grizzly at first, or later contact? The lodge manager had informed me that lodge people were drawn to the trap at 1:00 am when they heard something and went to the trap to find the grizzly. Wouldn't this be very basic vital information as part of a report to determine what was going on from 1:00 am until early morning before WG&F arrived? Again, very basic but important information, was the captured grizzly bear alive or dead, at 1:00 am when first, or later visited, and by whom? Our second conversation ended with *F&G* agreeing to call me after he spoke with his large carnivore biologist and reviewed the lab reports. I was now under a growing feeling that perhaps *F&G's* biologist was actually in charge and participated in the trapping events at the lodge.

The Second "Never Before" Shoe Drops- Wyoming Game & Fish

Four days later, on November 8th I received a call from *F&G,* the October 30, 2019 lab report came back, and the bear died of "Capture Myopathy." That was a new and foreign term to me. It was described as elevated body temperature and muscle stress. According to *F&G*, capture myopathy was very rare with bears, and never heard of a bear dying with it. It was more common to see this with other stressed ungulates as prey being chased. When asked if any signs of poisoning, *F&G* stated there was nothing in the organs or necropsy to indicate that and was following up with (name withheld) "large carnivore biologist, and again confirmed they had no previous history with this grizzly bear. It was further stated that the bear first came to the lodge on the 26th and was chased off from s'mores at the campfire. The bear was again chased off on both the 27th and 28th. The bear trap was set by WG&F on Sept 29th (time not revealed.) This was the same afternoon we arrived at the Shoshone Lodge from the Grand Tetons.

Due to the fact they had prior represented that no statements or interviews were taken, I asked who was the first person(s) that went to their bear trap at 1:00 am. As directly stated to me by the lodge manager, "They got the bear." Was the grizzly alive or dead when first visited by lodge person(s)? Or perhaps, did someone else go to the captured bear trap? I further inquired, "Why wouldn't you want to know, or even ask some questions on the scene or later on, when WG&F went to your trap and found a dead grizzly inside the trap? Even more puzzling was the incredible issue that this bear was the first ever to die in WG&F's traps in recorded history and was federally protected by the ESA. Stacked on top of that, the cause of death was something that you never heard of involving a bear. This amounted to two "never before happened" events involving the same grizzly, both within a couple of hours and the state wildlife agency responsible for this entire event never conducted any fact investigation, nor any apparent interest in what happened. Inexplicably, they merely hauled the dead grizzly away to their lab. Not to mention the irresponsible and dangerous setting of the bear trap without any identity, warnings, etc. on or near the active trap, nor any public postings or warnings anywhere on the lodge premises or elsewhere. None of this made any sense to me. *F&G* did not respond to my question, but went on to state, "They were not called or notified of a trapped grizzly and had no knowledge if it was alive or dead. For safety, we wait until first light to check traps." In our parting final telephone conversation, I was asked by F&G, "What was my concern about all this?" I reiterated that I first called as a guest at the lodge, to find out if WG&F was aware of the trapped dead grizzly at the Shoshone Lodge and now, I am hearing some things that just don't sound right. After expressing my thanks and appreciation for all they do, our conversation cordially ended.

Following the verbal representation that the Shoshone Lodge grizzly died of capture myopathy, which had never happened before and was exceedingly rare with bears, I embarked on some research on this condition and specifically, its relationship as a cause of death with grizzly bears and in particular to the SL grizzly. Generally, as I understood the condition, capture myopathy (CM), aka exertional myopathy (EM), is a disease created by the stresses of fight or flight, found mainly in ungulates as prey animals, i.e., deer, antelope, etc. This condition is rarely seen in carnivores, as predators chase the prey animals subjecting them to the stresses of flight and capture. The disease was documented in red foxes, American river otters, mountain lions, badgers, and black-footed ferrets.

There is only one other case in all literature of EM in a grizzly bear.

In an article in the *Journal of Wildlife Diseases*, 2008, entitled: Exertional Myopathy in a Grizzly Bear (Ursus arctos) Captured by Leghold Snare by Marc Cattet, Gordon Stenhouse, and Trent Bollinger of the Canadian Cooperative Wildlife Health Centre, Dept of Veterinary Pathology, University of Saskatchewan, Canada, only one such case was ever documented. However, it is important to note that the facts and circumstances of this only one case, *are not similar, nor apples to apples*, with that of the SL grizzly.

In the article Abstract, the authors diagnosed EM in the death of a grizzly bear captured by a leghold snare in Alberta in June 2003.

The facts of capture are as follows. On June 2, 2003, a free-ranging, ten-year-old adult grizzly weighing 540 lbs. with normal body condition, was captured along the Berland River in Alberta, Canada. The bear was captured by an Aldrich leghold snare. The bear was restrained by the left forelimb between a 5- and 15-hour range before the capture team arrived. It was anesthetized by remote drug delivery. Various lab and blood samples were taken, as well as a premolar tooth extraction for age determination. A small 2.5cm laceration was noted on the snared wrist. A radio GPS collar was applied, and medications were administered to reverse the anesthetic state. The bear was then released. The capture team twice sighted the grizzly by helicopter, over 5 days after release. The team was unable to observe the bear again, until 15 days after the capture date. GPS data from the collar indicated the bear died around 10 days after capture in the same general area.

The bear carcass was recovered and transported to Western College Veterinary Medicine, Saskatchewan for pathological examination. The snare trap did substantially more left-front damage than the exam at the capture site. The laceration was deep, with a metacarpal bone fracture with the distal 1cm missing. Based upon multiple capture events, a diagnosis of Exertional Myopathy (EM) was supported. However, the report concluded that they were <u>unable to determine if EM was the primary cause of death</u>. The findings led to a diagnosis of **"nonfatal" EM** in this bear. The report further concluded that a comparison with 127 leghold snare captures of grizzly bears in a Foothills Model Forest Grizzly Bear Research Project from 1999 to 2006 concluded that **EM is not generally a cause of mortality** for grizzlies. Also, this was the first report of EM in a snared grizzly bear.

Based on this and other reported information, suggested to me that the contrasts and distinctions between the SL dead grizzly versus the only ever reported case of a non-fatal EM diagnosis in the Canadian grizzly were profoundly different. Consider for example; the SL bear died inside a box trap without indications of trap injuries and died within a few hours of capture. The Canadian grizzly was captured in a painful, traumatic leg snare with resulting significant morbidity and did not die until 10 days later, not within a few hours. Therefore, by all recognized research and studies involving EM with grizzly bears, it appears that no grizzly has ever been diagnosed with capture myopathy as a Cause of Death. Yet here, with the Shoshone Lodge grizzly, WG&F's laboratory concluded that capture myopathy was the cause of death. If that internal representation is true, unbiased, and accurate, without other independent pathological studies and reviews, this would make the SL bear the first grizzly bear ever to die from this condition. That's even more amazing, considering the experts in grizzly bear capture myopathy opine that report of EM in carnivores are few and the only diagnosis of EM in a grizzly was "non-lethal."

The bottom line of the 2019 Shoshone Lodge event directly embodies two "first-time, never before happened" results. The first result: Never before in WG&F's entire history of culvert trapping grizzlies, has a bear died inside of one of their traps. The second result: This is the only grizzly bear ever to die, due to capture myopathy. How ironic or statistically implausible are these two "first-time ever" events coinciding within a mere few hours? Given the foregoing, and the total absence of any factual investigation, as well as inconsistent information; transparency was becoming quite bothersome. With our presence and observations at the Lodge during this incident, the question of lagging transparency was now foremost on my mind.

WG&F Public Records and Documents Production Phase

After I had an opportunity to digest and process the events at the Lodge along with subsequent conversations with *F&G*, I realized that I needed official records from WG&F to better understand what took place that night at the lodge and thereafter. I must readily admit when again viewing the gruesome picture of the agonal death of the grizzly in the trap only a few hundred feet from my cabin window, that image urged me to seek transparency and answers.

On November 14, 2019, I submitted a formal Public Request for Records and Document Production via certified mail receipt to Cody Regional Wildlife Supervisor, Wyoming Game & Fish Department, Cody, Wyoming. My request included the production of all: Copies of all original WG&F reports, investigations, communications, documents, photographs, and diagrams during the entire period of WG&F's involvement. Also requested, were all grizzly bear post-mortem records, tests, and findings, including laboratory, pathology, morphology, necropsy, etc. While I have never done so before or was involved in a situation like this, I felt comfortable that I did the right ethical thing, for the right reasons. I remain steadfast with that very decision today. With receipt and full disclosure of all records, etc., my anticipatory hope was those documents would satisfactorily settle all questions and inquiries and would help to prevent future occurrences and promote public safety when live trapping grizzly bears.

In mid-December 2019 I received a certified mail packet, without a cover letter from WG&F. The total produced official records contained 39 pages; the majority of the official records were various email communications. These emails revealed both WG&F inter and intra-agency communications, often with multiple official parties, either forwarding or in response. A number of the pages were redundant copies. I have no way of knowing if what was produced, included all requested documents, communications, etc. The scope of the provided records appeared somewhat sparse in my initial opinion. However, these official documents opened my eyes with an entirely new lens, into questioning what happened and full transparency of same. With my personal guest experience at the lodge and prior conversations with WG&F, it became abundantly clear, something simply just didn't look right. This new information created far more questions than answers, with gaping inconsistencies. Independently, my son Michael harbored similar opinions. All I wanted to do was simply report and find out if WG&F was aware of the trapped/dead bear. Due to transparency issues and produced handling records by WG&F, matters had now evolved into an unexplained mystery of "who, what, and when."

Upon my initial review of the records, I felt that perhaps, I may have been misled or misdirected by WG&F during my initial and follow-up telephone conversations.

The email documents that WG&F submitted to me included communications from the following WY Wildlife officials with knowledge of the Shoshone grizzly. None of the emails or documents were marked or designated as confidential communications. Listed below (names withheld) are the official titles.

WG&F Large Carnivore Section Supervisor. Lander, WY.

WG&F Large Carnivore Conflict Coordinator. Lander, WY.

WG&F Large Carnivore Biologist. Cody, WY.

USGS Northern Rocky Mountain Science Center, Interagency Grizzly Bear Study Team. Bozeman, MT.

Wildlife Biologist, Forest Service Shoshone National Forest. Cody, WY.

WG&F Wildlife Disease Specialist, WY State Veterinary Lab. Laramie, WY

*In addition to the above, seven other Wy. gov individuals were forwarded messaged.

Of critical importance, none of the provided records revealed any investigation information, other than later lab findings, concerning the facts and circumstances of the discovery of the grizzly bear after it was first trapped on the premises of the Shoshone Lodge. According to my review of WG&F's records, they did not conduct any on-site, or later investigation, interviews, or questions when they first discovered the dreadful condition of the dead captured grizzly bear. No diagrams, notes, or references of where they found the trap or the position of the remains inside the trap when they arrived. No photographs were taken. The documents are completely void of any relevant factual information of what, did or did not, take place with their trap or the bear at the time (1:00 am per lodge manager) it was trapped; including, the next morning when three WG&F personnel arrived to check on the trap. In my personal view, this makes no responsible sense whatsoever. Furthermore, the emails from top WG&F supervisory officials, do not reveal at any point, did they question or requested any follow-up information, insight, or questions relative to the bear's death. Their records suggest just the opposite and may further reflect their preference to keep this quiet, away from the public's right to know.

On Oct 10, 2019, the WG&F Large Carnivore Section Supervisor authored an email to the three-game officials (with cc to four other officials) who found the bear dead, which reads in part," (name withheld) is asking about the bear that died in the trap, obviously someone from the paparazzi alerted her to the situation as it's not listed that way on the IGBST or anywhere else.....anywhoo {sic} wanted to start on some talking points *should this gain some attention. I included Admin as we chatted about this yesterday at my PMI. I don't feel we need to do any kind of release as that will likely just fuel an unnecessary discussion*, but wanted to share these for consistency."

The above email appears to be generated from an Oct 8, 2019 email to the above Section Supervisor from the Executive Director of Wyoming Wildlife Advocates stating in part," I'm trying to find out more information on a grizzly that was found dead in a culvert trap near the Shoshone Lodge in Cody. Is there a report that has a narrative attached that you would be able to send me?" This information was the first that I knew that someone else before me had inquired about this incident.

The only non-WY laboratory documents produced were three pages; WGFD Wildlife Capture/Immobilization Form, Bear Measurement Form, and WG&F Grizzly Bear Mortality Report. Again, no factual investigation reports, notes, or references.

The <u>WGFD Wildlife Capture Form</u> was authored on 9-30-19 by the WG&F Cody Large Carnivore Biologist. It now appeared to me that this person was likely the WG&F official responsible for setting, baiting, and retrieving the bear trap. Based upon representations and now supporting records, it appeared to me that the initial WG&F Cody Regional Supervisor that I had spoken with, was the supervisor, not the direct hands-on official, involved with the trapping operations. This Capture Form does not reveal any important times from arrival to departure after the WG&F three members arrived or departed. Nor does it list or reference any communications between the team and anyone else. One would reasonably think, given the discovery of a never-before-dead grizzly in their trap, with three experienced wildlife officers present, they had both the time and resources to at least take and document some sort of investigation and seek information from third parties. The Handwritten notations on the form are the words "Not Drugged" however, this entry only applies to the Immobilization Procedures block on the form. The form further shows the adult male grizzly had an estimated age of seven years old, 300 lbs., without tags, markers, radio transmitters, etc., to indicate any prior capture or relocation. The specific report entry confirming that this ***bear was unknown to wildlife management, without any prior relocations***, immediately drew my attention to what the Lodge desk manager directly told me at our check-in to the Lodge stating "***This bear had been relocated once before.***" Where, when, and from whom did the manager get that important conflicting information to advise a checking-in guest? Please recall, WG&F statistics exposed a substantial pattern of "management" killing of grizzlies with a prior relocation history.

The Capture Report also revealed conflicting information concerning the bear's condition and appearance. According to the onsite report, the grizzly was described as; "being in good condition, nice dark coat and a high body condition score of 4 out of 5." This documented information, once again, is in stark opposition to the Oct 11th statement to me by the Cody Supervisor stating, "The grizzly was in poor condition and emaciated, they were waiting for toxicology/lab reports. But then, we may never know what, or why the bear was dead." The lab report confirms the Shoshone Lodge grizzly was not in poor condition or emaciated, just the opposite. Reflecting on these important representations and subsequent official record discovery, I can't help but feel now, from the onset with WG&F, I was being misguided to influence my interest in what happened that night. A nudge toward "move on, nothing to see here." Additional information also reinforced my perceptions that something just wasn't right about the uninvestigated facts and circumstances of another dead ESA-protected grizzly. The Remarks section of the report states the bear was captured for frequenting a guest lodge, bold behavior, and food rewards. The bear died in a culvert trap of unknown cause and was sent to the WGFD lab.

I don't have the least bit of concern, nor question the necessity for the Lodge to contact WG&F with a grizzly bear drawn to their premises by the enticing smells drifting from their outdoor grill for several nights. Unquestionably, that was the right and reasonable action to take. As to the grizzly bear, this was its first incident and was without causing any injury or property damage. It should have been humanely captured and relocated. But, from the beginning, was this the mindset and intent of the stakeholders?

The Bear Measurements Form indicates that no measurements were taken. The form itself identifies under the Samples Taken captions, with devoted attention to blocks: Tooth, Blood, Hair, and Tissue. The Cody Large Carnivore Biologist in charge of the trapping operation wrote on the form that Tooth, Hair, and Tissue samples were taken. However, and perhaps very relative, for some unexplained reasons, blood samples were not taken. Why not? If the controlling biologist takes the time to yank out teeth from the carcass and remove both hair and tissue samples, why wouldn't an experienced biologist logically take a blood sample, as referenced in the samples to be taken? If blood samples are important enough by WG&F standards to specifically list to avoid oversight in obtaining, why were they acknowledged and marked, "No" by the state wildlife official in charge of obtaining the samples?

The remaining form produced was the Wyoming Game & Fish Department/Grizzly Bear Mortality Report. The report is identified as IGBST Mort: 201930, dated 9-30-2019. Diagnostic Case Coordinator: (name withheld) The captions, Reporting Party, and Investigated By are listed as; WG&F Cody Large Carnivore Biologist and another (name withheld). Another caption identified as KILLED BY: reads Unknown. The mortality report goes on to state the adult, male grizzly bear estimated age is 7 years and is described as being in "*Good Condition*, dark color." Disposition of Parts caption names WGFD Lab.

The final produced form is entitled: Diagnostic Report, date submitted 9/30/19 and Date Reported 10/27/19, from Wyoming State Veterinary Laboratory. Laramie, WY. Submitted by: (name withheld) Wy.gov.

The produced complete three-page report contains seven Summary Captions: Clinical History, Diagnosis Summary, Necropsy, Bacteriology, Histology, Parasitology, and Virology, with several sub-summary captions. A sub caption entitled Morphologic Diagnosis, read in part with various findings......., "with *possible* early exertional myopathy." The Comments subsection, reads in part, "The gross lesions suggest **significant struggle in the culvert trap** with *possible* exertional hyperthermia/exertional myopathy."

The Diagnostic Summary Performed on **10/27/19** by (performing pathologist) under Final Diagnosis reads as: "Pulmonary congestion/edema/peripheral emphysema and acute (skeletal) degenerative myopathy consistent with early exertional hyperthermia/myopathy. Mild GI endoparasitism (Baylisascaris transfuga). Mixed bacteria isolated (nothing that looks significant). Negative for rabies.

While studying these reports as a layperson, something in the WG&F uninvestigated handling and retrieval of the dead grizzly, linked with WG&F's own Wildlife Laboratory process, caught my attention. Nowhere in these produced lab studies or reports is there any mention, of a **Toxicology** screen or study. Why wasn't an important blood sample, especially heart blood, examined for possible signs or traces of poisoning? Per WG&F records, their on-site Large Carnivore Biologist in charge of the trapping & retrieval process, inexplicably never took a blood sample(s) from the bear. Veterinary College of Medicine information refers to Toxicology, defined in part as the "science of poisons". Blood was referred to as one of the most important specimens of toxicology interest, along with all gathered samples. Yet, this suggests it wasn't done in this case because the officials in charge of retrieving the trapped dead bear, failed to obtain any blood samples. Keep in mind, this grizzly died an agonal death while in the trap evident by both the 9-30-19 photograph and the lab's necropsy findings and comments that gross lesions suggest significant struggle in the culvert trap.

Several other things concerning the lab reports also drew my interest and attention beyond the words, "possible, consistent, and suggest" concerning the Cause of Death. The produced lab records themselves are void of the word "poisoning" nor any specific efforts, questions, or comments to inquire, or rule out, the possibility that a toxic substance may have played any role in the death of this bear. The records suggest the possibility that exertional or capture myopathy, as a never before, exceedingly rare condition, alone caused the death of the Shoshone Lodge grizzly bear.

Another lab finding directed my further questioning remarks made by WG&F Large Carnivore Biologist on the WGFD Wildlife Capture Form. The handwritten form reveals the bear was captured in part for "food rewards" at the lodge, directly indicating it was habituated to human food rewards. On 10/1/19 the Necropsy Gross Description states the following, "The stomach contained 1.8 kg of intact and macerated chokecherries, with abundant chokecherries present in the proximal small intestine with chokecherry pits present in the colon, rectum and comprising much of the fecal matter." These GI tract lab findings in my mind, establish an important fact, this bear was feeding on all-natural food sources in the wild. Furthermore, there were no physical or laboratory findings/evidence at all, to establish this bear had consumed s'mores, or any other human food at the lodge, or before the time of its trapped death. Likewise, WG&F records confirm they had no prior record, complaints, or encounters with this healthy grizzly to suggest any history of food habituation, or human contact. With this important laboratory finding of only natural food found in the GI tract, in my opinion; it stands very reasonable and quite possible that the Shoshone Lodge grizzly was roaming the wilderness during fall's hyperphagia stage feasting on chokecherries, one of grizzly bears' natural fall food sources. While passing through the unfamiliar ground, with its incredible sense of smell, it was drawn directly to the lodge's "BBQ pit" as the desk manager described it, when we first checked into the lodge.

According to other produced email documents, on 10/4/2019 an email string reveals that the Large Carnivore Section Supervisor, Lander, WY emailed USGS Interagency Grizzly Bear Study Team, Bozeman stating, "This is the interim report for the bear that died in the culvert. We won't know the final until the histo tests etc. are done. Never seen anything like this, but I don't know if you want to call it accidental or results pending or something?" Less than half an hour later, USGS replied, "I had talked to (Large Carnivore Biologist, Cody, WY) regarding this and we put it up on the web list as under investigation until the lab results come back. We can revise the list once we know the cause. Accidental, capture-related myopathy can be indicated if no other reason is found."

Six days later, the above 10/10/19 email was prepared as WG&F "didn't want any kind of release that would likely just fuel an unnecessary discussion and admonishment to the "Cody guys" to make sure that all things are correct in regards to conflict activities for this particular bear." This email further initiated the creation of Talking Points, "If this should gain some attention." The email references an Attachment entitled, "TALKING POINTS FOR CAPTURE MYOPATHY IN A BOX." The attachment produced on or before 10/10/19 reveals VI bullet point topics for public disclosure if this event gained some attention.

Of notable importance, Bullet point II of the Talking Points states in part, "We are awaiting final pending laboratory results in regards to an adult male grizzly bear that was captured and subsequently died in the trap...final lab results will help final assessment of this very unique mortality situation." This sentence is immediately followed by the entry: Final Results were indicative of a rare capture myopathy event. Another entry states, "There were multiple rumors of human foul play, but those were unfounded based on the final necropsy and investigation."

Bullet point III asserts, "This is a very unique and extremely rare occurrence, in fact, this is the first time this type of mortality has been documented in over 1,500 captures (n=>_ 1,573 captures in box/culvert traps in GYE) using these types of capture devices."

The Talking Points for Capture Myopathy, including the Final Results of rare capture myopathy as the Cause of Death, were created by WG&F on Oct 10th. However, WG&F emails and records reveal that the Final Report by WY State Veterinary Laboratory was not completed and communicated until weeks later, on 10-31st. On that date, the Final Report was submitted by the Lab, Wildlife Disease Specialist to the Large Carnivore Coordinator along with a string of WY wildlife officials. The reporting email states, "It looks like your bear really got stressed out in the culvert trap." On Nov 1st the Large carnivore Coordinator replied via email, "Well, I guess there is a first time for everything." I must ask myself, "How can you have a predetermined Final Report of the Cause of Death when the actual Final Report is not yet completed or communicated?

Why is it, that wildlife officials predetermined the Final Results of a never before cause of death (capture myopathy) in their Talking Points, well in advance of the actual Final Report? Their Talking Points themselves were created as they didn't want any public awareness or scrutiny of a dead grizzly in their trap. Recall that their Oct 10th intra-department email declared they didn't need to do any kind of media release as that would likely just fuel an unnecessary discussion and were concerned this could gain some attention. Furthermore, after the bear's death, they chose to discredit anyone even asking about this bear as "paparazzi." What was it during this entire event that WG&F wanted to keep quiet and away from the public's right to know? But for a single laboratory study by their laboratory, the records reveal there's no finding or evidence of an "investigation" even though some of their communications refer to that word. Common sense alone dictates that some form of factual investigation was not only justified but warranted in this exceptionally rare and unexplained sequence of events involving

WGF's trapping and death of an ESA-protected healthy grizzly bear.

In December 2019, I was contacted by Angus M. Thuermer Jr. Mr. Thuermer is a seasoned Wyoming reporter, journalist, and photographer. His biography indicates that he has served as the president of the Wyoming Press Association and an advocate for access to public documents and meetings. At the time he reached out to me, Mr. Thuermer was the natural resources reporter for *WyoFile*, with more than 35 years of experience in Wyoming. He had become aware of the Shoshone Lodge grizzly bear death and interviewed me by telephone concerning my knowledge as a guest at the lodge during the entire incident. I shared with him; factual information I collectively knew from both my personal experiences at the lodge and follow-up contact and records.

A news article was to follow. Thuermer Jr, Angus M. "Game and Fish documents first agency trap-related grizzly death. *WyoFile,* 28 Jan. 2020. In the article, the reporter indicates that he had contacted the same Cody, Large Carnivore Section Supervisor that I had spoken with. Regrettably, the article omitted some important issues that I had brought to his attention, and in my personal opinion, portions are less than factually correct. On the other side, for the first time, the article brought to light other statements and events by WG&F that were not revealed in discussion with me and most importantly, are nowhere to be found or validated in WGF's official reports and documents.

Case in Point I. In the 1/28/20 article, *F&G* states, "Game and Fish notified the lodge and guests of the operation in advance and we warned them to stay away. We made sure to talk with the lodge and the people who run the lodge, employees, and owners who are well versed in grizzly bear behavior."

I don't know about any others, but we were not warned. My son and I checked into the lodge the day the trap was set.

We were not warned to stay away, in fact just the opposite. At the time we checked in, we had no knowledge of an active WG&F bear trap on, or near the premises. The front desk manager who checked us in, casually mentioned there was a bear trap somewhere out there, but it was ok for us to go find it if we wanted to take a look. We did so, only to discover the trap itself and the entire area around the trap and premises did not have any posted public warnings or identity of the trap.

Of greater importance to the lack of warning at the SL trap site, it appears as if WG&F may have violated their own policy and procedures for bear trap capture operations. On May 14, 2019, Cody WG&FD posted on their website an article entitled, "Game and Fish to begin grizzly bear trapping for monitoring purposes in Northwest Wyoming. Public reminded to heed warning signs."

The public was advised as follows: "Department biologists will conduct grizzly bear trappings in both front and backcountry areas. <u>All areas where trapping is being conducted</u> will have major access points marked with <u>warning signs</u>. <u>All trap sites will be posted with area closure signs</u> in the direct vicinity of the trap sites. It is critical that all members of the public heed these signs."

Below is a screenshot excerpt from WG&FD. Atkinson, Clint, et al."*2016 Wyoming Grizzly Bear Job Completion Report.*" *Wyoming Game and Fish Department Large Carnivore Section,* 1 Jul. 2017, p.4. You will note the agency's block description with an arrow pointing to a closure sign. You will further note the wording in the blocked caption, "<u>Capture sites are closed to all human presence</u>." No such closure signs or warnings were posted at or during the Shoshone Lodge trapping site. *The multiple WG&F authors of this report, specifically include the name of the Cody Large Carnivore Biologist in charge of the SL trapping site.

678	7/5/16	Adult female	Grouse Cr	GPS collar
859	7/6/16	Subadult male	Kettle Cr	GPS collar
861	7/12/16	Subadult female	Kettle Cr	GPS collar
819	7/13/16	Subadult male	Poison Bench	GPS collar
G217	7/15/16	Subadult male	Grouse Cr	No collar
506	7/17/16	Adult male	Kettle Cr	GPS collar
863	7/17/16	Subadult female	Poison Bench	VHF collar
867	7/20/16	Subadult female	Kettle Cr	VHF collar

A grizzly bear checks out the area closure sign at a capture site – capture sites are closed to all human presence.

Evident by photos of the unmarked bear trap and the surrounding vicinity and my observation of the lodge premises on 9-30-19, the Cody Large Carnivore Biologist in charge of actually setting the SL trap, along with supervisors, completely neglected to post any public warnings. Furthermore, official WG&F records fail to show those important warnings were applied.

Case in Point II: In the WyoFile article, apparently in response to my observation that WG&F didn't make any attempt to determine what happened. *F&G* now claimed to the reporter, "We did stop and talk to the wranglers-seven or eight of them- and let them know that we were pulling out now and had a unique situation. Game and Fish checked the trap to ensure it was working correctly. Because the incident was unprecedented, G&F decided to order a necropsy."

If that statement is true, then it begs a host of sensible questions. Who were the eight "wranglers" they spoke with? What did they say? Did they ever go to trap before, during, or after capture? Where were they and what were they doing when you stopped to talk? What time did this talk place and for how long? (WG&F pickup & departure times are not recorded.) What was their relationship, if any, to the lodge where the trapping death occurred? Did any of them see the bear, dead or alive, in the trap, and if so, what time, and circumstances? Did any of the three WG&F biologists that hauled off the bear record or document any information of this exchange whatsoever? Did WG&F take any notes or memorialize the talk? In other words, what information was exchanged during this new claim of a "stop & talk?" Once again, WG&F's actions from my personal experience and limited interaction with them, created more questions than answers.

Of critical importance, nowhere is any of this information contained or reflected in the produced official WG&F records. Objectively, the official WGF records do not validate or support any such position.

Case in Point III: Lastly, the WG&F statement in the WyoFile article claims, "Trappers found snow on the ground when they arrived at the trap the morning of Sept. 30th. There was fresh snow-there were no tracks around the trap, we have several techniques where we can tell if somebody has tampered with the trap. To our knowledge nobody went up and tampered with the bear-nobody did anything to harass that bear while it was in the trap."

You may now know why I pointed out my previous personal observations and photos, drawing attention to the fact there was no snow at the trapping site, or anywhere nearby. It appears WG&F would have the public believe that nobody went to or appeared at the trap after the grizzly was captured or while in captivity, until found dead the next morning because there were no footprints in the snow around the trap. The plain and simple fact is there wasn't any snow on the ground at or near that trap. That position is clearly evident from my photographs and my personal presence at the trap both late afternoon after it was set, until the next morning when WG&F removed it. The ground at both times was simply wet and muddy, just as they were when my son and I arrived. No snow, old or fresh, was present at the trap nor on the lodge grounds. Once again, nowhere in WGF's records is the "snow claim" reported. The undisputable fact remains that for reasons still unknown, WG&F never conducted a factual investigation, except their own lab study.

Several months passed by after the WyoFile article. It was clear to me that my scrutiny of the WG&F records was now amplified, by yet more inconsistencies revealed in the WyoFile article. One common indisputable fact remained: The entirety of events that occurred at the lodge were all related to WG&F's bear trap. Admittedly, they set the unmarked trap, baited & positioned it, and retrieved it along with the dead bear which they sent to their laboratory. Therefore, all events which took place, known and unknown, occurred while the trap along with the captured grizzly bear was within the care, custody, and control of WG&F. They alone were responsible. How is it then, that the very same government state wildlife agency responsible for their actions in this specific case, could unbiasedly self-investigate, without any evidence or record of an investigation? The only thing they did; fully knowing that these were first time, never happened before, unprecedented occurrences, was immediately transport the bear to their lab. Under the shroud of non-transparency, I wondered if this was like the old axiom of the fox guarding the hen house.

In any event, with this growing mysterious handling, I had hoped perhaps further official records would provide insight or answers to bring factual integrity and transparency. After all, the only focus here is the trapped ESA dead grizzly bear and what took place during and after the captivity. It's my understanding that the USF&WS retains federal control whenever an ESA-protected grizzly bear is killed, as in this case. It was described to me that USF&WS delegates state wildlife agencies to conduct investigations of grizzly bear deaths and report to them. If unsettled, they may then intervene. It stood logically to me that if WG&F timely reported the dead SL grizzly, there would be inter-agency communications between the WG&F

and USF&WS associated with the SL grizzly. Especially so, as this event and the listed cause of death were both unprecedented.

On Feb. 4, 2020, via certified mail, I submitted to USF&WS, a Public Request for Records and Document Production, along with a cover letter requesting the production of a relative expanse of documents, records, reports, intra & inter-agency communications, etc. My certified letter and enclosures were received and signed for by USF&WS on Feb 12, 2020. Though my public request was received by the agency, I never received a response. Not even an acknowledgment form or letter. My formal request was met with complete silence and non-compliance. Inter-agency open disclosure and transparency? Well, you be the judge.

Final Phase-Mystery Shoshone Lodge Grizzly

I never expected, nor desired whatsoever, to find myself entwined with a confusing, unexplained death of a grizzly bear a couple hundred feet away from my cabin door in the middle of night. Nevertheless, convoluted circumstances and skepticism both found me. The confluence of perhaps, my naivety to newly discovered state wildlife grizzly bear management and my ultraistic newcomer perceptions had raised my awareness to a never before questioning and uncomfortable level. One final unsettling development that I could not have imagined, was just around the corner.

As previously indicated, only through the discovery of the WG&F records was I able to learn that there was a Large Carnivore Biologist from Cody, who was actually in charge of the entire WG&F trapping and was on scene at the Shoshone Lodge to set the unmarked trap. This biologist also led the three-member WG&F recovery team to remove the trap and the dead bear. I've already shared observations from the disclosed WG&F records that did not support this biologist had conducted any investigation, interviews, questions, etc. into the totality of his direct involvement, with this grizzly bear. The same biologist on site, failed to obtain blood samples, though the WG&F Wildlife

Capture Form called for blood samples. The same individual is identified in the WG&F Grizzly Bear Mortality Report, as the Reporting Party with one other individual. They are also listed as "Investigated By."

After reaching a dead end with my formal request for records with the USF&WS, I was drawn to a revealing article involving the shooting killing of a grizzly bear off the North Fork of the Shoshone River. Baker, CJ. "Costly Mistake: G&F employee must pay $10,000 for misidentifying, killing grizzly." *Powell Tribune*, 14 Oct. 2014. Before my discovery, I did not know about this event or the article.

According to the published *Powell Tribune* article, this matter was about a court case in Park County Circuit Court involving a Cody-based Large Carnivore Biologist. He was charged with killing a grizzly bear and firing at it from a spot 23 feet from the edge of the North Fork Highway.

According to the news report in part; On September 2013, the LCB had spotted a large black bear while checking bruin activity in the Sweetwater Creek drainage along the North Fork of the Shoshone River. After completing his Game and Fish work, LCB bought a black bear license, returned to the area, and spotted what he thought was the same bear. Once he discovered that he had shot and killed a grizzly bear, he immediately notified authorities. He later told wildlife investigators he believed the bear had no hump, tall ears, a straight face, and appeared solid black as it passed through an opening in the brush on a rainy day. According to the charging documents, the Game & Fish investigator wrote," (name withheld) said he had just the one opening before the bear would be gone. He only had a couple of seconds to judge if it was a black bear or a grizzly bear." He recalled being 100 percent certain the animal was a black bear until approaching the carcass and seeing the blond tips and long claws characteristic of grizzlies.

Another news article reported on the court case. Ellison, Greg. "Killer of Grizzly fined $10,000." *CodyEnterprise.com/news*, 9 Oct. 2014. This article presented some additional information. In part, the article states, "The shooting took place on Sept. 6, 2013, about 10 miles east of Yellowstone Park. Earlier in the day, (name withheld) had been tracking a black bear and returned that evening to continue the hunt. He watched the bear for more than 10 minutes from a distance of about 130 yards. When the bear started to leave the area, he said he had to make a split-second decision to shoot."

"Park County Circuit Judge Bruce Waters granted (name withheld) a deferral on two charges: taking a grizzly bear without a license and shooting across a roadway." The article reveals," Wyoming Game & Fish biologist (name withheld), who shot a grizzly bear, will pay $10,000 in restitution. Besides restitution, the judge ordered him to pay $260 in fines and costs." The state had determined the value of the grizzly to be $25,000. The news article goes on to state," (Name withheld) was given first-time offender status and granted a 7-13-301 disposition. He will be on probation for one year. The case will be dismissed upon successful completion of probation." *G&F* suspended (name withheld) for two weeks without pay, with a letter detailing the incident was put in his permanent file.

In my personal opinion, there is no distinction, relevancy, or bearing whatsoever, between the WG&F, captured dead grizzly bear at the Shoshone Lodge and the above unrelated 2014 court-reported case of a shot and killed grizzly, with the court finding of taking a grizzly bear without a license. However, the only commonalities are two dead ESA-protected grizzly bears, with two distinctively different events and facts; and both events involved the same WG&F Large Carnivore Biologist.

After an extended factual-based chapter; as both a fact witness and grizzly bear advocate, I believe this was a relevant chapter to convey. It wasn't pleasant, but necessary. It created my first-time personal experience and light of day, into a perplexing story and state wildlife management practices with grizzly bear management. The entirety of events followed by transparency concerns, shaped my narrow lens into local state management of our nation's once near-extinct, iconic grizzly bear. It's my hope and desire that this incident will promote WG&F's future trappings to be safely conducted and that investigations into the death of ESA protected grizzly bears under their handling will be thorough, transparent, and unbiased.

In conclusion, the mystery of what events took place during the entirety of WG&F's trapping event at the Shoshone Lodge on Sept 30 and Oct 1, 2019, continues or perhaps ends. Would a rare, unprecedented final Cause of Death "capture myopathy" conveniently be listed? Evident by the earliest WG&F emails replying "Perfect" to "if no other reason is found." Could it be that no other reasons were found because WG&F officials weren't looking for, or investigating their own first-ever grizzly trapping death?

One of the first statements made to me on October 11, 2018, by the Cody Large Carnivore Supervisor was, "We may never know what, or why the bear was dead." This extraordinary prophetic, or perhaps predetermined statement, may have commenced the very moment the heavy steel trap gate slammed shut, sealing the grizzly's fate.

Chapter Fourteen

The Tri-State Agreement

"Trophy" Grizzly Bear Hunts, or Not?

My personal experiences during and after, the Shoshone Lodge grizzly bear trapping death, were my first direct insight into Wyoming's state wildlife management, operational policies, attitudes; and most of all, WG&F's alarming grizzly bear mortality record of "Management Captures." My favorable preconception beliefs were shattered, assuming their efforts, resources, law enforcement, and policies, were all in unbiased favor of protecting endangered grizzlies under the ESA and controlling auspices by the United States Fish & Wildlife Services. I decided to educate myself with research, testing if my newly formed opinions were based upon fact, rather than emotion as a grizzly bear advocate and enthusiast. I also needed to gauge, how or if, state management's operational history and current policies would affect both my own and the public's ability and rewarding success of seeing grizzly bears in the wild. Please note that my opinions and statistical findings pertain exclusively to grizzly bear management and no other, vital state wildlife services or management policies. I commend the agency for those other well-deserved programs and successes.

I was taken back by WG&F's openly self-stated policy and purpose for the monitoring of grizzly bear information. The Cody Regional Office of WG&F posted on their website Nov 25, 2019, an article unequivocally declaring, "Game and Fish is committed to monitoring grizzly bears and demonstrating recovery to support future delisting." This statement of purpose is openly biased and distorted in only one direction, the agency's pursuit to remove grizzly bear ESA status and protection. One huge element of their biased support for their past and future ESA delisting was proved to be a race to enact Trophy grizzly bear hunting. How is it that a state agency, with public and private funding, would not unbiasedly monitor grizzly bears, rather than a biased one-way policy that will unquestionably result in Trophy killing, on top of their excessive "removal" mortality history of the same bears they are monitoring? Based on this policy, one has to question: "Is this a trusted reliable state wildlife grizzly bear management agency, or something far less?"

WG&F produces an annual report entitled: *Wyoming Game and Fish Department Grizzly Bear Management Captures, Relocations, and Removals in Northwest Wyoming*. The report is prepared by the Large Carnivore Conflict Coordinator, Large Carnivore Section. Data for the report is supplied by the Large Carnivore Section biologists.

The contents of this annual Wyoming grizzly bear mortality report are stunning, and not in a good way. In my book for fluency, I try to avoid numbing statistical information. Rather, I broadly focus on the import of meaningful statistics. However, I suggest that my review and analysis of this eye-opening report is a worthy exception, having direct relevance to WG&F and USF&WS-sponsored "grizzly bear removal." I take no pleasure, but rather discomfort, in objectively revealing what the report data indicates.

The assimilated data below obtained from the WG&F report embodies the past seven-year history (2022-2016) of mortality of "Removed" grizzly bears at the hands of WG&F. The term "Removal" designates captured grizzlies that were killed. The term "Captured" refers to grizzlies that were trapped by WG&F.

*2022 Captured (21) Removed (15) = 71.4% Mortality

*2021 Captured (45) Removed (30) = 66.6% Mortality

*2020 Captured (26) Removed (18) = **69.2%** Mortality

*2019 Captured (33) Removed (18) = **54.5%** Mortality

*2018 Captured (59) Removed (32) = **54.2%** Mortality

*2017 Captured (31) Removed (13) = **42.0%** Mortality

*2016 Captured (40) Removed (22) = **55.0%** Mortality

During these seven years, WG&F Removed (killed) 148 grizzly bears out of 255 bears Captured (trapped). Thus, the annual averages during these seven years, reflect that on average, each year (36) bears are Captured/trapped and (21) are Removed/killed. Therefore, based on their data, on average **WG&F has a 58% average annual Mortality Rate**, with three years appreciably exceeding the 58% average. Interestingly, I noted that WG&F never indicated, nor published any Mortality Rate information as reflected in my research. Presumably, when your own managing agency's data and policies, expose the alarming fact that 7 out of 10 captured/trapped grizzlies are killed by WG&F; is something you would prefer to statistically omit from public review and scrutiny.

To test if WG&F's own collected data entertained any other mortality trends, I randomly examined the same reports for the years 2012 and 2005. Indeed, the same criteria of the earlier reports compared to the most recent seven years revealed an alarming variation in captured grizzly bear mortality.

*2012 Captured (48) Removed (12) = 25% Mortality

*2005 Captured (21) Removed (4) = 19% Mortality

A total of 69 grizzly bears were Captured/trapped, of which 16 were Removed/killed, presenting an average **23% Mortality Rate**. Compare these earlier years' 23% average annual mortality rate to, WG&F's current 58% average annual mortality rate. The data suggest that a major troubling grizzly bear management trend is evident. Statistics from their reports support the observation that WG&F Large Carnivore

Management has adversely evolved from a low mortality rate; into a highly aggressive rate, pattern, and practice of removing, or killing (the words are synonymous) of the very same grizzly bears they should be monitoring. And I should also again reference the alarming fact that WG&F openly states, their only purpose in monitoring grizzly bears is to delist them from ESA federal protection. Translated these patterns and trends end game: Yellowstone Trophy grizzly hunting.

Sadly, the USF&WS not only supports the same ESA delisting, but persistently drives the charge; bowing to federal and state political whims and pressures of a public minority, and the high heeled, deep pocket special interest groups eager for the Trophy kills. According to *WG&F Grizzly Bear Management Captures, Relocations and Removals Reports*, "Removal of grizzly bears in Wyoming is dependent upon authorization from the U.S. Fish and Wildlife Service after careful and thorough deliberation taking into account multiple factors unique to each conflict situation." The report fails to identify the authorization process and the type and nature of deliberations. Furthermore, there is no information revealing the actual counts or percentages of "Removal" collaborative submissions by state wildlife agencies to USFWS. How many, if any, state submissions are rejected or remanded back to the states for reconsideration? Based upon the miserable statistics of state killings of captured grizzlies, I suggest that it is simply a lockstep process to satiate their mutual goals and objectives to terminate ESA protection, thus swinging the door wide open to Yellowstone Trophy grizzly bear hunting.

The current history of grizzly bear ESA Delisting and Reinstatement of ESA, is helpful to understand the assault against America's most treasured iconic wilderness species. This continuing assault is nonpartisan. Both Democrat and Republican Administrations under their appointed Secretaries of the Interior, have and are currently (2023) endorsing and sponsoring grizzly bear removal. The USFWS delisted the grizzly bear two times and is seeking a third attempt, to do so.

The first delisting occurred on March 22, 2007. In September 2009 a federal judge in Missoula, MT restored federal protections, placing the grizzly bear back on the ESA list. The court held that USFWS did not follow its own science in delisting. The white bark pine a diet staple of grizzlies, had dramatically declined due in part to climate change impact. The court further opined that the conservation strategy in place to protect the grizzly bears was largely unenforceable and inadequate.

The second USFWS Delisting of the Yellowstone GYE grizzly bears took place on June 22, 2017. Under Republican Administration, then under Interior Secretary, Ryan Zinke announced the Delisting of the Yellowstone GYE area grizzly bear from ESA federal protection and the transfer of grizzly bear management back to the individual states of WY, MT, and ID. Republican Montana Senator Daines announced, "I look forward to continuing with the state of Montana as they take the lead in the management of the grizzly." The Order was highly contested by the majority of the public. Conservation groups and Tribal Nations filed lawsuits to prevent Delisting and the handover to the states. The Delisting Order, imposing its adverse impact on the preservation of grizzly bears, was vigorously and soundly opposed by the Humane Society of the United States and many other organizations. Among their opposing contentions was the position that the grizzly bear population had not recovered. Furthermore, the population was far from being recovered. Statistical data revealed that in the past three years, record-high grizzly mortality was recorded and 175 bears were killed because of the actions of poachers, cattle ranchers, and elk hunters. The bears also faced a host of threats to their habitat and food sources.

Enter the 2017 Tri-State Agreement

Before the ink was even dry on the federal Delisting Order, handing federal protection and grizzly bear management back to the states, a document had been drafted and agreed upon by the only three states in the lower forty-eight blessed with a grizzly bear population. That document was known as the

Tri-State Agreement, collaboratively enacted by the states of WY, MT, and ID. As part of the new state management takeover, the Agreement specifically introduced "TROPHY" Grizzly Bear Hunting Seasons as a means of state management. The last time Wyoming held grizzly bear hunting was 1974, the very same year that ESA protection was enacted to afford federal protection and enforcement of the utter collapse of the few remaining grizzly bears. Incredibly, the Agreement created two (spring and fall) annual Trophy grizzly hunts. The provisions also included hunting collared research bears.

The cat was now officially out of the bag. It becomes rather evident why, Wyoming Game and Fish, Montana Fish and Parks, and Idaho Fish and Game collectively clamored for ESA delisting and turning over management back to themselves. The driving force was the pervasive thirst to Trophy hunt and kill grizzly bears. This was their management end game, along with the Trophy hunting special interest groups who support the recreational killing of grizzlies. It also explains their bias in "monitoring" the grizzly bear populations in their respective states to advance questionable recovery numbers suitable to legally start killing the bears once again. How credible is the proposition as a state grizzly bear management technique, to immediately start Trophy hunting and killing the very same national resource that was twice on the very edge of virtual extinction?

How ironic is the fact, that at the very same time Wyoming was about to unleash a restricted number of Trophy grizzly bear hunters to what now, would become killing grounds with proximity outside Yellowstone National Park and Grand Teton National Park; when the government in British Columbia ended all grizzly bear hunting. Effective immediately on Dec. 18, 2017, a complete ban was enacted in British Columbia on all grizzly bear hunting, with only one exception. First Nations hunters would be allowed to hunt the bears for food, social or ceremonial reasons. This would likely be a very small group. That order comes from a Canadian Province that has a grizzly population over 15 times the highest number of GYE grizzly bears, exceeding the GYE population by approximately 15,000 grizzlies.

Joy Foy of the Wilderness Committee environmental group labeled the measure as "tremendous news" that sets a global standard. Foy went on to say, "Some nations still allow trophy hunting for big beautiful creatures. This is a word out to the world that says times are changing and changing because so many creatures are in decline. We've got to start to look out for them, not kill them for fun." Another NDP official remarked to hunters that he knows hunting is important to many British Columbians, but "this is not the thin edge of the wedge, this is a specific species, an iconic species." The ministry advised that illegally killing grizzly bears in more extreme cases, as a first court conviction can lead to a fine of $100,000 or a one-year jail sentence.

It appears very reasonable that we should look to and monitor our northern Canadian neighbors for grizzly bear management policy results, insight, and wisdom rather than by, our state certifications to manage our scarce population of grizzlies by Trophy hunting them.

After the Tri-State Agreement was signed by the member states, Wyoming and Idaho immediately jumped to the forefront to aggressively enact the first fall GYE Trophy grizzly bear in 2018. Idaho jumped in the Trophy hunting fray along with Wyoming by ridiculously allowing one, yes one (1) single grizzly to be Trophy killed in the entire state. This was a politically run decision, completely void of any common operational grizzly bear management sense; much less an ounce of common sense. At first, I applauded Montana for its position to defer grizzly bear hunting for a year. Were their reasons predicated upon; public sentiment against Trophy killing, or perhaps, their suspicion of the accuracy of the *estimated* grizzly bear population? After all, the very same state wildlife agencies announced mission for monitoring the number of bears, was to delist ESA protection, knowing all too well this would unleash the grizzly bear hunting industry. My words above, "I applauded Montana," soon came to a screeching and disappointing halt. Montana's further actions unmistakably revealed their misguided appetite to not only promote Trophy kill grizzly bears but later advanced draconian policies to do so with other wildlife.

With the advance of the September 2018 Wyoming Trophy Grizzly Bear Hunt, WG&F announced an Application Process for an opportunity to "harvest" a Trophy grizzly. This would be the first grizzly bear hunt in 40 years; the period of which ESA protection first came into law, removing state grizzly bear management from the states to federal ESA management. It's critically important to historically observe that prior grizzly bear management under state management (WY, MT, ID) miserably failed. State actions were irresponsible and ineffective. Grizzly hunting was a key destructive component, resulting in the collapse and near extinction of the few surviving 136 grizzly bears within thousands of square miles. The estimated total GYE grizzly population is 700 bears. Each year, approximately 60 grizzlies are killed by some form of human interaction. That's a 9% mortality rate, excluding loss from natural sources. Now in 2018, add state management plans to conduct two Trophy hunting seasons and well, you can see the grizzly's future.

Illustrating the extent of the hunting community's massive assault with now having a chance to kill a WY grizzly, over 7,000 Applications flocked to WG&F from near and afar to seek a tag. The staggering number of Applicants took place during a very brief period before the hunt was to take place. It's more than reasonable to assume this number would be greatly higher, if more time to file was available before the Sept. 15 and Nov. 15 hunting period. If an applicant was granted a license, WY residents would pay $600 and $6,000 for all others. Never mind the additional excessive hunt expenses for outfitters, guides, taxidermy, firearms, equipment, travel, lodging, and other expenses. At the expense of dead Trophy grizzly bears and displacement of remaining bear habitat; the unconscionable assault of big money from the Trophy hunting industry would soon descend on the entire Greater Yellowstone Ecosystem. The cost of killing a WY grizzly bear close to YNP & GNP boundaries would run well into the tens of thousands of dollars. Quite a bounty tag to hang a Yellowstone grizzly's head on the wall, pelt on the floor, or a standing stuffed Trophy to impress visitors at the door.

Following the USFWS Order delisting the grizzly bear from the Endangered Species Act list, various conservation, and environmental groups, and Native American Tribes filed lawsuits in late 2017 seeking the GYE grizzly bear reinstatement of ESA protection and Administrative Procedures Act. Six federal lawsuits were filed in the District of Montana. These lawsuits were later consolidated into a single Case No: CV 17-89-M-DLC *Crow Indian Tribe; et al., Plaintiffs vs. United States of America; et al., Federal Defendants and the State of Wyoming; et al., Defendant and Intervenors.*

On September 24, 2018, Chief District Judge, United States District Court, Dana L. Christensen; in a 47-page Order, ruled in favor of the Plaintiffs and vacated the June 30, 2017, Final Rule of USFWS delisting the GYE population of grizzly bears, and restored ESA status to the GYE grizzly.

In the Order, the court found in favor of the Plaintiffs on both grounds. USFWS exceeded its legal authority when it delisted GYE grizzly bear without consideration of the impact of other members of the lower forty-eight grizzly designation and USFWS application of ESA threats analysis was "arbitrary and capricious." Further finding that by dropping a key commitment to ensure that any population estimator adopted in the future is calibrated to the estimator used to justify delisting, USFWS "illegally negotiated" away its obligation to apply the best available science to reach an accommodation with the states of Wyoming, Idaho, and Montana.

Before the Court's Final Order on 9/24/18, with the proposed GYE trophy grizzly bear hunt scheduled to start in two days, Judge Christensen issued a 14-day restraining order, halting the hunts. The court desired to carefully weigh arguments from both sides of the ESA delisting lawsuit. As accepted with the Final Order restoring ESA protection, public and special interest organizations' emotions were running high, and often quite contentious and uncompromising. As expected, the red lines greatly centered on state management plans for Trophy killing.

I would be remiss, if not presenting an unrelated reported 2018 non-litigated, nor involved parallel Montana grizzly bear management mortality warning report. MFW&P reported that 2018 had been the deadliest year for grizzly bear mortality since scientists started keeping track of grizzlies in Northwest Montana. This report exclusively focused on a large tract of grizzly bear habitat around Glacier National Park, referred to as the Northern Continental Divide Ecosystem (NCDE.) During Montana's record-setting year, it was reported that at least 46 grizzly bears died within the NCDE. This number had never exceeded 35 deaths in the past decade. An MFW&P grizzly bear research biologist responded by stating, "She wasn't worried and that the numbers themselves are not alarming." Well, if a decades-old grizzly mortality report was shattered and the official management response is "not worried or alarmed," there appears to be a disconnected or lacking state grizzly bear management attitude and concern.

In May 2019 USFWS filed an appeal to the Ninth Circuit Court of Appeals seeking to overturn the U.S. District Court Order reinstating ESA protection status to the GYE grizzly population. This would be the second appeal by USFWS to remove GYE grizzlies from ESA protection. In 2011 the Ninth Circuit rejected the federal agency's attempt to ESA delist the GYE grizzly bear on grounds that there was no evidence to support the Service's position, that decline in the whitebark pine (a major grizzly bear food source) did not threaten the GYE grizzly bear population.

Now in July 2020, for the second time, the U.S. Court of Appeals for the Ninth Circuit, affirmed the 2018 Montana U.S.

District Court decision to restore ESA status to the GYE grizzly, thus sparing the WY Yellowstone grizzlies and one incredibly fortunate token Idaho quota grizzly bear of certain death and habitat disruption by hunters. The Ninth Circuit concluded, affirming the district court in all respects, with one exception of the order requiring USFWS to conduct a "comprehensive review" of the remaining grizzly population. This item was remanded to the district court to order further examination of the delisting's effect on the remnant grizzly population consistent with this opinion. As Andrea Zaccardi, a senior attorney with the Center for Biological Diversity artfully opined, "Grizzlies still have a long way to go before recovery. Hunting these beautiful animals around America's most treasured national park should never again be an option."

However, the hard-fought legal victories thus far preserving ESA delisting of the GYE grizzly would not be over, just the opposite. Was this second court victory, in favor of sustaining GYE grizzly ESA status, the termination of the state wildlife agency's misguided drive for delisting and Trophy hunting? As many feared, sadly not. Predictably, it merely reignited the renewal of vigorous further efforts by the collective heavily financed, well-heeled federal, state, and special interest pro-delisting/Trophy hunting affiliations.

In March 2021, both federal Senate and House Bills were introduced as the *Grizzly Bear State Management Act of 2021*. The bills would once again attempt to remove GYE grizzlies from the ESA and transfer management back to the states. The GBSMA also prevents further judicial review of the delisting. The House companion bill was previously filed by former U.S. Rep. Liz Cheney (R-Wy). In response to U.S. District Court reinstating ESA status to the grizzly an article by: Brufke, Juliegrace. "Cheney blasts court decision to place grizzly bear back on the endangered species list." The Hill. 30 July 2019. Cheney said, "The court-ordered relisting of the grizzly was not based on science or facts, but was rather the result of excessive litigation pursued by radical environmentalists' intent on destroying our Western way of life." Cheney further said, "Placing the bears on the endangered species list — which prevents hunters from targeting the animals — could have a negative impact on the ecosystem."

The 2021 Senate bill was introduced by Senator Cynthia Lummis (R-WY) together with Senator John Barrasso (R-WY), Senators Mike Crapo (R-ID) and James Risch (R-ID) and Senator Steve Daines (R-MT.)

Interestingly, Senator Barrasso commented that Wyoming's good work and sound management practices should be allowed to demonstrate success. I might add, well ok. However, was WG&F's 2019 grizzly bear management record of 55% mortality of "removed" i.e., killed" grizzlies, reflective of good work and sound management? What about successive years of escalating, not leveling or decreasing, WY management grizzly bear mortality rates as stunningly high as 71% for 2021?

Likewise, sponsoring Senator Crapo commented that Idaho's local wildlife managers have a history of successful species management practices based on sound science and collaborative efforts among federal, state, and tribal agencies. Well again ok, but was that body of work complimentary to the foolish fact that Idaho, pursuant to the agreed Tri-State Agreement, had a Trophy grizzly bear hunting quota of just one grizzly that could be killed in the entire state for the entire grizzly bear hunting season? Idaho, according to published grizzly bear habitat data, has 8% of suitable grizzly habitat in the GYE. How is it then, that within thousands of ID/GYE square miles of bear habitat, according to the TSA Trophy hunting rules; the moment a hunter killed the first Idaho grizzly, the state's Trophy hunting season was over.

Incomprehensively, ID unleashed a Trophy grizzly hunting season that could last less than an hour. Is Idaho's bewildering action reflective of" successful state species management practices" and a precursor of what's next to come? With Idaho being proportionately bound to exclusively present one sacrificial grizzly bear for the proposed 2018 inaugural GYE Trophy hunt; will Idaho's future Tri-State Agreement provisions for Trophy kill quotas, be further reduced to less than its one obligatory sacrificial grizzly? As nonsensical as that sounds; it's no less illogical than their race with Wyoming for the first Yellowstone Trophy grizzly bear kill.

Chapter Fifteen

Black Bear Hunter "Mistaken Identity" Grizzly Bears Pay the Price

A rash of killing ESA-protected grizzly bears by black bear hunters allegedly claiming "mistaken identity" of a grizzly bear for a black bear, further demonstrates the precarious and skeptical recovery numbers promoted by state wildlife grizzly bear managers for the express purpose of delisting Yellowstone grizzlies ESA protection status, furthered by Trophy grizzly bear hunting. As to reported or prosecuted cases, these are not simply isolated cases and are void of, all but certain, unreported similar cases. In any event, there appears to be a recent growing trend of this nature with the end result of more dead grizzly bears at the hands of humans, namely hunters.

Generally, within the Tri State area of ID, WY, and MT there are two black bear hunting season, spring and fall. Generally, with slight state variations, the spring season is April 15 to June 15. The fall season runs from September 1 to Oct 31 or longer. Depending on the state, most, if not all black bear hunting is conducted with tree stands over baited and electronically monitored bait stations and/or with hounds. Most noteworthy, a high percentage of black bear shootings/kills occur in grizzly bear habitat. Needless to say, this potentially places the ESA protected grizzly bear in the direct line of fire of eager black bear hunters, experienced or otherwise. With the black bear spring hunting season overlapping into June, this also places mating grizzly bears in harms way. Grizzlies generally mate in early to mid-June.

To factually illustrate the "mistaken identity" manner of black bear hunters shooting and killing grizzly bears, rather than black bears of which they may be licensed to hunt, let's briefly examine some very recent reported cases in which grizzly bears were shot and killed, with the trophy hunters afterwards claiming as a defense, mistaken identity or black hunters simply killing protected grizzlies.

According to an article by, Heinz, Mark. "Wyoming Bear Hunter Who Accidently Killed Grizzly Fined $10,000." *Cowboy StateDaily*, 11 May 2023. A Cody man (name withheld) was charged with a misdemeanor count of being an accessory before and after the fact in taking a grizzly bear that was shot on a spring black bear hunt on May 22, 2022. The illegal shooting place in the North Fork near Cody. After the shooting, the defendant immediately contacted WG&F that his son had mistakenly shot a grizzly, not a black bear. The man pleaded no contest to the charges and prosecutors waived the normal penalty of a $10,000. fine and a year in jail. The Circuit Court judge ordered that he must pay $10,000 in restitution to WG&F for telling his son to shoot the grizzly bear.

Another MT black bear hunter shot and killed a grizzly bear on June 5, 2003. In an article, Staff, Chronicle. "Hunter kills grizzly in Madison Range south of Ennis." *Bozeman Daily Chronicle.com.*, 12 Jun 2023. A black bear hunter, while on Madison private land, claimed he was charged by a grizzly bear. The hunter killed the bear with a pistol and claimed self-defense. He wasn't injured. He reported the incident to MFW&P the same day. A field investigation was conducted by three agencies that were helped by the landowner. The investigation is ongoing.

The grizzly bear killed was a 15-year-old female, without cubs. In 2013 this bear was researched and captured and had no known conflict history with humans. The grizzly was killed outside the Greater Yellowstone Ecosystem (GYE) grizzly bear recovery zone, however, the shooting occurred within the (DME) demographic monitoring area.

In the above incident, I can't help but notice there is no mention whatsoever of the hunter having or using bear spray as a first line of defense. That same adult bear without any history of adverse behavior might be alive, productive, and well today. Rather, hunter bullets brought about its finality while within its habitat.

An Idaho grizzly bear was shot and killed by black bear hunters in the spring of 2022. According to a June 16, 2022 article by Idaho Fish and Game, two hunters were actively hunting black bears and in fact, had just shot and killed one black bear in the Ruby Creek drainage. The hunters claimed a grizzly bear "appeared" and "approached" them. Backing up and yelling at the bear, it continued to "approach" when one of them shot and killed the sub-adult grizzly. The state investigators concluded it was self-defense. End result, another killed grizzly by black bear hunters in grizzly bear habitat. Once again, there is no mention of either hunter having or using bear spray. According to the brief incident description, this bear did not charge, rather it simply "approached" them. In my opinion and direct experience, if that is truly the reason to shoot and kill any bear, then hundreds of bears (black & grizzly alike) that make a curiosity approach or a non-threatening advance would unjustifiably suffer the same ill-intended fate.

Another current Idaho case exemplifies the danger black bear hunters pose to protected grizzly bears. According to a recent article by Buley, Bill. *Cour d' Alene Post Falls Press*, 14 Jun 2023. A non-resident black bear hunter shot and killed a grizzly bear north of Upper Priest Lake. IF&G officials reported that the hunter had good visibility when he shot a male grizzly, he mistook for a black bear at a distance of 170 yards. The hunter reported the incident. In another related article by: Clouse, Thomas. "Hunter mistakenly kills grizzly bear north of Priest Lake." *The Spokesman Review*, 13 Jun 2023 reports that on June 8, 2023 the hunter killed an endangered grizzly bear and told officials that he mistakenly identified the bruin as a black bear. He was issued a citation because he was legally responsible to identify his target before shooting. The case was sent to the county prosecutor. He faces a misdemeanor charge of taking a game animal during a closed season. He also faces a maximum $1,000 fine, up to six months in jail and a civil penalty up to $10,000. All penalties are subject to a judge's discretion.

This Idaho grizzly bear killing came a week after environmentalists called on officials in Idaho and Wyoming to require hunters to pass tests showing they can discern the difference between black and grizzly bears. Bear hunters in Washington and Montana must pass these tests to secure a tag. Interestingly, and perhaps ironically, I observed that the black bear hunter in this shooting is a resident of Washington. Therefore, as a non-resident black bear hunter in Idaho; did he take and pass the bear identity tests in Washington, and if so, would that impact if any, the citation against him?

An unrelated, but companion 2021 article from Idaho Fish and Game, announces a multi-funded $40,000 reward for information to help solve the cases of three very disturbingly illegal killings of grizzlies in one general area. An adult female was shot and killed between March 15 -23, near the Pole Bridge Campground in Island Park. This was a reproductive female. The agency received a mortality signal from its collar. Officials discovered her body submerged in the Little Warm River. Investigation revealed it died from multiple gunshot wounds. Even more disturbing, her den site revealed a 6–8-week-old cub that perished as a result of her death.

Within eight weeks, two other grizzly bears were shot and killed in the same area. In September 2020, an adult male was killed in Coyote Meadows. A third young male grizzly was killed in November near Cold Springs Road. It's unknown what the status is of the three investigations.

A very current and publicized legal case of alleged "black bear mistaken identity" remains back again to the North Fork Highway (U.S. Highway 14/16/20W) and just miles from Yellowstone's East Entrance.

According to an article by: Baker, C.J. "Hunter pleads not guilty in North Fork grizzly case." *Powell Tribune*, 23 May

2023. On May 1, 2023 (the opening day for spring black bear season) passersby on the North Fork Highway spotted a very large dead bear close to the road. Photographs were taken and the matter was reported to WG&F. The finding went viral on social media and drew national attention. A necropsy revealed the adult male grizzly bear of 530 pounds was shot at least four times. The carcass was left where it was shot and killed, 30 yards from the road and near a picnic area on the Shoshone River.

On May 2, (20 hours after WG&F received notice of the dead bear, and the photos went public on social media, a 65-year-old Wapiti, WY man (name withheld) called WG&F to report he had mistakenly identified a black bear and while going to the body, discovered it was a grizzly bear. He did not immediately report the incident to wildlife officials. In a charging affidavit, a North Cody Game Warden sated that (he) should have immediately turned himself in.

Other information revealed he spotted the bear at 100 yards and was sure it was a black bear roaming on the North Fork Highway. The hunter fired seven shots at the bear, hitting it four times. After examining the bear, he discovered it was a grizzly. He abandoned the scene and did not report to wildlife officials. At the time of this writing, his court case remains open with status conference and trial dates pending.

Following this North Fork mistaken identity case, on June 1, 2023 an impressive nine-member coalition of grizzly bear and animal rights organizations wrote to Brian Nesvik, Director, Wyoming Game and Fish Department, Rick King, Wildlife Division Chief and WG&F Commissioners respectfully requesting that; "In light of the continued killings of grizzly bears by black bear hunters claiming mistaken identity, we are writing to ask the (WGFD) revise black bear hunting regulations to *require* all black bear hunters to complete the WGFD bear identification course that is already in place and available from the Department. The killing of large male grizzly bear west of Cody in the North Fork area on May 1, 2023 is only the latest example of one more grizzly bear that could be alive if black bear hunters were required to undergo training to properly identify the species of a bear. This is a common- sense solution to a preventable problem."

Alarmingly, the letter goes on to state, "From 2010 to 2022, the Interagency Grizzly Bear Study Team identified 14 grizzly bears in the Greater Yellowstone region that were killed because of mistaken identity, but a total of 113 mortalities remains "under investigation." Over those 12 years, there were a total of 113 in the database that remains "under investigation." Seventy-one percent of those mortalities under investigation were in Wyoming. Without knowing how many of those are mistaken identity, the incident of grizzly bears being killed by black bear hunters is likely higher."

The above paragraph draws direct awareness to the fact that are 113 uninvestigated cases of grizzly bear mortalities over a current 12-year period, which is alarming to the very agencies that are charged with safeguarding and managing our national treasure of remaining grizzly bear populations. In my opinion, the astounding number of basically, uninvestigated or under-investigated dead grizzly bear cases, draws serious questions as to the accurate, unbiased estimated counts of GYE grizzly bears and the numbers claimed to support the passion of the Tri-States to overturn ESA protection and regain state management of grizzly bears. Furthermore, this long overdue, deficient data glaringly leaves the facts and causes of deaths unaccounted for. How is anyone to trust, much less rely on the integrity of the numbers? The tax-paying public, independent government, and oversight agencies deserve transparency and accountability.

In summation, it is quite obvious and accurate that black bear hunters are killing federally protected grizzly bears at an accelerated, unacceptable pace. Along with required black bear hunter species identification education, stricter laws along with effective and timely law enforcement, are all necessary factors to help control preventable grizzly bear killings by hunters.

Chapter Sixteen

2023 and Beyond

Political Scorched Earth Policies

Fast forward to the current 2023. On January 18, 2023, factions of the pro-ESA community went on the offensive side, with three wildlife conservation groups filing a 70-page suit in U.S. District Court for the District of Montana, Missoula, MT, USDC docket (No. 9-23-cv-00010) over the *Wildlife Services Predator Removal Program*. Federal Defendants include; the United States Dept. of Agriculture APHIS-Wildlife Services, USDA, and the U.S. Department of the Interior for violations under the ESA and Administrative Procedure Act. The lawsuit was filed as a challenge to a May 2021 USFWS decision to continue the Montana Predator Removal Program. The Complaint also contests USFWS environmental assessment (EA) and its finding of No Significant Impact (FONSI) of their biological opinion, was not likely to jeopardize the continued existence of grizzly bears. The suit further contends that Wildlife Services contracts and cooperates with states, other federal agencies, and others to carry out predator removal in MT. Wildlife Services coordinates MT predator removal work with the MT Dept. of Livestock (MDOL) in the killing of MT predators. Significantly, MDOL defines a "predator" as a coyote, red fox, or "any other animal causing livestock losses." Wolves and grizzly bears qualify as "other animals." Predator removals by MDOL are unregulated.

The excess means by which Wildlife Services uses or authorizes predator removal including wolves and grizzly bears are astonishingly barbaric and cruel beyond any measure of wildlife management. The Complaint contends that in addition to the use of cage, box, and culvert traps in MT, Wildlife Services authorizes and uses the following predator removal tactics and objects; body-gripping, quick kill traps when triggered kill the animal. They are indiscriminate killers of smaller/mid-sized animals, including dogs. Body-gripping traps have also captured and killed grizzlies. Also indiscriminate are foothold traps that capture and kill non-target species such as the grizzly. Also employed in MT are foot, neck, and body snares, with arbitrary consequences. Trained dog pursuits, dart guns, and use of baits, scents, and attractants are utilized in MT.

The most egregious MT predator removal means of Wildlife Services is aerial shooting from fixed-wing aircraft and helicopters. Aerial shooting is used to kill grizzlies. Additionally, night vision, thermal imaging for night shooting, decoy dogs, predator calling, stalking, and bait are all used to kill. Chemical repellants are also used. Disgustingly, Wildlife Services in MT engages in a practice known as "Denning." This practice involves locating a predator's den and killing both adults and young alike with sodium nitrate cartridge. When ignited, the sodium nitrate burns to produce poisonous carbon monoxide. "Denning" may also involve the use of gasoline and fire to burn animal occupants alive in their den.

If the above practices aren't enough to recoil one's senses; the suit contends that Wildlife Services in MT used or authorized indiscriminate, spring-activated device of sodium cyanide M-44 for lethal removal. The Complaint contends M-44 has poisoned and killed humans, as well as grizzly bears. Between 2018 and 2021 more than 950 animals were unintentionally killed by Wildlife Services. Most states have banned M-44 on public lands, while 15 states including MT allow their use.

While my book is solely focused on grizzly bear management concerns, you cannot separate or divorce the current MT war against predators including wolves; without consideration of what may ultimately cross over to a threatened delisted grizzly population. In this regard, I decided it was time to shed some light on Montana's unrelenting assault of killing wolves with just about every available fashion. The majority are inhumane, and completely void of which hunters claim they are "sportsman-like" in nature.

Results speak louder than claims. To test my ever-growing perceptions and observations that state wildlife management was not a sound, unbiased management approach, I proceeded to research Montana's dark statistical and political corners relating to wolf management. The source of the data was MFG&P's own annual *Wolf Harvest Report*. These reports reveal both statistical and financial information on the annual impact of both Hunter and Trapper wolf killing results. As described in the above 2023 lawsuit, in addition to the harsh killing tactics and devices, MT bills were introduced and passed to further allow reimbursement of wolf hunting costs, and other adverse wolf state legislative provisions.

The MT *Wolf Harvest Reports* research and discovery results affirmed the deleterious frequency and severity of killing off MT wolves as authorized by the *Wildlife Service's Predator Removal Program*. I decided to focus my study on collecting and analyzing MGF&P's own publicly published wolf mortality reports for the past three years. The state reports include annual wolf killing data in the form of Hunter and Trapper harvesting/kills and other financial and statistical information.

The following table on the next page, reveals the collected data.

Source Data: 2023 Montana Fish Game & Parks Wolf Harvest Reports

YEAR	HUNTER KILLED	TRAPPER KILLED	TOTAL KILLED	LICENSE SOLD	LIC REV	FEDERAL LAND KILLED
2021-22	148	125	273	38,018	$339K	58.3%
2020-21	170	159	329	18,508	$297K	39.9%
2019	163	130	293	20,406	$414K	39.9%
TOTALS	481	414	895	76,932	$1,050.M	46% Avg.

It's important to note that none of these numbers include wolves that were undoubtedly killed by poachers or otherwise non-reported. They do not reveal the number of wolves that were injured, escaped and eventually expired from all methods of lethal removal.

Still, the numbers are daunting. Currently (2023) it's estimated that MT has a wolf population of 800 to 1,200. Based upon an annual average of 300 wolves killed by firearms, poisoning, neck and foot trapping, etc., 37.5% of the MT wolf population are killed each year. I suggest the lower population estimate is more likely accurate, given the collective effect of killing methods, unreported killings, and injured wolves left to die unaccounted for.

Other observations from the data are the compounding effect of "killing begets killing" as the number of licenses sold more than doubled in 2022. Local and national word gets out fast in the Trophy hunting/trapping crowd; that it's now easier than ever, taking out multiple wolves in a single year. The fact indicating that nearly one million wolves, within a three-year period of time are killed off is staggering and sets the stage once again for wolf extinction in a matter of years. Some may claim the misguiding position that the 2022 data indicates that in spite of doubling licenses sold, the number of wolves killed is down and reflects sound predator removal policies. I however suggest, just the opposite may be in play. The doubling of sold licenses in contrast to a smaller killed number of wolves does not in any manner, reflect healthy MT wolf eradication policies and sustaining population numbers. Rather, the data now reflects that due to prior year(s) annual wolf killing practices and "harvested" numbers by Wildlife Services, have resulted in a decreasing wolf population. Simply stated, there are less wolves to hunt, trap or otherwise eradicate. I understand that the 2023 MT *Wolf Harvest Report* indicates continuation of the very same inverse mortality statistics. I'm unable at this time to view the report itself. However, if my understanding is correct, it would only further indicate advancement and perhaps a trend, supporting the position that less wolves remain available in the environment to Trophy kill. The data reveals that MT wolves are being Trophy killed off by an association of special interest policies and organizations.

My eye cannot further escape the fact that MGF&P garnered over One Million Dollars with license sales in the period of three short years. Adding big money to an agency hell-bent on predator elimination, predominately driven by the Trophy pelts of wolves and grizzlies, their population futures are easy to predict. Lastly, the data exhibits that the majority of MT wolves killed, occur on our national federal lands. The very same land where private livestock is situated and roams. That federal land is also the remnants of the prevailing natural habitat for predators and other native wildlife. MT state and private lands are distant second and third killing fields. The fact remains that Montana is slaughtering wolves overwhelmingly on federal land.

The harsh *Predator Removal Program* killing policies do not necessarily stop at the northern borders between MT and YNP. According to data provided by the NPS, Yellowstone Park's wolf population has substantially declined, much to the dismay of millions of YNP visitors and eco-wolf watchers' organizations. Individual wolves and wolf packs, as do grizzly bears, naturally move about in their remaining habitat, regardless of boundary lines and politics to eliminate them. Fact, in 2022 YNP area hunters/trappers killed 25 YNP wolves. That amounts to a 20% depletion of the park's wolves. One well-known YNP pack, the Phantom Lake Pack, was eliminated when the wolves were killed within two months starting in October.

Lone black wolf testing Mom's resolve to protect her newborn "little red."

If the wolf population is eradicated by the continuing efforts to accomplish just that objective, wolf encounters and photograph opportunities like the one I took on a recent spring outing, will no longer exist. By the way, the separated bison were able to escape the wolf's dinner plans by making it safely back with a mile sprint to the main herd.

Historically, it is important to note that wolves were nearly totally eradicated by hunters/trappers before being declared an ESA endangered species. In 1995, wolves were reintroduced with relocation to YNP from Canada. Other Canadian grey wolves also naturally migrated. However, in 2011 they were delisted from ESA status and turned back to state management, swinging the door once again to wide open hunting and trapping, which has evolved to current day dramatically exploding levels under the Wildlife Services, MT *Predator Removal Program*. Why do I opine this is historically important? Look no further, than the never-ceasing efforts by USFWS and Tri-States to strip away ESA status from the GYE grizzly bear. Is the potential for grizzly bears, in some form or fashion, to be subjected to the inevitable crash-and-burn wolf/predator policies? I certainly do. In my opinion, there is a similar correlation with the confluence merge of ill-advised intents, tactics, power, and politics.

Introduce MT Governor, Gregg Gianforte.

YNP Superintendent Cam Sholly, wrote to MT Gov. Greg Gianforte (R-MT) asking him to suspend the remainder of the wolf hunting season, created by the unprecedented loss of YNP wolves at the park's northern borders. Gianforte never responded. Was an apparent rude unresponsive silence by this governor, a disconnected uncaring response? Based on his questionable patterns of wildlife actions and history, it was almost predictable.

According to widely published articles, Gianforte was no stranger to discord and perpetual anti-wolf/grizzly policies. Within a very brief period since taking the governor's office, on Feb. 15, 2021, he trapped and shot/killed collared YNP research "Black Wolf 1155" on private ranch land owned by a political campaign donor near Tom Miner Basin in the Paradise Valley, several miles north of the YNP boundary near Gardiner, MT. Wolf 1155 was a member of the Wapiti and 8-Mile packs. As countless numbers of YNP wildlife seasonally cross that invisible line, Gianforte's wolf had sealed its fate, by crossing the YNP boundary seeking a mate. A day later after Trophy killing the wolf, wildlife officials determined Gianforte had broken the trapping certificate rule and was issued a warning. He had violated MT regulations by harvesting a wolf without first completing an important state-mandated trapping certificate. The trapping certificate requirement was also clearly indicated when applying for a license. After the citation, he described his failure to take the required trapping course, as a "slight mistake."

Regarding wildlife that naturally, exits YNP onto MT state lands, as with killing collared wolf 1155, Gianforte also legally shot and killed another iconic species. This time it was an elusive mountain lion. Not just any mountain lion, but once more a monitored research animal that was being tracked by the National Park Service. Paradoxically, the story of his mountain lion kill took place on the very day of Yellowstone's 150th anniversary as our nation's first national park.

Having stated that he's been in trapping for nearly 50 years, Gianforte further advised that in hindsight, he wouldn't have done anything differently. He also opined that trapping is an integral part of our heritage. Lest I forget, during a 2017 congressional run, Gianforte acknowledged he was fined $70 for mistakenly killing an immature elk that is illegal to hunt. Keeping in mind, that Gianforte was also the MT official that oversees MFW&P, I have to wonder: An attitude of self-entitlement and Rules and Laws for Thee, but not Me? By the way, the wildlife agency he controls, allowed him to keep his executed wolf's skull and hide.

2023 Here They Come Again.

Grizzly Bear State Management Act of 2023

House and Senate Versions.

As predictable as the morning's sunrise, the pro-Trophy killing coalition of state, federal, and special interest groups came back once again with vengeance to delist the grizzly from

ESA status and Trophy hunt/kill them. However, this time not only to resume but expands their assault against the precarious grizzly population for the third consecutive time after twice being defeated. The coalition efforts appear to be the perfect storm driven by the influential weights of money, political power, securing votes, and special state and national Trophy killing interests. Once again, the political forces at work are bipartisan in nature, with current elected Republican officials overwhelmingly leading the legislative charge to delist the grizzly from ESA protection.

On 2-15-2023, in the 118th Congress, Sen. Cynthia Lummins (R-WY) introduced S.445 cited as the: *Grizzly Bear State Management Act of 2023* in the United States Senate. The bill was also sponsored by Republican Senators: John Barrasso (WY), Mike Crapo & James Risch (ID), and Steve Daines (MT.)

S. 445

To direct the Secretary of the Interior to reissue a final rule relating to removing the Greater Yellowstone Ecosystem population of grizzly bears from the Federal list of endangered and threatened wildlife and for other purposes.

IN THE SENATE OF THE UNITED STATES

FEBRUARY 15, 2023

Ms. LUMMIS (for herself, Mr. BARRASSO, Mr. CRAPO, Mr. DAINES, and Mr. RISCH) introduced the following bill; which was read twice and referred to the Committee on Environment and Public Works

---

A BILL

To direct the Secretary of the Interior to reissue a final rule relating to removing the Greater Yellowstone Ecosystem population of grizzly bears from the Federal list of endangered and threatened wildlife and for other purposes.

Be it enacted by the Senate and House of Representatives of the United States of America in Congress assembled,

SECTION 1. SHORT TITLE.

This Act may be cited as the "Grizzly Bear State Management Act of 2023".

SEC. 2. REISSUANCE OF FINAL RULE RELATING TO GREATER YELLOWSTONE ECOSYSTEM POPULATION OF GRIZZLY BEARS.

(b) NO JUDICIAL REVIEW. —The reissuance of the final rule described in subsection (a) (including this section) shall not be subject to judicial review.

This bill would direct the Sec. of the Interior to reissue a final ruling to remove the Greater Yellowstone (GYE) population of grizzly bears from the Federal list of endangered and threatened wildlife, "and for other purposes." The bill would also transfer management of the grizzly to the states. Currently, the bill resides in the Committee on Environmental and Public Works. The troubled undefined words for "other purposes" deserve heightened scrutiny. *Furthermore, Sec. 2(b) would preclude judicial review. Obviously that provision is to prevent the courts from reviewing ESA delisting; which failed twice before, by reinstating ESA status to the GYE grizzly bear.

According to a 2-16-2023, article on Sen. Lummin's website, she claimed that grizzlies are essential to WY's ecosystem, but "keeping them listed hurts their population more than it helps them." Let me get this straight. By delisting the grizzly bear, which will free WY and the other states to then Trophy kill the GYE grizzly somehow, "helps them?" So, legislation that will lead to Trophy killing as a management policy, actually sustains and protects a natural wildlife population? Within the same article, Idaho Sen. Crapo claims that the GBSMA will restore responsibility to the right level. What "right level" is being referred to? Could that right level foreshadow a relationship to Idaho's one token Trophy grizzly bear to be hunted in the proposed Tri-State Agreement 2018 GYE grizzly hunt? The "right level" when in 2021, the state's own Idaho Fish and Game estimated a meager count as low as 40 grizzly bears battle for survival in the entire state and you're eager to sponsor Trophy killing?

Hot on the heels of the Senate's drive to strip away protection for GYE grizzly bears the House of Representatives is in lockstep with the Senate, also targeting the grizzly bears future. On 2/28, 2023, H.R. 1245 was introduced by newly elected Harriet Hageman (R-WY-At Large) and cosponsored by familiar pro delisting and Trophy grizzly bear hunting elected representatives; Ryan Zinke (R-MT) and Matthew Rosendale, Sr. (R-MT-2). The House bill is identical and cited in title and context with the Senate bill. H.R. 1245 was referred to the House Committee on Environmental and Public Works. As identical to the S.455 bill, House Bill H.R. 1245 also recites the same "and for other reasons."

H.R 1245 cosponsor Rep. Ryan Zinke (R-MT) is the same official who previously was appointed in 2017 as U.S. Secretary of the Interior under Republican administration. He resigned two years later due to continuing alleged ethics scandals. Perhaps, most notably, shortly after his appointment June 2017, Zinke led the charge to delist the GYE grizzly bear. He succeeded in removing grizzlies from ESA protection. Moreso, with wild applaud by the Trophy hunting industry and politicians supporting them, the moment Zinke's Delisting Order was signed, the already cooked up Tri-State Agreement was off the launch pad to immediately start biannual Trophy killing.

Wyoming and Idaho wildlife agencies raced to make that a reality. By fall 2018 Yellowstone grizzly bears were now marked for death. Most fortunately, litigation in the MT Circuit Court stopped the hunt, days before the fevered WY and ID Trophy killers were to lock and load. The Ninth Circuit U.S. Court of Appeals upheld the District Court's Ruling and reinstated ESA status. As a 2023 cosponsor to H.R.1245, Zinke boasted, "As a Congressman, I am *demanding* the same thing I did as Secretary."

Trust the Science Act

Literally in 2023, a legislative scorched earth policy was unleashed against wildlife. At the same time Bills H.R.1245 and S. 445, both cited as the: *Grizzly Bear State Management Act of 2023;* another punitive anti-wolf and grizzly bill was introduced. On 2-2-2023 H.R.764 was introduced by U.S. Rep. Lauren Boebert (R-Co-3) cited as the: *Trust the Science Act.*

Introduced in House (02/02/2023)

118TH CONGRESS
1ST SESSION

H. R. 764

To require the Secretary of the Interior to reissue regulations removing the gray wolf from the list of endangered and threatened wildlife under the Endangered Species Act of 1973.

IN THE HOUSE OF REPRESENTATIVES

FEBRUARY 2, 2023

Mrs. BOEBERT (for herself, Mr. TIFFANY, Mr. BERGMAN, Mr. BIGGS, Mr. GALLAGHER, Mr. LAMALFA, Mr. MOYLAN, Mr. NEHLS, Mr. NEWHOUSE, Mr. OGLES, Mr. PERRY, Mr. ROSENDALE, Mr. STAUBER, Mr. ZINKE, Mr. GROTHMAN, Mr. GOSAR, Mr. CRANE, Mr. VAN ORDEN, Mr. STEIL, Mr. FITZGERALD, Mrs. FISCHBACH, Mr. BUCK, and Mr. MOOLENAAR) introduced the following bill; which was referred to the Committee on Natural Resources

A BILL

To require the Secretary of the Interior to reissue regulations removing the gray wolf from the list of endangered and threatened wildlife under the Endangered Species Act of 1973.

Be it enacted by the Senate and House of Representatives of the United States of America in Congress assembled,

SECTION 1. SHORT TITLE.

This Act may be cited as the "Trust the Science Act".

SEC. 2. REMOVING THE GRAY WOLF FROM THE LIST OF ENDANGERED AND THREATENED WILDLIFE.

Not later than 60 days after the date of enactment of this section, the Secretary of the Interior shall reissue the final rule entitled "Endangered and Threatened Wildlife and Plants; Removing the Gray Wolf (Canis lupus) From the List of Endangered and Threatened Wildlife" and published on November 3, 2020 (85 Fed. Reg. 69778).

SEC. 3. NO JUDICIAL REVIEW.

*Again, please note that Sec.3 of the bill would prevent any judicial review. This legislation would require the Sec. of the Interior to reissue regulations removing the grey wolf from the list of endangered and threatened wildlife under the Endangered

Species Act of 1973. H.R. 1245 was referred to the House Committee of Natural Resources. The Bill would reinstate federal wildlife officials' 2020 attempt to delist grey wolves in the entire contiguous United States. Cosponsoring the Trust the Science Act were 24 other Representatives, all Republican. Predictably cosponsored is Montana's, Ryan Zinke. However, as a Tennessean, I was very surprised to discover that first-year representative newcomer Andrew Ogles (R-TN-5) was also a cosponsor of this harsh bill.

Mr. Ogles, I'm unaware that TN has grey wolves. Could it be because we don't have any grey wolves, not a single one? And no sir, historically they weren't hunted off or eliminated in TN, because TN has never had any grey wolves. Strange to notice that Rep. Ogles is the one and only Southern representative sponsoring this bill.

Comprehensive Grizzly Bear Management Act of 2023.

Perhaps, the reader may recall an earlier chapter comment that I made alluding to the fact that after the pro Trophy grizzly bear coalition lost their 2017 bid to delist the GYE grizzly, they would come back again with vengeance. I suggest that the above 2023 legislative end around attempts to do so, more than validate my projected fears and concerns. However, lest I be less than inclusive; yet another bill to even further expand MT Trophy grizzly hunting is H.R. 1419, cited as the "*Comprehensive Grizzly Bear Management Act of 2023.*"

Introduced in House (03/07/2023)

        118TH CONGRESS
        1ST SESSION

H. R. 1419

To direct the Secretary of the Interior to issue a new rule removing the Northern Continental Divide Ecosystem population of grizzly bears from the Federal list of endangered and threatened wildlife.

IN THE HOUSE OF REPRESENTATIVES

MARCH 7, 2023

Mr. ROSENDALE (for himself, Mr. ZINKE, and Ms. HAGEMAN) introduced the following bill; which was referred to the Committee on Natural Resources

---

A BILL

To direct the Secretary of the Interior to issue a new rule removing the Northern Continental Divide Ecosystem population of grizzly bears from the Federal list of endangered and threatened wildlife.

Be it enacted by the Senate and House of Representatives of the United States of America in Congress assembled,

SECTION 1. SHORT TITLE.

This Act may be cited as the "Comprehensive Grizzly Bear Management Act of 2023".

SEC. 2. REMOVAL OF NORTHERN CONTINENTAL DIVIDE ECOSYSTEM POPULATION OF GRIZZLY BEARS FROM FEDERAL LIST OF ENDANGERED AND THREATENED WILDLIFE.

> Not later than 180 days after the date of the enactment of this Act, the Secretary of the Interior shall issue a final rule removing the Northern Continental Divide Ecosystem population of grizzly bears from the Federal list of endangered and threatened wildlife without regard to any other provision of law that applies to the issuance of such rule. Such issuance and this section shall not be subject to judicial review.

As with all the delisting bills, Sec. 2 specifies the bill in a final ruling would preclude judicial or court review. The bill was sponsored and introduced on 3-7-2023, by Matthew Rosendale Sr.(R-MT-2) This bill was introduced to the 118th Congress. 1st Session and directs the Secretary of the Interior to issue a new rule removing the Northern Continental Divide Ecosystem population of grizzly bears from the list of endangered and threatened wildlife. Of course, the passage of this bill as with the others, would also be immediately followed by Trophy grizzly killing. Rosendale's bill was also sponsored by Rep. Hageman and surprise, Ryan Zinke. Please note that Sec 2. Of the bill, delisting the NCDE grizzly population specifically would prevent judicial review.

Expectedly and with good cause, opposition statements and opinions followed in various forums from opposing wildlife management, attorneys, and conservation groups. I'm of the opinion that a committee hearing statement by Chris Servheen was the most compelling, merging context coupled with professional credentials and experience. Mr. Servheen is a bear biologist with 35 years of experience. In 2016 he retired from his position with U.S. Fish and Wildlife Service as grizzly bear recovery coordinator. During the 2017 attempt to delist the grizzly, he was a strong proponent and voice in favor of delisting. However, he no longer supports delisting, just the very opposite, he opposes it. What changed such an immediate and forceful reversal? Servheen opines his shift was related to the legislative bills promoting aggressive, indiscriminate wildlife killing methods into grizzly bear habitat. He further cited that protecting grizzlies and wolves is inadequate due to political interference of wildlife management.

According to a recent article referring to the same committee testimony by Mr. Servheen: Heinz, Mark. "Bad Predator Policies in Montana, Idaho Could Derail Delisting Wyoming Grizzlies, Bear Expert Says." *Cowboy State Daily*, 29 Mar. 2023. Servheen further stated in particular, Montana and Idaho, changed his mind to not delist due to overall terrible state-level predator management. Wildlife in those two states is handled largely by "anti-predator paranoia" rather than sound management. He further continued that heavy-handed and unnecessary wolf-killing policies in Montana can also affect grizzlies. Snares for wolves also kill grizzlies, with people responsible for doing so, having little incentive to report grizzly snare deaths. Also snared bears may go off and die elsewhere without nobody knowing about it.

According to Servheen's expertise, public unfounded fears could hurt hunting. The fear that grizzlies and wolves will attack and kill livestock and ruin big game herds is largely unfounded. While wolves and bears do kill some livestock and draw attention, in the larger picture that is not a problem. The livestock numbers don't add too much. In support of his positions, Servheen cites that in the period of 2018 and 2020, roughly 113 cattle and sheep were lost to wolves each year. However, by comparison to 2015 alone, 40,000 cattle and sheep were killed by weather in Idaho alone. The bottom line of this extraordinarily experienced grizzly bear expert and federal wildlife servant is the learned position that the grizzly bear should not be delisted from ESA protective status, at least not yet.

Whatever happens in the future with these delisting bills and other political, legislative, and judicial involvement, remains to be seen. History appears to be on the side of future ESA protection. Nevertheless, with a skeptical estimate of increasing numbers of grizzly bears and all but admitted bias by WG&F to monitor the grizzly bear population only to delist them, any increasing numbers of bears create a perch to advance delisting and ensuing Trophy hunting. Some 2023 proponents of delisting believe their chances are good because the number of GYE grizzly bears has increased. That may be true, but are the actual derived numbers of grizzlies unaffected by a thumb on the scales, from the very agencies whose stated purpose is to delist the GYE grizzly bear?

Author's Thoughts for a Solution.

In conclusion, I believe it's important to not just offer a critical view, as wholly justified as they are; but within my ability and own evaluation, offer some solution or compromise position in an attempt to better secure balance between two polar opposite grizzly bear management provisions. The results of this will have a profound influence on the near and long-term sustainability of the irreplaceable Yellowstone grizzly bear.

In my evaluation, two profoundly decisive issues are both independent and dependent on each other. The first issue is delisting the grizzly bear from ESA protection, thus transferring federal grizzly bear management and protection back to the states. This issue presents itself as a potential conditional pathway for giving the states another opportunity or chance to validate that their new state management plans are productive, unbiased, and most of all; successful results are obtained. This factual observation is evident by the calamitous results of prior state grizzly bear management, with the mid-1970 grizzly population on the precarious edge of extinction with 136 GYE surviving bears. For the most part, after years of state-sponsored Trophy hunting, it's undisputed that the grizzly bear population plummeted which then invoked federal ESA status.

The second issue, which in my opinion would be <u>initially</u> non-negotiable is the reintroduction of state management Trophy grizzly bear hunting. I need not rehash the historically destructive results for a sustainable grizzly population. Furthermore, not to be overlooked is the intensity of the state's ongoing predator removal programs and abominable methods employed to hunt, trap and kill wolves which may spill over to grizzly bears. This ongoing policy is illustrative of extreme hostility and abhorrent eradication of predators. The 2023 legislative (House and Senate bills) promoting a scorched earth predator assault on "other animals" which includes wolves and grizzlies, all tied in with bill provisions to prohibit judicial or court review; all but foreshadows hostile ill intent by new state wildlife management. For these issues alone, perhaps other viable and reasoned elements of return to state grizzly management are surpassed by Trophy killing.

As a grizzly bear advocate, alternatively, I would consider reserved support for ESA delisting, provided that Trophy hunting is initially off the table. If agreed upon, an ESA compromise would allow MT, WY, and ID a reasonable period to enact all other provisions of their state grizzly bear management programs. Such a compromise would provide a second chance by empowering the states' wildlife scientists, law enforcement, etc., to unbiasedly demonstrate they have the program capacity and good faith intents on overseeing sustainable grizzly bear population and habitat. After a reasonable period of state managing time, a negotiable period would be entertained for potential bear hunting if accurate comprehensive data proves to be achieved and a sustainable grizzly bear population and habitat are secured and independently verified. If this or other ESA/state management compromises are rejected out of hand by pro-delisting special interest groups, that would suggest their only purpose for ESA delisting is Trophy grizzly bear hunting. It would further test if other state program provisions were merely window dressings.

Grizzly inside YNP, traversing a high ridge as evening approaches.

    I recall one very exciting late afternoon while out alone in the field somewhere in the high country of the Washburn Range, when by good fortune this large grizzly appeared walking on top of a near ridgeline. In my eyes and lasting memory, this grizzly bear's powerful silhouette perfectly embodies and flawlessly represents my awe of Yellowstone Grizzlies in the Wild. As his silver-tipped hair slightly ruffled with the wind rushing over the ridge, his presence evoked many thoughts coalescing within me. I recall being captivated, by darting feelings of; wilderness, strength, beauty, fear, wonder, unfettered freedom, and my insignificance.

    Perhaps, unrecognized in my thoughts, this impressionable encounter on a Yellowstone backcountry ridge, was also an influencing moment for me to write this book and share insights into my journey.

Chapter Seventeen:

Closing

It's often said that there is no better place to end, than starting from the beginning. From my opening introduction remarks and successive chapters, we have journeyed together and experienced with an open window, glimpses into my path of discovering the Yellowstone grizzly bear. It's nearly, if not fully impossible to convey the level and degree of YNP's all-encompassing effects impacting those who visit and venture into her unspoiled wilderness. As personally meaningful and influencing those effects had propelled my journey, it was the captivating awe of searching for and locating grizzly bears in the wild that initially caught and now, progressively sustains my journey.

Each path and approach for those that may have similar interests, in whole or part, are highly personalized and without a roadmap. There is no one size fits all. For those who may be inclined, you will create and adjust your road forward on your terms. I am confident regardless of approach, you will experience as I did, many rewards, challenges, education, and adventures, tempered by your comfort level of risk. Whether or not, you choose to venture onto Yellowstone's trails and backcountry, is not exclusively important. Regardless of age or physical capacity, learning about the complex issues associated with grizzly bears and advocating on their behalf, is vitally important. I'm hopeful that I've shed some insight and recognition toward those objectives.

President Teddy Roosevelt, a staunch conservationist in 1903, commemorated and laid the cornerstone of the Roosevelt Arch at the north entrance into YNP. President Roosevelt was once quoted, "Believe you can and you're halfway there." In retrospect at the beginning, I had a cautious belief, but I don't know if I was "halfway" there, or in fact "halfway" anywhere. That measurement level itself didn't matter to me, simply acting upon that belief was my catalyst.

My pathway first began in my senior years and continues to this day. Now, well into my seventies and soundly within my second Yellowstone decade, my journey continues unabated with zeal and determination. Maturing well beyond that of when I first discovered the majestic bounty and adventure of the Minnetaree tribal named, Mi tse a-da-zi or translated, Yellow Rock River, and our more modern identity Yellowstone; the journey itself was my inspiration. It is never too late to become involved, inspired, and encourage others.

In the opening of my book, I critically referred to the majority (myself included) of YNP visitors often disappointed in failing to see a grizzly bear. In the early years, that was my very same sentiment. That same feeling remained with me after I started to educate myself and guardedly ventured into Yellowstone. As reflected in my book, given time and experience, I turned that disappointment into well over a decade of searching for GYE grizzly bears in their habitat. Why do I now feel compelled to again draw attention to that issue? Having brought attention to the many natural and human elements adversely impacting grizzlies, primarily look no further than chapters 14 and 15 for the answers. Solutions will remain elusive and contested at individual, local, state, and federal levels.

I took no pleasure in unveiling troubling state grizzly bear wildlife management statistics and operational policies, many of which are destructive to wolves and grizzlies alike. However, this is where my journey took me and could not be ignored. The impacts are profound. However, retreating to a basic opening tenant of my book, expressed by a majority of YNP visitors, "Where are all the grizzly bears?" Does society want to go back to the mid-1970s with a total of 136 GYE surviving grizzly bears in thousands of square miles of habitat? Will ESA delisting and Trophy grizzly bear hunting sustain, much less increase, the odds that current and future YNP visitors and adventurers, will even have an opportunity to see a Yellowstone grizzly bear? This is a question and issue for the public to confront and evaluate. My faith in doing the collective right thing rests with the experiences and knowledge we shared together in these pages and beyond.

Lastly, wherever your relationship with Yellowstone may take or lead you, either short or long-term; always respect her great wildlife, both large and small. Remain good stewards of their irreplaceable habitat. Leave Yellowstone history undisturbed and above all else, enjoy and take wonder with God's hand creating this earthly marvel we call Yellowstone.

As I conclude writing my book, I'm drawn to the physical realization that my remaining years hiking about the GYE and photographing Yellowstone grizzly bears will be approaching an end at some time in the not-too-far-distant years. Knowing what I now know and have so richly experienced; my only regret is that I first commenced with this journey late in life. Through that retrospective lens, I lost some valuable exploring years. I don't look back though, with any feelings of loss. Starting the way my journey unfolded and expanded was a source of my determination and inspiration. Above all, I am blessed to have had the opportunity, starting well into my senior years, to have accomplished some of the most exciting years of my life. I hope my story may encourage others, regardless of age, to seek out in their very own personal ways, your path, and pace with Yellowstone, whatever your passion may be. The future of the Yellowstone grizzly bear needs our immediate and committed support. Imagine YNP without the last trace of a true wilderness: the Yellowstone grizzly bear. Thank you for joining me, it has been my true pleasure and honor.

The author hiking in the GYE, outside YNP.

About the Author

    Robert Nevens, Sr. resides in Brentwood, TN, and is proudly married to his wife Anita, in over five decades of marriage and with his best buddy, Daisy the Beagle. They have three adult children, two grandchildren, and two great-grandchildren. He is a first-time author at the young age of 76 years old.

    Bob is a graduate of the University of Arkansas-Little Rock and is a six-year United States Air Force veteran. He served with USAF Strategic Air Command (SAC) and U.S. Pacific Air Forces (PACAF) in Korea. Bob retired in 2012 after a three-decade-year professional career serving as Vice President and Director of Claims for a large international hospital organization.

    Well into his senior years, he was drawn to Yellowstone where he developed his talents for GYE hiking with amateur grizzly bear photography. Through his education and experience with the land and the grizzly, Bob focused his passion and efforts as a developing grizzly bear advocate and preservationist. Approaching two decades of active engagement, he remains steadfast to those principles and challenges.

Printed in Great Britain
by Amazon